Probation, Parole, and Community Corrections Work in Theory and Practice

Probation, Parole, and Community Corrections Work in Theory and Practice

Preparing Students for Careers in Probation and Parole Agencies

Kathryn Morgan

CAROLINA ACADEMIC PRESS
Durham, North Carolina

Library of Congress Cataloging-in-Publication Data

Names: Morgan, Kathryn, 1953-
Title: Probation, parole, and community corrections work in theory and
  practice : preparing students for careers in probation and parole agencies
  / Kathryn Morgan.
Description: Durham : Carolina Academic Press, 2015. | Includes
  bibliographical references and index.
Identifiers: LCCN 2015037793 | ISBN 9781611637939 (alk. paper)
Subjects: LCSH: Community-based corrections--United States. |
  Probation--United States. | Parole--United States. | Vocational
  guidance--United States.
Classification: LCC HV9304 .M667 2015 | DDC 364.6023/073--dc23
LC record available at http://lccn.loc.gov/2015037793

Carolina Academic Press
700 Kent Street
Durham, North Carolina 27701
Phone (919) 489-7486
Fax (919) 493-5668
www.cap-press.com

Printed in the United States of America
2021 Printing

Contents

Probation, Parole, and Community Corrections Work in Theory and Practice

Chapter 1

Probation, Parole, and Community Corrections

Key Terms

Bail	Parole
Determinate sentencing	Probation
Deterrence	Rehabilitation
Flat-time sentences	Retribution
General deterrence	*Roper v. Simmons*
Jury nullification	Sanction stacking
Incapacitation	Selective incapacitation
Indeterminate sentencing	Specific deterrence
Lex talionis	*Thompson v. Oklahoma*
Mandatory sentence	Time served
Net-widening	Truth-in-sentencing

Learning Objectives
1. Outline the criminal justice system process.
2. Identify the purposes of corrections.
3. Summarize the strategies of community corrections.
4. Discuss major controversies in community corrections.

Probation, Parole, and Community Corrections in the Criminal Justice System

Despite the attacks on rehabilitation and the shift away from the rehabilitative ideal in the 1970s, community-based corrections have continued to proliferate in the United States correctional system. Correctional data indicate that at the end of 2013, there were approximately 4.7 million offenders being supervised in community corrections programs. Although there has been a decline in the number of offenders under community supervision since 2008, there are almost 5 million who are still being supervised in community correctional programs.[1] Many of those in community correctional programs are on probation and parole; probationers make up 84% or 4.2 million, and parolees account for over 800,000 or 16%.[2] From 2009–2011, probation populations declined but still remained at more than four million offenders.[3] Despite the fact that 16 states and the federal government abolished parole, the Bureau of Justice Statistics reported that at the end of 2013, 800,000 parolees were supervised by parole agencies.[4] Statistics for adjudicated juveniles reveal a similar pattern. Probation is the most common disposition for juveniles who have been adjudicated as delinquent. Recent data indicate that about 56% of delinquent juveniles receive probation.[5]

The Criminal Justice Offender and the Criminal Justice System

Potentially, a criminal case may flow through five phases in the criminal justice process. At any of the phases, the offender may be diverted out of the system and will not be subject to further prosecution.

Phases of Criminal Justice Processing

Phase 1: The Legislative Phase

The first phase of the criminal justice system process is the legislative phase. Because it is not a formal phase of the criminal justice process, it may not always be recognized. The laws passed by state legislatures and the U.S. Congress have an important impact on corrections, especially through the sentencing

---

1. Erinn J. Herberman and Thomas P. Bonczar (2014, October). *Probation and Parole in the United States, 2013*. Washington, DC: U.S. Department of Justice, Office of Justice Programs, Bureau of Justice Statistics, 1.

2. Lauren Glaze and Thomas P. Bonczar (2009, December). *Probation and Parole in the United States, 2008*. Washington, DC: U.S. Department of Justice, Office of Justice Programs, Bureau of Justice Statistics, 1.

3. Laura Maruschak and Erika Parks (2012, November). *Probation and Parole in the United States, 2011*. Washington, DC: U.S. Department of Justice, Office of Justice Programs, Bureau of Justice Statistics, 1.

4. Herberman and Bonczar, *Probation and Parole in the United States, 2013*, 1.

5. Sarah Livsey (2010, June). *Juvenile Delinquency Probation Caseload, 2007*. Washington, DC: U.S. Department of Justice, Office of Justice Programs, Bureau of Justice Statistics.

system. Sentencing laws affect the actions and behaviors of judges and correctional administrators. There are two main types of sentencing systems:

  a. determinate sentencing
  b. indeterminate sentencing

Under determinate sentencing systems, the sentence is "fixed" at the time of sentencing. Release is based on **time served**.[6] Judges fix sentences within a minimum and maximum range established by the legislature. Although the judge may have some discretion regarding the sentence, it cannot be changed once it has been given. The offender serves the entire sentence minus any "good time" built into the sentence. Under this sentencing structure, the inmate will "max out" or be released from prison after serving the entire sentence minus the good time.[7] Recently, many states have passed truth-in-sentencing legislation that requires the offender to serve most of their sentence before being released.[8]

The indeterminate sentencing system allows flexibility in the time of release. The judge sets the minimum and maximum sentence, and the time served is determined by an administrative agency such as the parole board.

Phase 2: Entry into the System

Initial contact is made with the system when an act makes a person the subject of interest to law enforcement agencies. Police may observe a person acting suspiciously or may be called to the scene of a crime. A victim may report a crime. Once police have investigated the illegal activity and gained sufficient evidence to identify the violator and justify an arrest, an arrest is made. Police take the suspect into custody, where he or she may be interrogated, photographed, and fingerprinted. Many who commit crimes may never enter the system because crimes

Determinate — The type of sentence that is fixed at the time of sentencing. **Flat-time sentences** and **mandatory sentences** are types of determinate sentences.

Flat-time sentences are sentences where the length of the sentence is fixed by law and cannot be changed by the trial judge or the parole board. Judges have no discretion; the offender serves the entire sentence minus any "good time" built into the sentence. Under this sentencing structure, the inmate will "max out."

Indeterminate — A sentence where there is a minimum and maximum. The sentence is not fixed, but there is flexibility in the time of release.

Time served is the amount of time that an offender spends in confinement either awaiting trial or serving a sentence in the custody of correctional authorities.

Truth-in-sentencing laws — Laws passed in most states that require convicted offenders to serve a significant portion of their sentence.

---

6. Frank Schmallenger and John Smykla (2011). *Corrections in the 21st Century*. New York, NY: McGraw-Hill, 71.

7. Todd Clear and George Cole (2000). *American Corrections*. Belmont, CA: Wadsworth Publishing, 348.

8. Dean Champion (2008). *Probation, Parole and Community Corrections*. 6th Edition. Upper Saddle River, NJ: Pearson/Prentice-Hall.

may go undetected and unreported. Police may exercise discretion and decide against arresting a suspect.

Phase 3: Prosecution and Pretrial

Once the suspect has been arrested, the case and the evidence are turned over to the prosecutor for further processing. The prosecutor makes two crucial decisions: (a) if charges will be filed and (b) what charges will be filed. If the case goes to the grand jury, the prosecutor decides what evidence to send. The prosecutor may choose to drop a case for several reasons, including insufficient evidence, witness problems, victim behavior and characteristics, prosecution caseloads, and deciding to try a more serious case pending against the suspect.[9]

Prior to trial, many states still use a grand jury to determine if there is probable cause or enough evidence to justify a trial. If the evidence is sufficient to justify the case going to trial, the grand jury will return a "true bill of indictment." In some instances, attorneys present the case in open court in a preliminary hearing before the judge who makes a decision about the evidence. A finding of "probable cause" indicates that the evidence is sufficient for the suspect to stand trial. During the arraignment, the defendant appears in court to hear formal charges and be informed of rights including the right to trial by jury, right to an attorney, protection from self-incrimination, and the right to confront and cross-examine witnesses. The defendant enters a plea and informs the court of the desire for an appointed attorney. If the defendant is declared indigent, an attorney will be appointed.[10]

Bail is a type of pretrial where the defendant puts up a surety to guarantee that he or she will show up for trial. The defendant is required to pay 10% of the bail amount.

Bail and detention decisions will determine if bail will be set and how much. Bail guarantees that the defendant will return for trial and allows the defendant the freedom to participate in his or her defense while awaiting trial. Research has shown that the money bail system discriminates against the poor, who remain in jail prior to trial, plead guilty more often, and receive a more severe sentence.[11] Minorities are less likely to receive bail or will be assessed higher bail amounts, making it impossible to be released or to participate in their defense. Some states have instituted "bail schedules" to keep judges from ar-

---

9. Joseph Sienna & Larry Siegel (1995). *Essentials of Criminal Justice.* St. Paul, MN: West Publishing Company, p 25.

10. Ibid. pp. 27–28.

11. Samuel Walker, Cassia Spohn, and Miriam DeLeone (2004). *The Color of Justice.* California: Wadsworth Publishing Company.

bitrarily setting higher bail amounts. The schedule identifies the offense and the bail amount that is appropriate for that offense. Even with the existence of the schedule, judges deviate from the suggested bail amounts, often giving lower than the scheduled amounts for white females and higher amounts for black males.[12]

Plea-bargaining is an important pretrial decision that allows the defendant to plead guilty to a lesser offense in exchange for a less severe sentence. Cases move through the court system more quickly and save the cost of a trial. It is estimated that approximately 90% of all cases end in a plea bargain rather than a criminal trial.[13]

Phase 4: Adjudication

If the defendant does not plead guilty, the case continues to court and is heard by a judge or jury. This phase is the adversarial component of the process where evidence is presented by both prosecuting and defense attorneys and witnesses are confronted and cross-examined. The judge or jury hearing the case must decide that the evidence beyond a reasonable doubt proves that the defendant did commit the crime. A jury may not be able to reach a decision and becomes "hung." Jury deadlock may leave the case unresolved and open for a possible retrial. If the individual is convicted, the standard of proof must be "proof beyond a reasonable doubt." In recent years, there has been increased emphasis on jury nullification. In such a case, a jury may refuse to convict a defendant despite the evidence that proves guilt beyond a reasonable doubt and members of the jury believe that the defendant is guilty of the charges.

> The standard of proof in criminal court is proof beyond a reasonable doubt. In civil cases, the standard of proof is preponderance of the evidence.

If the defendant has not been diverted out of the system, and has been tried and convicted of the crime, the defendant must face sentencing and punishment. Following conviction, a number of questions must be answered regarding the disposition of the case. Should the defendant be incarcerated or supervised in the community? What are the special conditions that should be assigned if the defendant is placed in a community correctional program? Often, the judge will request a presentence investigation report (PSI) to address these ques-

> **Jury nullification** — The jury votes to acquit the defendant despite evidence that proves the defendant's guilt beyond a reasonable doubt.

---

12. Ibid.

13. Bureau of Justice Statistics (2005). *State Court Sentencing of Convicted Felons.* Washington, DC: U.S. Department of Justice, Office of Justice Programs.

tions and assist in sentencing. (A more complete discussion of the PSI and its role in the criminal justice process will be discussed in chapter 3.)

Phase 5: Corrections

The next and final phase of the criminal justice process is corrections. The corrections system is responsible for carrying out the sentence that has been imposed by the court. The defendant may be placed in an institutional correctional facility or a community-based corrections program.

> Community-based corrections refer to those programs that provide punishment for the offender in the community.[14]

A review of correctional populations reveals that community corrections programs have become the panacea for the overcrowding and related costs of prisons. Statistics from the 2010 survey of correctional populations by the Bureau of Justice Statistics indicate that offenders sentenced to community corrections programs have surpassed prison admissions. At year's end, approximately 1.6 million offenders were confined to the nation's state and federal facilities.[15] At the same time, the Bureau of Justice Statistics reported that almost five million offenders were supervised in a community-based correctional program. Escalating prison costs and prison overcrowding have been two main factors related to the growth of community-based corrections programs. The difference in the daily cost of housing an offender in prison versus supervising that person in the community is worth noting.[16] The national average for the daily supervision of a probationer or parolee is approximately $4.00. In Alabama, the daily cost of supervising an offender on probation or parole is $1.96.[17] The daily cost for supervising an inmate in prison may range from $36 (Mississippi) to $198 (New York). In a time when states and corrections departments are called upon to do more with less, community corrections programs become very practical alternatives. Community corrections represent an important aspect of the criminal justice system.[18]

---

14. Dean Champion (2008). *Probation, Parole and Community Corrections*, 68.

15. Paul Guerino, Paige M. Harrison, and William J. Sabol (2012). *Prisoners in 2010*. Washington, DC: U.S. Department of Justice, Office of Justice Programs, Bureau of Justice Statistics.

16. Lauren Glaze (2011, December). *Correctional Populations in the United States, 2010*. Washington, DC: Department of Justice, Office of Justice Programs, Bureau of Justice Statistics.

17. Alabama Board of Pardon and Paroles (2010). *Fiscal Annual Report.*

18. Todd Clear & George Cole (2000). *Corrections in America*. Fifth Edition. Belmont, CA: Wadsworth Publishing Company.

Community-Based Corrections: A Definition

Community corrections is a strategy for managing offenders by reducing institutional confinement in favor of community supervision.[19] In the 1980s, a number of "get tough" strategies increased the number of prison admissions and caused prison populations to grow beyond what most facilities could handle. In response, many states passed community corrections acts to increase the number of alternatives to incarceration available to judges for sentencing. In addition to probation, parole, and other community-based correctional programs already in existence, there was the creation of intermediate sanctions to reduce prison overcrowding while maintaining the purposes of punishment. These newly passed laws allowed local communities to implement community corrections programs to supervise convicted offenders at the community level. These programs promoted rehabilitation and reintegration back into society while reducing prison populations and prison costs.[20]

Purposes of Corrections

There are four major purposes of punishment and corrections: retribution, incapacitation, deterrence, and rehabilitation.

Retribution

A major emphasis of corrections is retribution. Retribution is derived from the idea of *lex talionis*, an ancient form of justice and revenge which literally meant "eye for an eye and tooth for a tooth." According to the retribution perspective, the offender must pay his or her debt to society.[21]

Incapacitation

Incapacitation emphasizes that incarcerating the offender protects society from the offender's potential criminal activities. As crime rates continued to increase during the 1960s and

Retribution is the philosophy and purpose of punishment that advocates punishment for revenge against the offender.

Lex talionis, incorporated into the Code of Hammurabi, referred to "equality of revenge." The amount of revenge taken against an offender could not exceed that of the harm caused by the offender.

Incapacitation — The philosophy of punishment advocating confinement for the criminal to limit the capability to commit more crimes.

---

19. Dean Champion (2008). *Probation, Parole and Community Corrections*, 69.
20. Ibid., 71–72.
21. Dean Champion (2001). *The American Dictionary of Criminal Justice*. 2nd Edition. Los Angeles, CA: Roxbury Publishing Company, 81.

1970s, there was growing awareness that crime prevention and rehabilitation programs had not worked. Robert Martinson (1973) and his colleagues published the results of a controversial study in which he reviewed 231 evaluations of rehabilitation programs. He concluded that all of the 231 evaluations ended with the same finding: "The program shows no appreciable effect on recidivism"; thus leading Martinson to conclude that "nothing works."[22] Criminologists began to challenge the rehabilitation philosophy that had dominated criminal justice policy for over 70 years.

Following Martinson's controversial findings about rehabilitation programs, Charles Murray and Louis Cox published *Beyond Probation*, challenging the belief that rehabilitation and treatment efforts reduced future criminal behavior. Instead, they suggested that punishment, not treatment, was more effective in reducing recidivism.[23] During the 1970s and 1980s, James Q. Wilson's *Thinking About Crime* promoted a new approach to thinking about crime that suggested that criminals are cold calculators with a low stake in conformity who are willing to commit crime for the perceived benefits. Therefore, severe punishment is the only way to deal with those who engage in criminal behavior.[24] Embracing Wilson's conservative ideas regarding crime and criminal justice policy, politicians promoted a "get tough on crime" agenda. Laws were passed that instituted "sentencing guidelines," set mandatory sentencing for certain offenses, and set mandatory prison sentences for drug offenders.[25] The United States Supreme Court demanded harsher treatment of ordinary street crime, limited rights for those arrested for crimes, limited last-minute appeals by death row inmates and mandated the execution of violent teenage killers. In a 1988 decision, the U.S. Supreme Court ruled that juveniles who committed capital offenses at 16 could be eligible for the death penalty (*Thompson v. Oklahoma* 487. U.S. 815, 1988).[26] *Thompson v. Oklahoma* was struck down in

Thompson v. Oklahoma — A 1988 landmark decision by the United States Court that execution of a juvenile under age 16 violated the Eighth Amendment and constituted cruel and unusual punishment.

---

22. Robert Martinson (1974). "What Works? Questions and Answers about Prison Reform," *Public Interest 35*: 22–54.

23. Charles Murray and Louis Cox (1979). *Beyond Probation*. Beverly Hills, CA: Sage Publishing.

24. James Q. Wilson (1983). *Thinking About Crime. Revised Edition*. New York, NY: Basic Books.

25. Michael Tonry (1995). *Malign Neglect: Race, Crime and Punishment in America*. New York: Oxford University Press.

26. Thompson v. Oklahoma, 487. U.S. 815 (1988).

2005 by the Supreme Court's ruling in *Roper v. Simmons* (543 U.S. 551, 2005)[27] that banned capital punishment for juvenile offenders under age 18.

Increased incarceration of convicted criminals was viewed as an important strategy for deterring criminals and reducing crime rates. By the end of 2009, approximately two million adult offenders were supervised in jails and prisons, making the United States' incarceration rate the highest in the world.[28]

Proponents of **selective incapacitation** advocated reducing crime by focusing on chronic offenders or the small percentage of the population that commits a large percentage of the crimes. Keeping chronic offenders and potentially chronic offenders (identified by crime history, employment history, and history of substance abuse) incapacitated or incarcerated for long periods could reduce the amount of crime.[29] The "three strikes and you're out" policy was popularized as a "get tough" mechanism that required repeated offenders convicted of three violent offenses to receive a mandatory sentence of "life without parole."[30] Several states, including the federal government, abolished discretionary parole, passed truth-in-sentencing legislation, and mandated that offenders serve all of their sentences minus good time.[31]

> **Roper v. Simmons —** A landmark ruling by the Supreme Court in 2005 that struck down Thompson v. Oklahoma and prohibited capital punishment for juveniles under age 18.

> **Selective incapacitation** was a policy that advocated identifying potential chronic offenders and locking them up for long periods. As a result, crime rates would decrease.

Critical Thinking Box 1.1

Advocates of selective incapacitation argue that we should identify potentially chronic offenders by criminal history, employment history, and substance abuse history and incarcerate them for long periods of time to reduce crime. Others argue that this promotes labeling, which could lead to more criminal behavior. Are labeling theorists correct? Does labeling potential chronic offenders as such and incarcerating them for an extended periods lead to more criminal behavior?

---

27. Roper v. Simmons, 543 U.S. 551 (2005).

28. International Centre for Prison Studies (2010, March 18). "Prison Brief—Highest to Lowest Rates," *World Prison Brief.* London: King's College London School of Law.

29. Peter Greenwood (1982). *Selective Incapacitation.* Santa Monica, CA: Rand Corporation.

30. Dean Champion (2001). *The American Dictionary of Criminal Justice.* 2nd Edition. Los Angeles, CA: Roxbury Publishing Company, 134.

31. Doris Mackenzie (2001, July). "Sentencing and Corrections in the 21st Century: Setting the Stage for the Future," https://www.ncjrs.gov/pdffiles1/nij/189106-2.pdf.

Deterrence

The goal of **deterrence** is to put an end to future criminal actions. Deterrence is accomplished on two levels:

General deterrence is the philosophy of punishment that promotes swift and certain punishment to discourage the criminal behavior of others.

a. *General Deterrence* pursues the goal of discouraging potential offenders through punishment of criminal offenders. The celerity, severity, and certainty of punishment are important factors related to general deterrence, which suggests that if individuals fear being caught and punished, they are unlikely to commit crime. Fear of punishment leads to a reduction in crime.[32]

Specific deterrence — The punishment of the offender to prevent future criminal behavior.

b. *Specific Deterrence* presumes that once the offender has been punished, he or she will not return to criminal activity because the punishment experience has been swift and severe.

Rehabilitation

Rehabilitation emphasizes the treatment of the offender rather than the punishment of the act. The goal of rehabilitation is to modify the offender's behavior to reduce the risk and occurrence of criminal behavior while encouraging a productive lifestyle. The emphasis on rehabilitation grew out of the progressive movement in the United States. Progressives were upper class, benevolent men and women who were opposed to institutionalizing the deviant, the delinquent, and the mentally ill. Reformers advocated searching for the causes of crime and curing crime, delinquency, and mental illness on a case-by-case basis. From this perspective, offenders should be treated with case-specific remedies.[33] Early initiatives associated with rehabilitation included probation, parole, and juvenile courts. Group counseling programs, diversion programs, drug treatment programs, and vocational educational programs all followed as reformers of the penal system continued their crusade to cure. Rehabilitation of offenders became the primary focus of the criminal justice system.[34]

---

32. Larry Siegel (2013). *Criminology: Theories, Patterns, and Typologies.* 11th Edition. Mason, OH: Wadsworth, Cengage Learning.

33. David Rothman (1980). *Conscience and Convenience: The Asylum and Its Alternatives in Progressive America.* Boston: Scott, Foresman.

34. Todd Clear, George Cole, and Michael Reisig (2010). *American Corrections. 10th Edition.* Mason, OH: Wadsworth Cengage.

> ### Critical Thinking Box 1.2
>
> How would you respond to the following statement?
>
> Community corrections programs are liberal solutions that do little to punish the offender and control and reduce crime. These programs treat criminals too leniently and are not effective in reducing crime and protecting society. Therefore, our policies must be driven by efforts to control crime through the effective use of punishment and not concerns for rehabilitation of the offender. We must "get tough" on crime and criminals. What is your position on this subject?

Strategies of Community Corrections

There are several different community-based corrections strategies.

Diversion

The diversion strategy permits the offender to participate in an alternative program and avoid formal processing. The alternative program may be treatment, counseling, educational, or other programs designed to influence behavior. It is often in the best interest of the offender and the community to avoid formal prosecution of the case.[35] Juvenile offenders, drug offenders, or the mentally ill who have committed minor offenses are candidates for diversion.

Probation

Probation is an alternative sentence to incarceration imposed by the court on a convicted offender or a person who has pled guilty to a crime. The offender remains in the community under supervision with conditions given by the court. By remaining in the community, the offender is able to support dependents, make restitution, maintain employment, and participate in treatment programs.

Intermediate Sanctions

Intermediate sanctions are punishments that fall in severity between prison and probation. These programs are more restrictive than probation but less

---

35. Schmalleger and Smykla (2013). *Corrections in the 21st Century*. Sixth Edition. New York, NY: McGraw-Hill.

severe and less expensive than prison.[36] Intermediate sanctions include intensive probation, electronic monitoring, home confinement, and shock incarceration. These programs are characterized by small caseload sizes, intensive surveillance and supervision, community service, restitution, curfews, and electronic monitoring.[37] They were created with the primary goals of reducing prison overcrowding and prison costs.

Parole

Discretionary parole is the original early release program. The inmate is released from prison prior to the completion of the prison term. In most states, after a person has served one-third of the prison term, he or she is eligible for release under parole supervision. Under the supervision of parole officers, the parolee must abide by conditions of parole and will be subject to revocation if the conditions of release are not followed.[38]

Unresolved Issues in Community Corrections

Even though community corrections have become a staple in the criminal justice system, there are unanswered questions associated with the administration of these programs.

The first issue is **sanction stacking**. Sanctions are stacked when a number of different punishments are heaped upon the offender. An offender may be given one year of jail time and three years of intensive probation, to be followed by 10 years of regular probation. In addition, the person will have monetary assessments including fines, supervision fees, and/or restitution. None of these punishments are standalone but are given in conjunction with other punishments. Some researchers indicate that this practice may be related an increase in technical violations.[39] A second question focuses on **net-widening**, which occurs when individuals who would not

> **Net-widening** is targeting someone for treatment or control that otherwise would not be targeted.

---

36. Joan Petersilia (1998). *Community Corrections: Probation, Parole, and Intermediate Sanctions*. Oxford: Oxford University Press.

37. Ibid.

38. Kathryn Morgan and Brent Smith (2005). "Parole Release Decisions Revisited: An Analysis of Parole Release Decisions for Violent Inmates in a Southeastern State," *Journal of Criminal Justice 33*: 277–287.

39. David May, Kevin Minor, Rick Ruddell, and Betsy Matthews (2008). *Corrections and the Criminal Justice System*. Burlington, MA: Jones & Bartlett Learning, 330.

have been targeted for a program are placed under social control. Austin and Krisberg (1982) suggest that many correctional alternatives, such as diversion programs and intermediate sanctions, have unintended consequences. They may create:

- Wider Nets: The correctional alternatives increase the number of people under state control. Often, these people would not have been subject to control.
- Stronger Nets: The alternatives increase the state's control over more people.
- Different Nets: Alternatives shift the control from one agency to another.[40]

Thirdly, many question the severity of these punishments. Community-based corrections are viewed as too lenient or little more than a "slap on the wrist" for offenders who have committed serious crimes.[41] Even offenders may view these punishments as "getting off." In an effort to convince a skeptical public that the justice system is tough on crime and criminals, criminal justice agencies may impose a number of very strict requirements, including curfews, random drug tests, and intensive surveillance. Finally, community-based corrections may be viewed as promoting bias in decision-making regarding who is selected for these programs. Race/ethnicity and social class bias may exist in the selection process for these programs. Racial and ethnic bias in the selection process is especially troubling. Black and Hispanic offenders are more likely to be incarcerated and less likely to be selected for participation in community-based corrections programs. Correctional data from 2012 indicate that blacks and Hispanics are disproportionately incarcerated in federal and state prisons in the United States. Thirty-three percent of those incarcerated were whites, 36% were black, and 22% were Hispanic; blacks and Hispanics represent approximately 13% and 15% of the U.S. population respectively. At the end of 2012, the Bureau of Justice Statistics reported that 54% of probationers in the United States were white; 31% were black and approximately 13% were Hispanic. This pattern has remained stable since 2000.[42] The pattern is similar for parole. Recent data by the Bureau of Justice Statistics indicate that in 2012, whites comprised 41% of the parole population, while blacks made up 40% of the parole

---

40. James Austin and Barry Krisberg (1982, July). "The Unmet Promise of Alternatives to Incarceration," *Crime and Delinquency* 28(3): 374–409.

41. Todd Clear and Harry Dammer (2000). *The Offender in the Community.* Belmont, CA: Wadsworth.

42. Laura M. Maruschak and Thomas P. Bonczar. *Probation and Parole in the United States, 2012.*

population and Hispanics comprise approximately 17% of the parole population in the United States.[43] Social class bias may be a problem associated with selection for community-based corrections programs. Cole and Dammer (2000) state that:

> Middle-class offenders tend to look better on paper and have a better chance of being admitted than someone from the underclass. Middle-class offenders can show that they can work, can pay restitution and have strong family ties. Therefore, they are good candidates for these programs.[44]

Exclusion of minorities and the lower class from participation in community-based programs may not be intentional but the unanticipated consequence of decision-makers selecting offenders that are most likely to succeed in community supervision. Black and Hispanic males are often less skilled, less educated, less likely to be employed, and less stable economically. Many have serious criminal histories and are more likely to commit more serious crimes. These characteristics make them less suitable for participation in these discretionary programs. Therefore, unanticipated bias follows the natural selection of candidates who are most likely to succeed.[45]

Recap and Review

- The corrections system is an important sub-system of the criminal justice system; it carries out the sentence that has been given by the court.
- The number of offenders supervised in the community continues to increase each year. The majority of those supervised in the community are on probation and/or parole.
- Community corrections programs manage and supervise offenders in the community in order to reduce prison overcrowding.
- The two major purposes of punishment are the punishment and incapacitation offenders and the prevention of crime. The punishment orientation emphasizes increased use of incarceration, mandatory sentencing, less judicial discretion in sentencing, abolishing early release for inmates, and getting tough on juvenile criminals.

---

43. Ibid., p. 10.
44. Clear and Dammer, p. 41.
45. Clear and Dammer, 2000, p. 40.

- Prevention of crime emphasizes rehabilitation of the offender and deterrence of future criminal behavior. Probation, parole, juvenile court, and counseling programs are examples of rehabilitation programs.
- Community corrections strategies include probation, parole, intermediate sanctions, diversion, and early release programs.
- Community corrections programs have often been criticized for net-widening, which refers to giving some form of social control to an offender who would not otherwise be a part of the system. The program increases the state's formal control over more people.
- Community corrections programs have been criticized for being too lenient on convicted offenders and promoting a race/ethnic and class bias in the selection process for these programs.

Questions for Review

1. What is the role of the corrections sub-system in the criminal justice system?
2. Distinguish between institutional corrections and community corrections.
3. What is the role of community corrections in the criminal justice system?
4. What are major issues surrounding the use of community corrections?
5. Briefly describe the Martinson study and indicate its impact on rehabilitation and the rehabilitative ideal.
6. Identify and briefly describe the strategies of community corrections. How do intermediate sanctions differ from other community corrections programs?
7. What are the types of bias that might exist in the selection process for community corrections programs?

Questions for Discussion

Please use these questions for discussion. Choose the response that you think is most appropriate and explain your reasoning. Why are the other responses not appropriate?

1. Which of the following would *not* be compatible with rehabilitation?
   A. Placing an offender in a drug treatment program to deal with drug addiction problems.
   B. Recommending to the judge that the offender be given counseling for psychological problems that are associated with his offense.

    C. Referring an offender to a job training program to assist him or her in securing employment.

    D. Recommending that the offender be sent to prison to serve 100% of his or her sentence to "pay the debt to society."

2. "As an offender, you must pay your debt to society; you are going to get what you deserve." This statement would be consistent with what purpose of punishment?

    A. retribution

    B. incapacitation

    C. rehabilitation

    D. deterrence

3. In recent years, there has been an attack on rehabilitation as the public demands tougher punishment for criminals. Probation and parole have been viewed as too lenient or just a "slap on the wrist." As an advocate for community corrections in general and probation and parole in particular, how would you convince citizens that probation is really punishment for offenders? Which of the following statements would support your argument?

    A. Probationers are subjected to random drug tests, unannounced home and employment visits, and more control and enforcement of the conditions of probation.

    B. Many jurisdictions have dropped curfews as unnecessary and unenforceable.

    C. Because of limited resources and larger caseloads, there is less opportunity to provide adequate supervision for probationers.

    D. Because of overworked courts and crowded court dockets, judges are requesting that technical and even some new arrest violations be handled in the probation department.

4. You overhear a discussion about crime in your city. As they continue to talk, one person says that they should lock up criminals instead of leaving them in the community to commit more crime. Knowing that you are a criminal justice major at the local university, they proceed to ask you why offenders, even first-time offenders, are allowed to remain in the community in community programs. You respond by saying that:

    A. You agree with them; all convicted offenders should be locked up.

    B. Community corrections programs provide supervision while saving the state money. It is cheaper to supervise offenders in the community.

C. Since prisons are so expensive, community supervision should become the norm.

D. Community corrections programs do little to punish offenders and should be abolished.

5. You have been asked about the cost savings of community corrections and institutional corrections. As you speak to a community group, it is evident that they are not sure about how much community corrections save in supervision costs. What is your response?

A. There is really no difference in the cost savings for community and institutional corrections.

B. It is actually more expensive to supervise offenders in the community than in confined institutions.

C. In many states, the cost of community supervision is less than $2.00 a day compared to up to $100.00 for institutional supervision. As the prison population ages, there is also the cost of medical care.

D. Even though institutional confinement is more expensive, it is worth confining violent, property, and drug offenders and protecting the community.

Chapter 2

History and Development of Probation and Parole

History and Development of Probation

Probation is an alternative to incarceration in which the court delays the imposition of the sentence and places the offender under the supervision of the probation department. The court imposes conditions of probation to supervise the probationer. Probation is associated with the rehabilitation philosophy that refocused punishment to emphasize rehabilitation and reform of the offender rather than punishment of the offense. Although the modern era of probation began in the United States in the nineteenth century, there were several practices that served as antecedents of probation.[1]

---

1. Edward Latessa and Harry Allen (1999). *Corrections in the Community*. Cincinnati, OH: Anderson Publishing Company.

Precursors of Probation

Three historical practices served as precursors to modern probation: benefit of clergy, judicial reprieve, and recognizance.

- **Benefit of clergy.** This practice originated in twelfth-century England, when most crimes were punishable by death. It was used to lessen the severity of criminal law and exempt clerics from capital punishment. Clerics who had committed serious crimes, particularly rape and burglary, were exempt from prosecution in secular courts. Instead, their cases were tried in ecclesiastical courts where they would receive leniency. Initially, clerics had to appear before the secular court wearing ecclesiastical dress in order to plead benefit of clergy. This was later replaced by a literacy test that required defendants to read verse 1 of Psalm 51 ("Miserere me"), which came to be known as the "neck verse," because it literally saved the neck of the offender from hanging, the likely sentence. Gradually, the practice was extended to non-clerics who could prove their literacy by reciting a passage from this psalm. Many memorized passages, causing the practice to lose its meaning. Later, improvements in the criminal law and criminal sanctions and widespread abuse of the practice eventually led to benefit of clergy being abolished.[2]

- **Judicial reprieve.** Used in English courts, the judge would grant a temporary suspension of the sentence to allow the defendant time to appeal to the crown for a pardon. What started as a temporary suspension often became permanent because the sentence was usually never imposed. Today, the practice is largely limited to death penalty cases where defendants are given additional time for appeals.[3]

- **Recognizance.** In a Boston municipal court, Judge Peter Thatcher originated the practice of recognizance. He released a female defendant "upon her own recognizance" for her appearance in court whenever it was needed. The practice became law in Massachusetts

---

2. John Briggs, Christopher Harrison, Agnes McInnes & David Vincent (1996). *Crime & Punishment in England: An Introductory History*. Abingdon, OX: Routledge.

3. Dean Champion (2001). *The American Dictionary of Criminal Justice*. Los Angeles, CA: Roxbury Publishing.

in 1837.[4] What made it important was the implied supervision of the court. The court was responsible for knowing the actions and whereabouts of the defendant.[5] In the 1960s, there was renewed interest in the practice by bail reform advocates, who pointed out that the existing money bail system discriminates against the poor, encourages detained defendants to plead guilty, and results in harsher sentences for those who are not released on bail.[6] Believing that most defendants do appear for trial, bail reform proponents proposed release on recognizance as an alternative to the money bail system. The Manhattan Bail Project was the first bail reform experiment with release on recognizance. Because of its success, Congress passed the Bail Reform Act in 1966 that proclaimed release on recognizance as the principal form of pre-trial release.[7]

Manhattan Bail Project — Experiment in bail reform that introduced and implemented release on own recognizance.

John Augustus: Father of Probation

In the United States, John Augustus first used the term "probation" to refer to the practice of bailing offenders out of court followed by a period of supervised living in the community. The work of John Augustus ushered in the modern era of probation in the United States and laid the foundation for our modern probation system.[8]

Augustus, a Boston shoemaker, approached the judge in a Boston courtroom and requested permission to bail a defendant out of jail to supervise him for in the community and return to court to report on his progress. He was granted permission, and upon the return to court, the defendant received a fine instead of a commitment to Boston's House of Corrections. This began Augustus' work as the first probation officer — a volunteer.[9] For almost 20 years (1841–1859),

---

4. Todd Clear and Harry Dammer (2000). *The Offender in the Community*. Belmont, CA: Wadsworth, 57.

5. Ibid.

6. Samuel Walker, Cassia Spohn, and Miriam DeLone (2012). *The Color of Justice: Race, Ethnicity and Crime in America*. Belmont, CA: Wadsworth Cengage Learning.

7. Wayne Thomas (1976). *Bail Reform in America*. Berkeley, CA: University of California Press.

8. Charles Lindner (2007, December). "Thatcher, Augustus and Hill: The Path to Statutory Probation in the United States and England," *Federal Probation 71*(3):36–41.

9. Howard Abadinsky (1997). *Probation and Parole*, 30.

Augustus supervised approximately 2,000 offenders in the community.[10] Abadinsky (1997) notes that there are several aspects of his work have been retained as basic aspects of the probation practice. He:

1. Investigated the backgrounds of those he considered helping.
2. Took into account such factors as previous character of the defendant, the defendant's age, and the influences which surrounded him.
3. Kept extensive case records on each defendant, which he submitted to court.[11]

In 1878, Massachusetts passed a probation law authorizing the mayor of Boston to hire the first probation officer, Captain Savage, who was supervised by the superintendent of police. The officer's primary responsibility was to investigate cases and recommend probation sentences for all who could be reformed without punishment.[12]

Development of Probation

Vermont, Rhode Island, and Maryland followed the lead of Massachusetts by passing similar probation laws. Rhode Island's legislation placed restrictions on who could be granted probation. Offenders who had committed offenses of treason, murder, robbery, rape, or burglary were excluded from probation supervision. This model is currently used by most states in granting probation.[13] By the early 1900s, most states had passed laws that provided for the creation of probation departments. The development of a juvenile court in Cook County, Illinois, in 1899 influenced the rapid spread of probation throughout the United States. The juvenile court hired juvenile probation officers to investigate cases referred by the court. In the early 1900s, New York, Pennsylvania, Virginia, and Texas implemented adult probation programs to provide probation services for adults.[14]

These first probation officers were either volunteers or part-time workers who were paid extremely low salaries. For the few paid positions, probation officer appointments were often political. They worked primarily with juveniles, had no offices, and used their homes as the place where probationers reported. These officers received little or no training to perform their duties.[15]

---

10. Dean Champion (2008). *Probation, Parole and Community Corrections.* Upper Saddle: NJ: Pearson Publishing.

11. Howard Abadinsky (1997). *Probation and Parole: Theory & Practice.* 6th Edition. Upper Saddle River, NJ: Prentice Hall.

12. Champion, *Probation, Parole and Community Corrections*, pp. 170–171.

13. See Abadinsky (1997). *Probation and Parole: Theory and Practice*, 30.

14. Ibid., 32–33.

15. Ibid., 33.

Development of Federal Probation

The first federal probation law was introduced in Congress in 1909. It was not until 1925 that the federal probation legislation became law. The Probation Act of 1925 authorized courts to suspend the imposition of a sentence and place the offender on probation with appropriate conditions and for a specified length of supervision. Probation services were initially administered by the attorney general in the Department of Justice. The superintendent of the Federal Bureau of Prisons was responsible for direct supervision of federal probation officers. In 1940, administration and supervision were transferred to the Administrative Office of the U.S. Courts.[16] Decades later, President Ronald Reagan signed the Pre-trial Services Act of 1982 that authorized (a) the expansion of 10 experimental pre-trial programs and (b) the creation of separate pre-trial services offices through the probation department. Most districts chose to develop pretrial services out of probation agencies, thus creating a combined federal probation and pretrial services system to save money.[17]

The Administration of Probation

The administration of probation varies from state to state and often between jurisdictions within states. Probation may be administered in a variety of ways. These include juvenile probation, city probation, county probation, state probation, state combined, and federal probation. The most common model for the administration of juvenile probation is through the local juvenile court. However, in recent years, some states now administer juvenile probation services through a statewide agency.[18] At the federal level, U.S. district courts administer probation and pre-trial services. Federal probation services enjoy a greater degree of uniformity across probation agencies.[19] The third method of administration is county level administration. Surveys

County probation is a method of probation administration where each county in the state develops probation departments under state guidelines. These counties have more autonomy over budgets and programming with less bureaucratic control.

---

16. See "History of Probation and Pretrial Services," http://www.uscourts.gov/Federal Courts/ProbationPretrialServices/History.aspx.

17. Ibid.

18. Patricia Torbet (1996, March). "Juvenile Probation: The Workhorse of the Juvenile Justice System," *Juvenile Justice Bulletin*. U.S. Department of Justice, Office of Justice Programs.

19. Abadinsky, *Probation and Parole: Theory and Practice*, 34.

indicate that this is the most common method of probation administration at the state level. Under guidelines established by the state, a county operates its own probation agency. There are major advantages to this method of administration. First, probation departments have greater control over budgets. Rather than sending supervision fees to a central state agency that disburses the funds, probation departments keep these funds. Second, programming can be implemented more easily because there is a shorter line of bureaucratic control. Finally, probation departments can more easily adapt to change.[20]

The **state method of administration** involves one state central agency that administers probation services throughout the state, and the **state combined method** stipulates that probation be administered by a statewide agency that administers both probation and parole services. In some states, such as Alabama, the Board of Probation and Parole administers probation and parole services throughout the state. Studies of this administrative model, especially those that examine fee collection practices, conclude that many probation departments throughout the state are concerned that they have no control over fees that they collect. Fees are collected from probation and parole clients but sent to the central administering agency.[21]

The **state method of probation** administration is the supervision of all probation departments in a state by a central governmental state agency. There is less autonomy for individual jurisdictions.

Probation in the Twenty-First Century —
Privatizing Probation

In 1975, Florida initiated the Salvation Army Misdemeanor Probation Program to supervise misdemeanor probationers.[22] In the 1990s, some states began to use private probation agencies to supervise low-risk and low-needs nonviolent offenders. Because of diminishing resources and increasing caseloads, jurisdictions turned to private probation. As resources became more scarce and probation departments were faced with "doing more with less," many states and municipalities turned to private organizations to supervise misdemeanor offenders. Although programs operated differently across states, general guidelines for the operation of private probation programs and service agreements

---

20. Ibid.

21. Kathryn Morgan (1995, Spring). "A Study of Probation and Parole Supervision Fee Collection in Alabama," *Criminal Justice Review 20*(1): 44–54.

22. Charles Lindquist (1980). "The Private Sector in Corrections: Contracting Probation Services from Community Organizations," *Federal Probation 44*: 58–64.

with private agencies usually specified details about officer qualifications and training, reporting, fee collection, and services to be provided.[23]

As use of these programs increased, there were increasing criticisms of private probation agencies. Although states were required to follow guidelines, review of many programs revealed that often these programs lacked standard guidelines or oversight.[24] Common criticisms of these programs include (a) illegally extending sentences in order to continue the collection of probation fees, (b) trolling or adding high surcharges and issuing arrest warrants for defendants who can't pay, (c) lack of educational and training requirements, and (d) discretion and inconsistencies in the application of treatment services.[25] Schmalleger and Smykla (2013) point out that the American Probation and Parole Association is hesitant to endorse the widespread use of private probation services. At the same time, the APPA recognizes that private probation services can provide new technologies and specialized services to assist probation officers in the supervision of offenders. By adhering to the same standards, laws, and regulations as probation departments, private probation agencies can assist probation departments in effectively providing services, supervising offenders and protecting the public.[26]

History and Development of Parole

Parole is the conditional release of prisoners prior to the expiration of the prison term. Unlike probation, the offender spends time in prison prior to release. Similar to probation, parole has a number of historical antecedents including transportation to America, transportation to Australia, and the ticket-of-leave system.

Transportation to America

In early seventeenth-century Great Britain, there was a dramatic increase in crime and unemployment rates. At the same time, colonial America was

---

23. Christine S. Schloss and Leann Alarid (2007, September). "Standards in the Privatization of Probation Services," *Criminal Justice Review* 2(3): 233–245.

24. Ibid., 242.

25. Ibid., 242.

26. Frank Schmalleger and John Smykla (2013). *Corrections in the 21st Century*. New York, NY: McGraw-Hill, 106.

experiencing a shortage of labor to work in the new colonies. As a result, English prisoners were given a choice of execution or transportation to the New World. Many of these offenders chose the more humane alternative and were transported by merchant companies who were paid by the English government. For over 150 years, English prisoners were pardoned by the English government and transported to America, where they became indentured servants. Initially, there were no conditions attached, but felons would avoid transportation or would return to England.[27] The Transportation Act of 1718 imposed conditions on the pardon and standardized transportation. The act specified that the pardon would be nullified if convicts failed to comply with the rules and regulations.[28] **Transportation to America** continued until about the 1780s. The American Revolution and England's loss of the war ended the transportation program to America.[29]

Transportation to Australia

After the transportation to America practice ended, England again experienced an increasing crime rate and crowded convict population. Following the end of the transportation program to America, **transportation to Australia** was implemented.[30]

After visiting the penal colony in Australia, **Alexander Maconochie** wrote a report that was highly critical of the prison conditions and the treatment of convicts at the prison. In his report, he suggested that cruelty to prisoners makes them bitter and resentful. In 1840, Maconochie was appointed as superintendent of the British Penal Colony in Australia. He introduced a number of reforms that had long-term effects on corrections. His philosophy of punishment was based on the idea of reforming the criminal: punish the convict for the past, but train him for the future. He opposed flat sentences and advocated sentences that were open-ended (we know this as the indeterminate sentence); and he established a system of marks where inmates could earn early release through good behavior and hard work. His reforms were designed to make prison life more humanitarian and give convicts some hope of release rather than serving flat sentences. However, his superiors ac-

---

27. Howard Abadinsky (1997). *Probation and Parole*. 6th Edition. Upper Saddle, NJ: Prentice Hall, 209.

28. Dean Champion (2005). *Corrections in the United States: A Contemporary Perspective*. 4th Edition. Upper Saddle, NJ: Prentice Hall.

29. Ibid.

30. Abadinsky, 210.

cused him of "coddling criminals" and rejected his reforms. He was removed from his post but returned to England and continued to advocate for penal reform. During his service as superintendent, over 1,400 convicts were released; many of them did not re-offend. He is known in corrections as the "Father of Parole."[31]

Ticket-of-Leave

In 1853, England passed the Penal Servitude Act, which allowed convicts to be released on a **ticket-of-leave** under the supervision of police. **Sir Walter Crofton** became the administrator of the Irish Prison System. Similar in philosophy to Maconochie, Crofton believed that sentences and time served in some way should be related to rehabilitation.[32] In 1854, he implemented the ticket-of-leave program in Ireland. This Irish system consisted of four stages that ultimately culminated in release of the prisoner: (1) strict imprisonment and forced solitary confinement; (2) placement in a special prison to work with other inmates earning marks to progress to the third stage; (3) transportation to an open institution where he could earn release on a ticket-of-leave; and (4) release on the ticket-of-leave under the supervision of police who would help the released offender seek employment.[33]

Parole in the United States: The Elmira Reformatory

The **Elmira Reformatory** opened in 1876 as America's first parole system. **Zebulon Brockway**, Elmira's first superintendent, was responsible for implementing the first parole system.[34] Brockway recommended that young male offenders be given indeterminate sentences not to exceed the maximum recommended by law. He implemented a "mark system" where the

> **Zebulon Brockway**, a penologist from Detroit, Michigan, attempted to implement the indeterminate sentence for first-time offenders. Even though the Michigan Legislature passed the statute, the courts later reversed the legislation. He later established the **Elmira Reformatory** for adult males in New York, where he introduced the indeterminate sentence. Because of his success at Elmira, the use of the indeterminate sentence spread to other states.

---

31. Dean Champion (2008). *Probation, Parole and Community Corrections*. 6th Edition. Upper Saddle, NJ: Prentice Hall/Pearson.

32. Abadinsky, *Probation and Parole*, 210.

33. Dean Champion (2008). *Probation, Parole and Community Corrections*. 6th Edition. Upper Saddle, NJ: Prentice Hall/Pearson.

34. Abadinsky, *Probation and Parole*, 212.

accumulation of marks could be used for rations or early release. The amount of time served was dependent upon the number of marks accumulated by the prisoner. Prisoners could receive marks for good conduct, progress in academic and vocational training, and good work performance. Once the inmate accumulated enough marks, the inmate was conditionally released by the reformatory's Board of Managers. Released inmates were supervised for six-month parole periods by appointed guardians. Parolees were required to report to the guardian once monthly and give an account of their conduct and situation. If there was actual or potential criminal behavior, the parolee could be returned to prison. By 1900, the foundation for parole in the United States had been laid with three underlying principles: (a) indeterminate sentences, (b) reduction of prison sentences based on good behavior, and (c) release of the parolee and supervision in the community. The use of parole as a correctional practice spread throughout the United States in the early 1900s, and by 1944, all states had implemented some form of conditional release.[35]

Critical Thinking Box 2.1

Historically, parole has always been associated with the rehabilitative ideal and the benefits that it provides for the restoration and rehabilitation of the offender. Despite parole being abolished in many states and attacked as ineffective in others, parole has persisted. Messinger and other criminologists point out that there are several non-rehabilitative benefits of parole that are attractive to managers and policy makers. How would you address those who argue that the non-rehabilitative aspects of parole rather than rehabilitative benefits justify the existence of parole?[36]

Parole in the Twenty-First Century

While there was opposition to parole as early as the 1930s, the increased focus on punishment in the 1980s and 1990s brought more criticism of discretionary parole. The Federal Sentencing Reform portion of the Comprehensive Crime Control Act of 1984 stipulated that discretionary parole at the federal level would be phased out. By 1992, discretionary parole at the federal level had been phased out. Twelve states followed the federal government in abol-

---

35. Ibid.

36. Sheldon Messinger (1985). "The Foundations of Parole in California," *Law and Society Review 19*: 69–106.

ishing parole. An additional four states abolished parole for certain violent offenses. In these states, released offenders are supervised under mandatory supervised release or controlled release.[37]

Criminologists identify three reasons that states abolished discretionary
parole:

a. The failure of indeterminate sentencing and rehabilitation to reduce
   recidivism rates.
b. Abolishing parole was compatible with the ideology of the "get tough
   on crime" movement.
c. The lack of transparency in parole board members.[38]

Morgan and Smith (2005) point out that discretionary parole boards have
come under attack because they are unclear about the criteria used in decision-
making or the variables that influence those decisions.[39]

Distinguishing between Probation and Parole

There has been a proliferation of programs designed to be community correctional programs. Probation and parole are two of those programs. Often,
they are viewed as identical programs even though they are very different. Probation is an alternative to corrections. During the sentencing phase, the Judge
decides to delay or suspend the imposition of the sentence and place the individual on probation for a specified period of time. Probation conditions reg-
ulate the behavior of the probationer, and the Probation Department enforces
these conditions. The Judge and probationer sign a probation order specifying the conditions of probation. This probation order constitutes a contractual
agreement between the court and the probationer. As such, probation is "judicial" because the probationer remains under the jurisdiction of the court
while being supervised. All amendments to probation supervision must go
back to the court from which the case originated. Violations are also handled
by the court. If the probationer fails to abide by the conditions of the contract,
he may be referred back to the courts for revocation proceedings.

While parole also represents conditional release, it is only granted after
an offender has served a specified period, usually one-third of the sentence,

---

37. Schmalleger and Smykla, *Corrections in the 21st Century*, 302.

38. Ibid.

39. Kathryn Morgan and Brent Smith (2005). "Parole Release Decisions Revisited: An
Analysis of Parole Release Decisions for Violent Inmates in a Southeastern State," *Journal of
Criminal Justice 33*: 277–287.

in prison. After meeting the time served requirement, the inmate is considered for parole and the case is brought before a parole board. If the parole board deems the inmate ready to return to society, members of the board will vote to release the inmate with rules and regulations known as conditions of parole. Unlike probation, parole is an administrative matter, where the Board of Pardons and Parole has jurisdiction over the inmate. Changes to parole conditions and violations of those conditions are handled by the parole board.

Critical Thinking Box 2.2

Advocates of probation and parole argue that these programs have both rehabilitation and deterrence functions. How would you support this argument?

Recap and Review

- Probation is an alternative to incarceration in which the court delays the imposition of the sentence and places the offender under the supervision of the probation department.
- There are historical practices that laid the foundation for our modern probation system. These historical antecedents include benefit of clergy, judicial reprieve, and release on recognizance.
- John Augustus supervised offenders and returned to the courts with reports of their progress.
- Augustus conducted offender background checks; considered factors such as age, previous behavior and the offender's environment; and kept extensive records for each offender.
- Rhode Island was the first state to restrict which offenders could be granted probation.
- The Probation Act of 1925 authorized courts to suspend the imposition of a sentence and place the offender under probation supervision.
- Administration of probation services varies across states and regions. It may be administered by juvenile courts, municipal courts, by the county, or by a state agency that administers both probation and parole services.

- Historical antecedents of parole in Great Britain and the United States include transportation to America, transportation to Australia, and the ticket-of-leave program. Alexander Maconochie is recognized as the Father of Parole.
- Elmira Reformatory is the first parole system in the United States, and Zebulon Brockway was the prison's first superintendent.
- Probation and parole are often used synonymously even though they are different correctional programs.
- Probation is an alternative to incarceration that allows the offender to serve the sentence in the community under the supervision of the probation department. Violation of probation conditions may result in the loss of the conditional release and the sentence imposed.
- Parole is granted by a parole board after the convicted offender has served time in prison, usually one-third of the sentence given in court. Decisions to parole are made by the parole board. After gaining early release, the parolee is supervised in the community by the parole department. Violation of parole may result in the loss of the conditional release and a return to prison.

Questions for Review

1. What are the historical precursors of probation and what features of these historical practices resemble modern probation practice?
2. Describe the work of John Augustus and the features of his supervision practices that influenced modern probation.
3. Identify the ways that probation may be administered.
4. Describe the transportation programs to America and Australia and the ticket-of-leave systems.
5. "Parole is a privilege and not a right." How would you explain that statement?
6. Explain the difference between mandatory release and discretionary release.
7. Probation is a judicial function and parole is an administrative function. How would you explain that statement?

Questions for Discussion

Please use these questions for discussion. Choose the response that you think is most appropriate and explain your reasoning. Why are the other responses not appropriate?

1. An alternative to incarceration that allows an offender to remain under supervision in the community with court-ordered conditions for which violation may result in revocation and the imposing of the sentence. This describes:

   A. parole
   B. commutation
   C. probation
   D. pardon

2. As director of community relations for your probation and parole agency, you are addressing a community action group that has raised the question, "Why probation and parole?" A member of the group points out that there are approximately four million persons under probation supervision. This group wants to know why there is extensive use of probation given the criticism of community-based corrections programs. Which of the following arguments would you make to this group?

   A. The overcrowding and high costs of incarceration make probation a reasonable alternative.
   B. Probation is more punitive than prison, so probation is a more severe alternative.
   C. Probation, as an alternative to incarceration, provides employment for many people who supervise probationers. By providing employment to many college graduates and many others, the economy benefits.
   D. Although probation does not reduce recidivism, it is unavoidable for the criminal justice system.

3. If you were making an argument about the advantages of probation, which of the following statements would *not* be included?

   A. Probation supervision is less expensive than incarceration.
   B. Releasing dangerous offenders in the community increases the risk of harm to the community.
   C. Probation allows offenders under supervision to be employed.
   D. It helps to avoid further criminalization of the offender.

4. Your director of probation and parole services has asked you to write a concept paper indicating the value of volunteers to probation and parole agencies. Which of the following arguments would you use to justify implementing a volunteer program for your agency?

A. Volunteer programs provide a way for well-meaning but bored upper-class housewives to do something with their time.

B. Volunteer programs give officers the opportunity to train citizen volunteers when they have little or no work to do.

C. Volunteer programs can train workers to replace ineffective or disgruntled officers.

D. Volunteer programs can assist in providing more necessary services to clients.

5. You have recently been appointed as the community outreach representative for your probation and parole agency. In your meeting with a community group, there seems to be some confusion about the difference between probation and parole. You realize that before you can talk to the group, you must explain the difference between the two. What do you tell them?

A. You tell them that there is no difference between the two — they are two different names for the same correctional program.

B. You tell them that it is too complicated and that they would not understand.

C. You take your time to explain that probation is an alternative to a prison sentence while parole is the release from prison prior to the expiration of the sentence. Both require supervision and conditions for the offender.

D. You explain that probation and parole are alternatives to prison that require the inmate to follow conditions to stay out of prison.

Chapter 3

The Presentence Investigation Report

Key Terms
  Gardner v. Florida
  Presentence investigation
  Private presentence investigation
  Williams v. New York

Learning Objectives
1. Describe the functions of the presentence investigation report.
2. Outline the history of the presentence investigation report.
3. Identify the correct form and content of a presentence investigation report.
4. Summarize the issues related to the presentence investigation report.

Functions of the Presentence Investigation Report

The presentence investigation (PSI) report is a document prepared by the probation department and used by the judge for sentencing purposes in felony criminal cases. The presentence investigation report uncovers circumstances that might increase or decrease the harshness of the sentence. Prepared after the defendant's conviction, the major goal of the PSI report is to provide objective, factually accurate information to the court for sentencing and other matters related to the disposition of the case. Whether conviction is obtained through plea-bargaining or trial, the **presentence investigation** is often conducted on instructions from the court. The PSI may be prepared within 30–60 days following conviction. According to the Administrative Office of the Courts (2006):

> The aim of the presentence investigation is to provide a timely, accurate, objective, and comprehensive report to the court. The report should have enough information to assist the court in making a fair

sentencing decision and to assist corrections and community corrections officials in managing offenders under their supervision.[1]

The PSI has several important functions. First, the PSI serves to assist the judge in making an informed decision regarding an appropriate sentence for the case. Second, the PSI assists probation officers with monitoring the offender's behavior if he or she is placed on probation. Third, it assists prison officials in prison programming and the parole board in supervision.[2]

The PSI through History

Growing out of the Positive School's individualized approach to dealing with the offender, the PSI has played a significant role in the sentencing process. The PSI originated with the work of John Augustus, who believed that law should assume the responsibility of reforming criminals to prevent crime, not only punishing them. As a volunteer probation officer, Augustus investigated offenders' past background, social history, and criminal history. Based on his investigation and report, Augustus made recommendations in the sentencing hearing regarding release. If granted release, he would provide money for bail.[3] With the introduction of the indeterminate sentencing structure, use of the PSI increased, making it a very valuable tool to assist judges in the sentencing process. Correctional personnel and parole boards use the PSI to develop individualized treatment programs for inmates and to evaluate that inmate's readiness for release back into the community.

In the early 1900s, social worker Mary Richmond and psychiatrist William Healy suggested an extensive investigation of offenders' backgrounds (a) to understand the offender's behavior before going to court and (b) to develop an individualized treatment plan for the offender. They suggested that this comprehensive investigation report should include family history, environmental and moral development, social data, physical and mental conditions, psychological data, social data, work history, religious affiliations, education, relations with others and community agencies, legal history and delinquency record for juveniles, and a case narrative that summarizes the information in the re-

---

1. Administrative Office of the United States Courts (2006). *The Presentence Investigation Report.*

2. Howard Abadinsky (2008). *Probation and Parole.* Englewood Cliffs, NJ: Prentice-Hall, Inc.

3. Center on Juvenile and Criminal Justice. "The History of the Pre-sentence Investigation Report," www.cjcj.org.

port.[4] In 1943, the Administrative Office of the United States Courts published the first manual detailing the appropriate content and format for the presentence investigation report. Later, in 1965, the office published a manual specifying the content, format, and procedures for conducting the investigation at the state and federal levels.[5]

After critics pointed out that those assessments by probation officers were overly influenced by extralegal factors, the emphasis shifted to legal factors. Factors surrounding the crime and offender's criminal history became more important than race, gender, and social class.[6] With the implementation of the Federal Sentencing Reform Act of 1984, sentencing shifted from indeterminate to determinate structures, creating less need for the PSI report and changing its format to comply with sentencing guidelines.[7] Under new determinate sentencing guidelines, an offense-based presentence investigation report is used to impose a pre-determined fixed sentence for punishment rather than rehabilitation. With the implementation of new sentencing guidelines, the presentence investigation report is a much shorter version of the PSI report and focuses on offense seriousness and criminal history to determine the sentence.[8]

Despite the transformations over the past decades, the presentence investigation report remains an essential document in the judicial process that aids in sentencing, correctional programming, and evaluation of an inmate's readiness for parole release.

Structuring the PSI Report: Form and Content

Over the years, the presentence investigation report has taken many different forms. Because the PSI is subject to the laws of the state or jurisdiction, the form, structure, and content of the PSI vary across states and jurisdictions. Whatever the form or structure of the PSI, the goal is to provide comprehen-

---

4. R. M. Carter (1978). *Prescriptive Package: Presentence Report Handbook.* Washington, DC: U.S. Government Printing Office, No. 027-0000577-2.

5. Ibid.

6. Donald Black (1976). *The Behavior of Law*; Stanton Wheeler, David Weisburd, and Nancy Bode (1987). "Sentencing the White Collar Offender: Rhetoric and Reality," *American Sociological Review 47*: 641–659.

7. Administrative Office of the United States Courts (2006). "The Presentence Investigation Report."

8. Dean Champion (2008). *Probation, Parole and Community Corrections.* Upper Saddle, NJ: Pearson, 146.

sive information to assist in the court's determination of a sentence and other matters. The PSI usually contains the following information.

Introductory Case Information

- Name
- Sex
- Marital Status
- Age
- Date of Birth
- Race, Offense
- Presiding Judge
- Name of Court — Docket Number
- Defense Attorney, Prosecuting Attorney
- Co-Defendants

Defendant's Case and Personal History

Official Version

These are the facts of the case taken from the police report. This section summarizes the details and circumstances of the offense.

Defendant's Version

Defendants are given the opportunity to provide their versions of the offense. Including the defendant's versions answers several crucial questions for the court:

- Does the defendant accept responsibility for his or her actions?
- What is the attitude of the defendant towards the offense, the victim, and the criminal justice process?

Victim Impact Statement

Victims are interviewed to provide some insight into the impact of the offense on their lives. Some jurisdictions have eliminated the Victim Impact Statement from the body of the presentence report since victims have the opportunity to speak at the sentencing hearing.

Criminal History

Juvenile History: This section includes offenses committed and case dispositions while the defendant was a juvenile.

Adult History: Listing of offender's offenses and dispositions. The court is especially interested in two things: (a) evidence of violent and drug-related behavior; and (b) previous incarcerations (could indicate that this person is not capable of being rehabilitated). This section should list other charges that might be pending.

Social History

Family History

Parents: The investigator seeks information regarding parental past or present criminal behavior and parents' relationship with offender.

Siblings: Is there evidence of criminality? What is the relationship with offender?

Marital Status: Description of the defendant's marital status as married, single (separated or divorced), co-habitating, or single never married. If married or living with someone, describes the adjustment, including problems.

Educational History

What is the highest level of educational attainment? Identifies adjustment issues in school, including problems, suspensions, and expulsions.

Employment History

The report should describe the defendant's employment history: places of employment, dates, nature of work, and reason for leaving. A sporadic employment history or chronic unemployment provides an insight into the defendant's sense of responsibility. There should also be some description of occupational skills or the lack of skills.

Physical and Mental Health

Descriptions of physical health and any health problems should be included. Description of mental health should include indications of emotional disorders or dysfunctions, substance abuse, treatment for mental illness, retardation, suicide attempts, and other mental health problems.

Financial History

This section provides a snapshot of the defendant's financial stability. The focus is on assets (what he or she owns) and liabilities (what he or she owes).

Narrative

The probation officer's narrative is a crucial component of the PSI report. It provides the officer's summary and evaluation or diagnosis of the offender's case along with sentencing and treatment recommendations. The narrative section includes three areas: Summary and Evaluation, Sentencing Recommendation, and Recommendations for Treatment.

The Summary and Evaluation section summarizes the information contained within the report. For example, the following information might be included in a summary for Mary:

> Mary is a 22-year-old white female who has been convicted of aggravated assault. She shows remorse for her actions and accepts responsibility for her behavior. She has above-average intelligence. She has maintained stable employment.

Recommendations

Sentencing Recommendations

In addition to the information contained in the report, the probation officer must consider other things before deciding to recommend either probation or incarceration. Factors for consideration might include the dangerousness of the offender, the attitude of the offender towards the offense, the victim, the defendant's emotional and mental ability to participate in the supervision process, and the person's attitude towards a probation sentence. The probation officer recommends a sentence with some justification for that recommendation.

Treatment Recommendations

The probation officer makes recommendations that will become the treatment plan for the offender while serving the sentence. Recommendations may be made for educational/vocational training, attendance at AA meetings, participation in counseling programs, curfew, or changing living arrangements.

Current Controversies and Legal Decisions

Disclosure

One controversy surrounding the use of the PSI relates to disclosure or confidentiality. Prior to 1975, the presentence investigation report was confidential and the contents of the report were only available to the judge. Probation officers who prepared reports were concerned that those being interviewed were less likely to be open and honest if there was anxiety about the defendant having access to the PSI report and its contents.[9] There were safety concerns related to victims, witnesses, and confidential informants if the report was given to the offender. Defense attorneys argued that failure to disclose the contents of the report to the defendant and defense counsel violated the due process rights of the defendant. Since the report contains information that is hearsay and may have inaccuracies, the defendant should have access to the contents in order to correct wrong information, and deny or explain information in the PSI.[10] Inaccurate information may affect the sentence given to the defendant. In two landmark cases, *Williams v. New York*, 337 U.S. 241 (1949), and *Williams v. Oklahoma*, 358 U.S. 576 (1959), the Supreme Court ruled that failure to disclose the contents of the PSI did not violate the defendant's due process rights. The 1949 case of **Williams v. New York** addressed the issue of disclosure and due process at the state level (337 U.S. 241, 1949).[11] Williams was convicted of murder by a jury in a New York criminal court and the jury recommended life in prison. After the presentence investigation report was submitted to the court, the judge imposed the death penalty. The judge's decision was based on the contents of the presentence investigation report that were discussed in open court. Williams had been connected to approximately 30 burglaries in the vicinity where the murder was committed. Additionally, the probation officer accused Williams of being "sexually morbid" and a "menace to society."[12] Williams and his attorney appealed the sentence and challenged the use of the PSI report for sentencing because it contained information from witnesses that the defendant did not have the opportunity to confront and cross examine. Williams and his attorneys claimed that using the contents of the PSI report as a basis of sentencing violated the due process clause of the Fourteenth Amendment. The New York Court of Appeals affirmed the decision of the lower court, referring to the PSI as a valuable tool that allows judges to impose sentences with the best available information rather than guesswork. Further, the court ruled that probation officers do not prosecute offenders but assist them; therefore, the PSI report is not designed to hurt defendants but to provide factual information for judges during the sentencing

---

9. Howard Abadinsky (1997). *Probation and Parole: Theory and Practice.* Upper Saddle, NJ: Pearson Publishing, 139.

10. Ibid.

11. Williams v. New York, 337 U.S. 241 (1949).

12. Ibid.

phase.[13] The appellate court affirmed the decision of the lower court and Williams was executed. Similarly, the U.S. Supreme Court in a landmark case (*Williams v. Oklahoma*, 358 U.S. 576, 1959)[14] ruled that a defendant is not denied due process when a court uses the PSI report without disclosing its contents.

In the 1977 case, ***Gardner v. Florida*** (430 U.S. 349, 1977), the Supreme Court overturned the *Williams* decision of 1949. Gardner was sentenced to death after a first-degree murder conviction. Similar to the *Williams* case, the contents of the presentence investigation report played a major role in the sentencing decision. Gardner and his defense counsel argued that the sentencing court made a mistake in sentencing him to death without the benefit of allowing him to review the contents of the PSI. The Supreme Court rejected the state's arguments that disclosure of the PSI will (a) make it more difficult for the investigators to get confidential information about the defendant's character and background if they cannot guarantee confidentiality and (b) disclosure of the PSI delays the proceeding and disrupts the process of rehabilitation. Instead, the Supreme Court ruled that defendants who are sentenced based on information contained in the PSI are denied due process when they have not had opportunity to explain or deny that information.[15]

Rule 32 of the Federal Rules of Criminal Procedure requires that the presentence report be provided to the prosecutor and defense counsel at least 35 days prior to sentencing so that information that is inaccurate can be corrected or disputed. If there are objections to any information in the presentence investigation report, the relevant parties must submit those objections in writing within 14 days of receiving the report. The probation officer must meet with all parties to resolve those objections and report to the court 14 days before sentencing any unresolved objections to the content of the presentence investigation report.[16] The federal rule governing disclosure of the contents of the PSI for federal offenders was upheld by the United States Court of Appeals, Sixth Circuit in the case of *United States v. Hamad* (858 F.2d 834).[17]

Private Presentence Investigation Report

Some defendants choose to hire a private agency to conduct a "defense-based presentence investigation" that addresses mitigating circumstances that

---

13. Ibid.
14. Williams v. Oklahoma, 358 U.S. 576 (1959).
15. Gardner v. Florida, 430 U.S. 349 (1977).
16. Legal Information Institute. *Federal Rules of Criminal Procedure.*
17. United States v. Hamad, 858 F.2d 834 (1988).

might reduce the severity of the sentence. The idea of a **private presentence investigation** report was first introduced by Dr. Thomas Gitchoff, who believed that a privately commissioned presentence investigation report would improve the quality of the defense presentation at the sentencing hearing. The private PSI provides a more comprehensive examination of the offender's background and motivations that would help to explain his or her behavior in a way that the PSI report, written by probation departments, did not.[18] By the 1980s, there was increased use of the private presentence investigation report for defendants who could afford the costs associated with the report.

While it is likely that the use of the private PSI will continue, many are opposed to its use. Charles Kulis (1983) argues that the proliferation of the private PSI report has been the result of bias in the criminal justice system, overcrowded prisons, and the court's limited resources to conduct public PSIs. Yet, he opposes this alternative format because it diminishes the credibility of the presentence function, exposes the private investigator to liability issues without the protection of judicial immunity, and reveals to the court those who have money versus those who don't.[19] The private PSI provides an advantage to those with money who can afford to pay a private investigator. The ability to point out mitigating circumstances can result in a less severe sentence for those who can afford it.

Critical Thinking Box 3.1

It has long been argued that the PSI is an "evaluative tool" and not a "weapon" to be used against the defendant. Are defendants entitled to due process protections during the investigation process? Justify your response.

Right to Counsel

A suspect in the legal custody of police must be informed of rights prior to interrogation, including the right to counsel, the right to remain silent, and protection from self-incrimination. If the defendant confesses to the crime, it

---

18. Robert Carter and Thomas Gitchoff (1970, February). "The Presentence Report: An Alternative Forma," *Criminology* 7(4): 58–67.

19. Charles Kulis (1983). "Profit in the Private Presentence Report," *Federal Probation* 47(4): 11–15.

must be proven that the *Miranda* warning was given prior to the confession. According to the Supreme Court, suspects must be warned of their rights prior to an interrogation (*Miranda v. Arizona*, 384 U.S. 436, 1966).[20] Recently, there has been a question regarding whether presentence investigation interviews are covered by Miranda rules. Court rulings have specified that probation officers are not required to provide Miranda warnings during presentence interviews (*Minnesota v. Murphy*, 465 U.S. 420, 1984).[21]

Another issue focuses on the right to counsel during the presentence interview. According to recent court rulings, defendants do not have the right to counsel during the presentence interview because the interview is not a critical stage of the proceedings and does not meet the requirements for Sixth Amendment protection. The Sixth Amendment only applies to prosecution.[22]

Critical Thinking Box 3.2

Many believe that money makes a difference in the punishment a defendant receives. Therefore, many question the fairness of the private presentence investigation report, arguing that it perpetuates economic bias in the criminal justice system. How would you justify the use of the private presentence investigation report and the fact that it promotes an inequality in justice?

Recap and Review

- The presentence investigation is ordered by the court prior to sentencing, after the defendant has been convicted or pled guilty.
- The PSI is prepared by the probation department 30–60 days following a conviction or guilty plea.
- The major goal of the PSI is to provide accurate and factual information to the court to assist in the sentencing process. The presentence investigation report has become a very valuable tool to assist the courts in the sentencing phase of the trial.

---

20. Miranda v. Arizona, 384 U.S. 436 (1966).
21. Minnesota v. Murphy, 465 U.S. 420 (1984).
22. United States v. Jackson, 886 F.2d 838, 7th Cir. (1989).

- Its value extends beyond the sentencing phase of the criminal justice process for it is also beneficial for correctional treatment, monitoring, and programming.
- The first PSIs were conducted by John Augustus, a volunteer probation officer, who investigated offenders' background, social history, and criminal history and made recommendations to the court regarding release.
- By the 1930s, use of the PSI was widespread throughout the United States. It was recognized as a valuable tool in the sentencing and correctional process.
- In 1943, the Administrative Office of the United States Courts published the first manual detailing the appropriate content and format for the presentence investigation report, and in 1965, the office published a manual specifying the content, format, and procedures for conducting the investigation at the state and federal levels.
- As sentencing guidelines changed in the 1980s, the format of the PSI also changed to comply with these changing sentencing guidelines.
- The goal of the PSI is to provide accurate and comprehensive information to the court to aid in sentencing.
- Although state laws determine the format of the presentence report, there are areas that should be covered in all reports, including details of the offense, defendant's version, victim's statements, prior criminal history, family, employment, educational history, physical and mental health, and financial status.
- The narrative section of the PSI is crucial in that it includes the sentencing and treatment recommendations to the court.
- Issues of confidentiality and disclosure of the contents of the PSI have been of major concern as many defendants complained that failure to allow them access to the PSI did not provide them the opportunity to explain or deny inaccurate information in the PSI.
- In the *Williams* case (1949) New York Appeals Court argued that the PSI is used for evaluation in the sentencing process and allowing defendants to view the contents makes it difficult to get information about the defendant.
- Later, the Supreme Court overturned the earlier case ruling that the PSI is a major tool for sentencing and defendants have the right to view the PSI to explain or deny information. Failure to do so denies them due process (*Gardner v. Florida*, 1977).
- Some defendants hire a private agency to conduct a private presentence investigation report that points out mitigating circumstances of the offense, which might help to reduce the severity of the sentence.

- Those who oppose the use of the private or defense-based PSI suggest that it promotes bias by providing an advantage to those with money, subjects the investigator to liability issues, and diminishes the credibility of the PSI.
- Criticisms of the PSI are the inclusion of hearsay and inaccurate information, lack of uniformity in the format, and lack of due process rights during the interview.

Questions for Review

1. What are some of the functions of the presentence investigation report?
2. How can the presentence investigation report be beneficial to correctional programming?
3. The PSI is used as an evaluative tool during the sentencing process. What does that mean?
4. How did the work of John Augustus influence our process of conducting the presentence investigation and writing the report?
5. How did the passage of the Federal Sentencing Reform Act of 1984 impact the use of the PSI?
6. What is the purpose of asking the defendant about the circumstance of the offense?
7. Discuss the *Williams* and *Gardner* legal decisions as they relate to disclosure and the confidentiality of the PSI.
8. What is the policy for disclosure of the contents of the PSI at the federal level?
9. What is the private presentence investigation report and how is it used in the sentencing process?
10. What are due process concerns associated with conducting the PSI?

Questions for Discussion

Please use these questions for discussion. Choose the response that you think is most appropriate and explain your reasoning. Why are the other responses not appropriate?

1. Which of the following statements is true of the presentence investigation (PSI) report?
   A. The PSI is prepared by the defendant and the defense attorney prior to the beginning of the trial.

B. The PSI is used to determine guilt or innocence.

C. The PSI assists in sentencing and treatment plans after the offender has pleaded guilty or been convicted of a crime.

D. The PSI is prepared by the district attorney's office for use in the trial.

2. Your supervisor has assigned you to the PSI Unit, which will require you to be in court as well as in the field conducting investigations. This will increase your workload tremendously, since you already manage an active caseload of 250 probationers. In the past year that you have been employed with the probation department, you have been recognized and have received merit raises for your "outstanding" work. Taking on such a major responsibility will likely reduce your effectiveness in your caseload management. After thinking about your dilemma, you decide to:

A. Inform your supervisor that you would like to decline the appointment to the PSI Unit.

B. Try to manage both caseload and PSI Unit responsibilities and wait to see if your work suffers.

C. Talk with your supervisor about reducing your caseload size so that the quality of your work with both assignments will not suffer.

D. Talk to the other officers about your displeasure with the new appointment and hope that it gets back to the supervisor.

3. You have been assigned to conduct a PSI of a 25-year-old female defendant convicted of three counts of forgery. As a part of the investigation, you are scheduled to interview her at the county jail. After introducing yourself and stating the purpose of your visit, you discover that she is hostile and refuses to cooperate. After 30 minutes of asking questions and getting answers such as "My daddy's name is Mickey Mouse and I was married to the Easter Bunny," you decide to:

A. Terminate the interview and attempt to reschedule it for a later time.

B. Terminate the interview and include your experience with the defendant as a part of your report, noting her attitude towards the process and the offense.

C. Approach the judge and request that he would force her to cooperate.

D. Completely omit the defendant's statement from the final report.

E. Contact the court psychiatrist and request an evaluation of the defendant's mental state.

4. As you review the defendant's criminal rap sheet, you notice that the defendant has 3 juvenile detentions, 10 arrests, and 6 convictions as an adult

for misdemeanor and felony assaults. He has just been convicted of aggravated assault with a deadly weapon. In your report, you:

A. Do not address the prior violent offenses because the court should have noticed that earlier.

B. Do not address the past cases because they have no relevance for the sentencing of the present offense.

C. Point out the pattern of aggressive behavior that began when he was a juvenile and has persisted to the present.

D. Recommend that the defendant not be incarcerated but placed under the care of a psychiatrist for intense counseling.

5. In interviewing the victim for your investigation of a defendant who has been convicted of robbery, the victim demands that you find the defendant guilty of the crime and send him to prison and "throw away the key." You respond by:

A. Lecturing the victim on her lack of understanding about the criminal justice process.

B. Explaining to her that the PSI is not designed to determine guilt or innocence but to provide the court with a picture of the defendant to assist in the sentencing process.

C. Informing her that she should take that issue up with the judge and the parole board.

D. Terminating the interview because it is obvious that she has nothing to contribute.

6. You have been assigned to conduct a PSI for a well-known attorney in the community who has been convicted of felony DUI and a vehicular assault. Before your interview with him, he smugly informs you that this is a waste of your and his time since he is not likely to get time even though he has been convicted. He has hired his paralegal to do a private PSI to be submitted to the court. He refuses to cooperate and tells friends, family, and co-workers not to cooperate as well. You:

A. Angrily confront him about his behavior and his cocky attitude.

B. Approach the judge to see if he can make the defendant cooperate.

C. Complete the report with the information that you have collected, noting that the defendant, his family, and co-workers refused to cooperate with the investigation.

D. Terminate the investigation and do not write or submit the report.

7. You are conducting an investigation for an 18-year-old male who has been convicted of 10 burglaries. As you interview him, he tells you that he now wants to identify the others involved in the burglary ring, including the leader. Although he refused to provide this information to his attorney, police investigators, or the court, he now wants to negotiate for a more lenient sentence. Not sure what to do, you consult your supervisor who suggests that you:
    A. Exclude the information because at this point it is irrelevant.
    B. Include the information as a part of the defendant's version.
    C. Advise him to contact his attorney with this information and they can decide the next move.
    D. Do nothing—act as if he never told you anything.

8. You have completed the presentence investigation report for Robert, who has been convicted in criminal court for robbery. You receive a call from his defense attorney demanding that you give him and his client a copy of the report before you submit it to the judge. You respond by:
    A. Telling him that he can pick a copy of the report immediately but only if he keeps it a secret.
    B. Telling him that you are new to the PSI Unit and will have to find out the rules of disclosure for contents of the PSI for your jurisdiction. You will get to back to him.
    C. Telling him that you will give him a copy of the report within 10 days on the promise that he must allow his defendant to read all of the report and give his opinion of the recommended sentence.
    D. Doing nothing and hoping to avoid his future calls.

Case Summaries and Recommendations

These exercises are designed to develop your ability to evaluate information and make decisions and recommendations based on your evaluation. Students will be given five presentence investigation reports for offenders who have been convicted of felony offenses. The report includes all of the information except the narrative section. Students will be required to write a summary and evaluation, and provide recommendations for sentencing and treatment.

Instructions:

1. For each case, you are to read and study the report carefully. Based on your evaluation of the information in the report you will complete the report to be submitted to the court. You should complete the:

    • Narrative
        ○ Evaluative Case Summary
    • Recommendations
        ○ Recommendations for Sentence (with justification)
        ○ Recommendation for Treatment (with justification)

2. Whatever recommendations you make for sentence and treatment, be sure that you justify the reason for the sentence and treatment recommendations. There are no right or wrong answers. If your recommendations are out of line with the information (i.e., a 10-year prison sentence for a first-time property offender with no priors, who is a college student, employed, and who poses no threat to society), then it is important that you explain the severe sentence.

3. There are two important questions that must always be addressed. (1) Why did you recommend this sentence? (2) Why this particular plan of treatment?

Case Study 1

Defendant: Debra Brown

Age: 41

Sex: Female

Offense

The defendant pleaded guilty to two counts of attempted murder and two counts of aggravated assault. Maximum punishment will include 20 years in prison and $50,000 in fines.

Official Version of Offense

The defendant was having an argument with her husband concerning an affair that he was having with another woman. Two other persons were observing this confrontation. As the argument heated up, the defendant pulled a gun from her pocket and shot him in the chest at close range. When another man in the room tried to take the gun from her, she shot him as well. Her husband was out of work for two months and required further surgery. The second victim suffered a fractured femur and right knee. He was out of work for six months.

Defendant's Version of Offense

The defendant states that she was extremely upset because her husband was having an affair with another woman. She had gotten a sexually transmitted disease that he picked up from the other woman. She stated that she only waved the gun around to scare him. The gun accidentally went off. When the other victim tried to take the gun away, it went off again. The defendant states that if she had wanted her husband dead, she could have run over him while he was lying in the parking lot waiting for an ambulance to take him to the hospital.

Prior Record

Juvenile Record

The defendant has three juvenile arrests for shoplifting and prostitution.

Adult Record

As an adult, the defendant has 10 arrests and 6 convictions for assault, assault and battery, receiving stolen property, forgery, prostitution, and disorderly conduct. Although she has six convictions, her longest period of incarceration was 60 days at the Gainesville Girls Correctional Farm.

Personal History

Family History

The defendant grew up in a home characterized as dysfunctional. Her father worked in oil refineries and made good money. He drank and gambled it away before he got home. He did not take care of his family and seldom lived with them. Her father has been incarcerated for failure to pay child support, assault, and domestic abuse. She has no contact with her father but heard that he had died.

The defendant does not remember her mother, who died when she was three years old. Some family members have said that she died because of injuries at the hands of her father. Her father remarried one year after her mother's death. The defendant went to live with her grandmother until she was 13. When her grandmother imposed rules on her, she ran away and spent the next five years living on the streets, prostituting.

She had an older brother that she hardly knew. He was murdered in prison while serving time for attempted murder.

Marital History

The defendant got married when she was 17. Her husband was a heroin addict and soon got her addicted. Her husband was killed while attempting to rob a store to get money for more drugs.

She met the victim two years ago and began living with him. The relationship between the victim and the defendant started out very good. After a while, he rarely came home; he also verbally abused her. After a year of living together, he started gambling and having numerous affairs with other women.

Educational Background

The defendant dropped out of school in the eighth grade. She missed a lot of school but got a GED while incarcerated at the Mumford Girls Correctional Farm. While incarcerated, the defendant received training and a license in beauty culture.

Employment History

The defendant has had a number of unskilled jobs (seven in the last eight years). Her longest period of employment is her current employment, where she has worked as a hotel housekeeper for the last two years. Her employer states that she is a good employee.

Health — Physical (Including Drug and Alcohol History)

The defendant was sickly as a child. She started to drink heavily at 15 and use drugs at 17. She was addicted to heroin by age 21. She claims that she has been drug free for the last 10 years. Her only problem now is that she has ulcers.

Health — Psychological

While incarcerated at Mumford, she was diagnosed with depression and an anxiety disorder. The psychologist did not think that they were serious enough for medication.

Military History

Financial History

The defendant has a weekly salary of $200 and a checking account balance of $350.00.

She also owns a 2000 Ford Focus.

Her liabilities include rent ($400 per month), a car payment ($200 per month), and a credit card debt of $1,100.

Case Study 2

Defendant: Roger Williams

Age: 32

Sex: Male

Offense

The defendant was convicted of robbery and attempted murder, which is punishable by up to 50 years in prison and $25,000 in fines.

Official Version of Offense

The defendant and another man entered the defendant's house to buy cocaine. After the defendant had paid the victims and gotten the drugs, he suspected that the victim had tricked him by giving him cocaine that had been tampered with. The defendant then pulled a gun and fired twice, hitting the victim with the second shot. The defendant threatened to kill the victim if he did not give him money and drugs stashed at the house. The defendant left the house with approximately $15,000 worth of marijuana and $10,000 in cash. The defendant was arrested the following day at the bus station. The victim suffered minor injuries and was arrested on outstanding warrants after being treated at the emergency room.

Defendant's Version of Offense

The defendant stated that he went to buy drugs from the victim, a known drug dealer in the community. He took the money promising to give the drugs that the defendant wanted. The defendant states that after taking the money, the victim made a comment about the drugs. The defendant states that he simply wanted to scare the victim with the gun. Initially, he had no intention of harming the victim. However, when the victim started to "talk trash" and threaten him, he got angry and took his money and drugs. He stated that he used to sell drugs with the victim, and the victim had a reputation for trying to cheat his customers. He does not believe that he should be sent to prison for this offense.

Prior Record

Juvenile Record

The defendant has no prior juvenile record.

Adult Record

As an adult, the defendant has 35 arrests and 20 convictions for receiving stolen property, burglary, and possession of drugs, robbery and assault, attempted murder, and parole violation. He has four prison commitments with his longest sentence being four years.

Personal History

Family History

The defendant was the younger of two children born to a single mother. The defendant never knew his biological father but was raised by his stepfather, whom his mother married when the defendant was three. The stepfather verbally and physically abused his wife and children. The abuse stopped after he spent time in jail for abuse. The defendant's mother is unemployed and receives disability for an injury received at the rubber plant. The defendant has an older brother and four younger stepbrothers and sisters. The family is close and all remain supportive of the defendant.

Marital History

The defendant has never married even though he lived with a woman for three years in a volatile relationship. She was hospitalized at least two times because of injuries caused by the defendant. She left him during one of his periods of incarceration. He has no contact with her and does not know her whereabouts. He has no children.

Educational Background

The defendant dropped out of school in the ninth grade. His school performance was extremely poor. He completed his GED while serving time in prison five years ago.

Employment History

The defendant has a poor employment record; he has not held a job for any length of time. He has received very favorable work records from his prison jobs, which suggests that he does have the capacity for responsible labor when he is not on drugs and receives proper supervision.

Health — Physical (Including Drug and Alcohol History)

The defendant is presently in good health.

He has an extensive drug and alcohol history beginning at age 14; he was addicted to heroin and LSD by age 20. He admits that he is a drug user addicted to alcohol, heroin, oxycodone, and Lortabs. While in prison, he faithfully attends drug therapy sessions and seeks other help for his addiction. He does not seek help for his problem when he is in the community.

Health — Psychological

The defendant is addicted to drugs.

Military History

The defendant has never served in the military. He tried to get into the army but was rejected because of his stab wounds.

Financial History

The defendant has no assets or liabilities.

Case Study 3

<u>Defendant</u>: Alice Brown

<u>Age</u>: 65

<u>Sex</u>: Female

<u>Offense</u>

The defendant was convicted of voluntary manslaughter. Maximum penalties include up to 10 years in prison and fines of $25,000.

<u>Official Version of Offense</u>

Police were called to the residence of the defendant on September 1 to investigate a shooting. Upon their arrival, they found the victim dead. The defendant and the victim, her husband, were having an argument. She shot him.

<u>Defendant's Version of Offense</u>

According to the defendant, the victim would get violent when he got mad. This time she went to the bedroom and got a .38 caliber pistol and shot him. She also stated that she had become fearful for her life because of his aggressive behavior. Shots were fired because of the confrontation. She has no idea why the shots were fired. She called and reported the incident to police. She feels that she acted in self-defense.

<u>Prior Record</u>

The defendant has no prior record. This is her first and only offense.

<u>Personal History</u>

Family History

The defendant's father was a sharecropper in Alabama. Both her parents are now dead. The defendant has four brothers and one sister. All are dead except the sister. She has little contact with her sister. Her early life consisted of extreme poverty in the rural South.

Marital History

The defendant married at age 16, but her husband died 6 months later. She married again at the age of 27; it was annulled when she found out that her husband was a bigamist. She began living with the victim 25 years ago. The relationship was good for the first eight years. For the last 17 years, the victim had become mean and threatening to the defendant. The victim was having an affair and was known to beat the defendant.

Educational Background

The defendant dropped out of school while in the tenth grade. She never received her GED.

Employment History

For the past 40 years, the defendant has worked as a domestic. She has had many different employers and some for a very long time. At the time of the offense, she was employed in the job that she has held for 35 years. They all describe her as honest, dependable, and reliable. They were all shocked that she could have shot anyone.

Health—Physical (Including Drug and Alcohol History)

The defendant is in good health given her age. She neither drinks nor uses illegal drugs.

Health—Psychological

Within the year before he died, the victim had begun to verbally and emotionally abuse her.

The defendant admits that recently she has suffered with bouts of depression and anxiety.

Military History

The defendant has never served in the military.

Financial History

The defendant has no assets.

Her debts amount to $750–1,000 due to lost wages while she has been in jail waiting for trial.

Case Study 4

Defendant: Gregory Harris

Age: 41

Sex: Male

Offense

Manslaughter and unlawful possession of a gun, which is punishable by up to 25 years in prison and fine of $10,000.

Official Version of Offense

Police were called to the residence of Gregory and Patricia Harris. When they arrived, they found the victim at the door, where she was dead after being shot by the defendant. The defendant was still in the house and called the police. The defendant and the victim had gotten into a fight and he pulled out the gun and shot her.

Defendant's Version of Offense

The defendant states that he and the victim were husband and wife after living together for 10 years; they had been married for 6 years. He states that he had heard around town that she was seeing somebody else and wanted to get rid of him. He states that he didn't start the fight but when he thought that she was going into her purse to get a knife or gun, he knew that he had to do something to defend himself.

Prior Record

Juvenile Record

The defendant has no juvenile record.

Adult Record

The defendant has had several misdemeanor charges of public intoxication and simple assault, where he was given misdemeanor probation for the assault and $50.00 fine for the public intoxication charge. He was also convicted of burglary and given a five-year probation term. He violated the conditions of probation and spent three years in state prison. Prior to the present offense, he was convicted of aggravated assault and spent two years in the county jail.

Personal History

Family History

The defendant's parents are deceased, but he remembers that his father had spent some time in prison for murder. He said that he never really got along with his father because his father was abusive to him and his mother. He believes that his father had something to do with his mother's illness (damaged kidneys) and ultimate death. He had one brother, who was killed by police during a robbery attempt.

Marital History

He was married when he was 18 but divorced one year later. He lived with the victim for 10 years prior to getting married. They had been married for the past six years. Police records indicate several calls to the address for domestic disputes. She always declined to press charges. The director of Turning Point, the domestic violence center, reported that a year ago, the victim sought help. At that time, she informed counselors that she was afraid for her life and that she thought that her husband would one day kill her. She never returned for a follow-up visit.

Educational Background

The defendant dropped out of school after the eighth grade. He admits that he never did well in school because he was absent from school most of the time and had problems at home.

Employment History

Because of limited education, the defendant has had only unskilled laboring jobs. He has worked construction but was laid off because of a lack of work. At the time of the offense, he had temporary employment with Manpower. He has been unemployed most of his adult life.

<u>Health — Physical (Including Drug and Alcohol History)</u>

Physical health is generally good. He says that he has back problems, but supporting medical information was not available.

<u>Health — Psychological</u>

Records show that he was admitted and treated as a patient at Brown Mental Health Center for depression and alcoholism in 1988.

<u>Military History</u>

The defendant reports that he enlisted in the army. Shortly after completing boot camp and being stationed at Fort Hood, he was arrested and convicted for a robbery that he committed while on a weekend pass. He was dishonorably discharged. However, a check of records at Fort Sill and Fort Hood did not show that the defendant was ever stationed in either place.

<u>Financial History</u>

The defendant owns a 2005 Mercury Sable. He has no bank account and no other assets.

The defendant has a monthly $250.00 car payment. He does admit that the car payment was usually made by his wife since he was unemployed most of the time.

Case Study 5

<u>Defendant</u>: James William Henry

<u>Age</u>: 31

<u>Sex</u>: Male

<u>Offense</u>

The defendant was convicted of four counts of robbery, simple assault, and four counts of aggravated assault, and receiving stolen property. These offenses are punishable by up to 40 years in prison and $25,000 in fines.

<u>Official Version of Offense</u>

The defendant and another man entered The Pantry Shop, and the defendant pulled a gun. The defendant took the store manager into the back room and forced her to lie down; he assaulted her with his fists and the butt of his pistol. He then took one hundred dollars from her purse. When he found that the cash drawer contained only a small amount of money, he and the co-defendant robbed another store employee and two customers. Defendants also took merchandise from the store. The employee and the customers were able to provide police with a description of the defendants and the car used in the crime. Shortly afterwards, police stopped the car with the defendants and stolen merchandise. The victims were able to identify the offenders in a police lineup.

Defendant's Version of Offense

The defendant admitted that he and the co-defendant were out riding around and getting high. The co-defendant suggested that they rob the shop since the clerks are usually female. They went in and robbed the store, but the defendant does not remember assaulting anyone. The defendant said that they needed money to buy more drugs. He says that he was under the influence of drugs when he committed the offense and does not remember much about the offense, especially the assaults.

Prior Record

Juvenile Record

The defendant has nine prior juvenile offenses with four adjudications and one commitment. Offenses included auto theft, burglary, larceny, possession of drugs, and assault and battery. He spent one year in Mt. Meigs Juvenile Prison and six months in the Aftercare Program of the Department of Youth Services.

Adult Record

As an adult, he has had 13 arrests, 10 convictions, and 8 incarcerations. These offenses included robbery, larceny, receiving stolen property, shoplifting, assault and battery, forgery, and illegal possession of a weapon. At age 17, he was incarcerated as an adult; he has spent most of his adult life in and out of prison.

Personal History

Family History

The defendant was the youngest of four sons born to his mother and father. They lived in a lower-class neighborhood where crime rates were high and there was easy access to alcohol and drugs. Unemployment was high and drug deals were made in the open in the public view. His parents spent long hours at work, leaving their sons to spend most of the time unsupervised. His father was distant from his sons and his mother was not able to discipline her sons. Two of the sons joined gangs and one was killed in a gang fight. He has always gotten along well with his remaining two brothers. Both of his brothers have long criminal careers. In fact, much of the crime in the neighborhood was the work of these three brothers. All three have had several incarcerations in state prisons—sometimes at the same time. When not in prison, the defendant and his brothers still live at home.

Marital History

The defendant has never been married and has no known children.

Educational Background

The defendant was a below average student. He had difficulty following directions. He was an angry and hostile student who was a constant discipline problem. He had several suspensions and eventually graduated from high school.

He played football and was team captain his senior year. He was recruited by the local university to play football but his grades were not good enough to be admitted under NCAA rules. After attending the local community college for a semester, he dropped out to get a job. While he was incarcerated, he took training as a machinist at a junior college.

Employment History

The defendant always manages to stay employed but only for short periods of time due to high absenteeism. At the time of his arrest, he was a machinist where he had worked for the past two years. When he was released on bond, he was able to return to his job. His employer says that he is satisfied with his work and attitude and will keep him if does not go to prison.

Health—Physical (Including Drug and Alcohol History)

The defendant's physical health is good. He has used heroin off and on for the past 15 years. He also uses cocaine and marijuana. At the time of his arrest, his habit required six to eight bags daily at a cost of $90–100. He drinks only moderately. He states that he has never received treatment for his addiction.

Health—Psychological

The defendant denies having any mental problems. During his incarcerations, he was diagnosed as having passive-aggressive tendencies with a moderate risk for assaultive behavior.

Military History

The defendant has never been in the military.

Financial History

The defendant has a good income from his job as a machinist but spends it all on drugs. He has no assets.

His liabilities include a $1,700 school loan and $200 that he owes the hospital for an emergency room visit.

Writing the Presentence Investigation Report

This exercise is designed to help students develop skills in writing the presentence investigation report. Below is the official version or official case data taken from police reports. Using that information, develop a PSI and make recommendations based on the contents of the PSI.

A. Official Version of the Offense — The Hit and Run

Police were called to the scene of a hit and run accident. When they arrived, they found that a female jogger had been killed by a hit and run driver. Witnesses described the car of the offender as a black 2005 Ford Taurus. When police spotted the vehicle and attempted to make a stop, the driver jumped from the vehicle and started to run. Police observed him throw something into the nearby shrubbery. The bags were retrieved and found to contain a large number of valium and Lortab pills. Another bag contained a white substance later determined to be cocaine. The defendant was arrested and transported to city jail, where he was charged with vehicular homicide, leaving the scene of an accident, and possession of drugs for resale.

B. Official Version of the Offense — Death and the Illegal Business

Firefighters were summoned to the scene of an explosion and building fire in a rural part of the county. When the fire was brought under the control, 15 bodies were discovered. Further examination of the building discovered that it was the location of an illegal fireworks factory owned by Mr. John Bart, a prominent local executive. Witnesses report that the business, located in nothing more than a shack, had operated for the past 10 years. Approximately two years ago, the business was closed briefly after an investigation by the ATF. Mr. Bart was arrested and charged with 15 counts of involuntary manslaughter.

C. Official Version of the Offense — Drugs for Sale

Police observed a 2007 Nissan Pathfinder driving erratically on a city street. Immediately, police attempted to stop the vehicle, which engaged them in a chase for approximately two miles. The Pathfinder crashed and the driver jumped out and attempted to run from the vehicle. After a five-minute foot chase by police, the suspect was apprehended. The suspect was identified as someone with an outstanding warrant for aggravated assault. Upon searching the vehicle, police discovered marijuana, $15,000 in cash, and two semiautomatic weapons. The marijuana had a street value of $20,000. The suspect was transported to jail and charged with possession of marijuana for resale and illegal possession of firearms.

Chapter 4

Probation Process and Supervision

Introduction

Probation, a community-based correctional program, continues to be the most popular alternative to incarceration. Despite the recent decline in the number of adults being sentenced to probation, probationers comprise 3.9 million of the 4.9 million offenders under community supervision.[1] This chapter examines the probation supervision process, including the selection process, conditions of probation, violation of probation conditions, and the revocation process.

---

1. Laura Maruschak and Thomas Bonczar (2013). *Probation and Parole in the United States, 2012*. Washington, DC: U.S. Department of Justice, Office of Justice Programs, Bureau of Justice Statistics.

Probation Process

Granting Probation

After a defendant has been convicted, decisions are made regarding the sentence to be imposed. The PSI report offers valuable and relevant information to assist the judge in making an informed decision regarding sentencing. It is still the judge's decision to accept or reject the sentencing recommendations made by the investigating probation officer. Studies suggest that there is a high correlation between officer sentencing recommendations and the judge's sentence.[2] Probation, a sentencing option and alternative to prison, allows the offender to remain in the community in lieu of incarceration. Defendants who may be restricted from probation supervision include offenders (1) who have been convicted of multiple offenses, (2) were on probation or parole at the time of the offense, (3) are addicted to drugs, (4) have a history of violent behavior, (5) seriously injured the victim, and (6) used a weapon in the offense.[3]

Critical Thinking Box 4.1

Mitigating circumstances may apply to individual cases. Consider the case of Robert. Robert was convicted of killing two individuals at a party. With two convictions for murder, he was not likely to receive a probation sentence. The officer conducting the investigation identified mitigating circumstances. Robert was attending a party. Two uninvited male guests came to the party and attacked some of the female guests. When he perceived that the lives of these women were in danger, and efforts to stop the attack failed, he pulled his gun and killed both men. While he could not argue self-defense at the time, the court did take into account the circumstances of the offense and decided to grant Robert a 10-year probation sentence. Was the court correct in placing Robert on probation? Was the sentence too lenient for the deaths of two people who posed no threat to the defendant?

In granting probation, judges consider the recommendations from the probation officer, but may take into account the recommendations of police and prosecutors. The judge may also be influenced by the geographic location of

---

2. Joan Petersilia (1998, Spring). "Probation in the United States, Part I," *Perspectives* (American Probation and Parole Association) Spring, pp. 30–41.

3. Petersilia, 32–41.

the court, the social and political attitudes of the area, and the overcrowded conditions in jails and prisons. The more overcrowded the jails and prisons are, the higher the number of plea bargains and probation sentences.[4] Other influences on the judge's decision are the judge's attitude towards a particular offense or offender, the quality of services provided by the probation department, whether or not the offender owes restitution to the victim, and if probation will allow the defendant to continue to take care of his or her family.[5]

There are factors that the judge must take into account. These include:

- the severity of the offense
- the seriousness of the prior criminal history and whether or not that history includes professional criminal behavior or violent, sex, and drug offenses
- sentencing guidelines
- the defendant's age
- rehabilitation potential
- the defendant's relationship with his family
- the attitude of the community towards the offender and the offense
- the attitude of the offender towards the offense
- remorse shown by the offender[6]

Questions are often asked about the impact of extralegal variables on the judge's sentencing decision. Do race/ethnicity, class, and gender influence judges' decisions to grant probation or incarcerate? Many studies have concluded that the strongest predictors of sentencing are severity of the offense and criminal history, not extralegal variables.[7] Other sentencing experts have argued that extralegal factors do affect judges' decisions in deciding to grant probation.[8] Petersilia and Turner (1985) studied probation and prison decisions for convicted felons in California. Their research revealed a number of findings:

---

4. Howard Abadinsky (1997). *Probation and Parole*. 6th Edition. Upper Saddle, NJ: Prentice Hall, 149.

5. Ibid., 149.

6. Howard Abadinsky (2005). *Probation and Parole: Theory and Practice. 8th Edition,* Upper Saddle, NJ: Prentice Hall, p. 36.

7. G. Kleck (1981). "Racial Discrimination in Criminal Sentencing: A Critical Evaluation of the Evidence with Additional Data on the Death Penalty," *American Sociological Review* 46: 783–805.

8. J. Hagan (1974). "Extra-Legal Attributes and Criminal Sentencing: An Assessment of a Sociological Viewpoint," *Law and Society Review 8*: 357–383; C. Spohn and S. Welch (1987). "The Effect of Prior Record in Sentencing Research: An Examination of the Assumption That Any Measure Is Adequate." *Justice Quarterly 4*: 287–302.

- Legal variables (conviction offense, prior record, offense related characteristics) have a significant impact on decisions to grant probation or sentence to prison.
- Demographic variables (age, education) do not do not influence probation decisions.
- Being Black and Hispanic significantly affects decisions. If felons were Black or Hispanic, they were more likely to receive a prison sentence.
- The type of attorney influences probation granting decisions. Those with private attorneys versus public defenders are more likely to get probation instead of prison.[9]

Probation Conditions

After probation is granted, the defendant must sign the probation order. The probation order specifies conditions that the probationer must follow while under supervision. The probationer's signature on the probation order indicates an agreement with the court-ordered conditions and a willingness to comply with the requirements of supervision. The probation order includes two types of conditions: **standard conditions**, given to all probationers, and **special conditions** that are designed for individual offenders. Special conditions may be punitive and/or treatment conditions. **Punitive conditions** usually reflect the seriousness of the offense and are intended to increase the punishment of the offender. Such conditions include community service, home confinement, restitution, and mandatory drug testing. **Treatment conditions** are designed to help the offender with problems that might be factors in the criminal behavior. The presentence investigation report serves as the source for many of the treatment conditions of probation. Approximately 55% of all probationers have additional special conditions beyond the standard conditions.[10]

Standard conditions typically include the following:

- Commit no other crime.
- Have no firearms in your possession.
- Report to the probation officer as ordered.

---

9. Joan Petersilia, Susan Turner, James kahan & Joyce Peterson (1985). *Granting Felons Probation: Public Risks and Alternatives. Prepared for the National Institute of Justice, U.S. Department of Justice (R-3186-NIJ)*, California: Rand Corporation, pp. 28–33.

10. Patrick Langan and Mark Cuniff (1992). *Recidivism of Felons on Probation*. Washington, DC: U.S. Department of Justice, Office of Justice Programs, Bureau of Justice Statistics.

- Allow your probation officer to visit you at home or at your place of employment.
- Support all dependents.
- Avoid association with known felons.
- Maintain employment.
- Do not change status without notifying the probation department (e.g., employment, residential, or marital status).
- Remain in the jurisdiction unless given written permission to leave.
- Pay all fees.
- Obey all laws.

Punitive conditions are given to show the seriousness of the offense.

- Be confined in county jail for three months.
- Do community service.
- Do not buy anything of value over $200 without permission.
- Submit to random drug testing.

Treatment conditions are designed to address problems that might be responsible for the criminal behavior.

- Attend AA meetings.
- Get psychological counseling.
- Attend school.
- Attend religious worship services.
- Participate in drug counseling.
- Get job training.

Judges may use their broad powers to impose any other conditions necessary to promote offender rehabilitation and protect the community. When imposing conditions, the basic principles are:

1. Conditions must be reasonably related to the two major purposes of probation:
   - the rehabilitation of the offender
   - the protection of the community
2. Conditions must not violate the U.S. Constitution.[11]

Conditions given by the court may not be changed except through court order. Probation conditions may be modified by the court at the request of the supervising officer. The probation officer may request that the probation

---

11. People v. Lent, 15 Cal.3d 48 (1975).

order be amended to change the conditions of probation temporarily (to allow travel out of the jurisdiction for a specific purpose) or permanently (removing a curfew for the duration of the supervision term). In *Principles of Criminology*, Sutherland, Cressey, and Luckenbill (1992) state that conditions of probation should not be too restrictive. When conditions are overly restrictive and inflexible, probation officers are inclined to overlook violations, causing the probationer to lose respect for the officer. When this happens, the supervision process becomes very difficult.[12]

Critical Thinking Box 4.2

How far should the courts go in regulating a person's life in the name of rehabilitation? Should there be limitations on the conditions imposed by judges for the purposes of rehabilitation of the offender, protection of the victim, and the safety of the community?

Probation Supervision

Types of Probation Supervision

There are several different types of probation supervision strategies that have evolved over the years.

Deferred Prosecution Probation

Deferred prosecution probation requires the accused to sign a contract accepting moral responsibility, not legal responsibility, for the offense in exchange for a probation term. The offender is assigned to a probation officer for a period of two to five years of supervision with conditions of probation to be followed while under supervision. The goal of this probation strategy is to give the offender a second chance while promoting rehabilitation and treatment.[13]

Deferred Adjudication Probation

The use of **deferred adjudication probation** is limited to first-time offenders. The defendant agrees to plead guilty, but the judge withholds or defers

---

12. Edwin Sutherland, Donald Cressey, and David Luckenbill (1992). *Principles of Criminology*. Lanham, MD: Rowman & Littlefield Publishers.
13. Joan Petersilia (1998). Probation in the United States, Part I. *Perspectives,(APPA)* Spring, p. 34.

the pronouncement of guilt and places the defendant on probation. If the probationer completes the probation term successfully, the offense is never entered as a conviction. Unlike standard or straight probation, a sentence of deferred adjudication probation is not treated as a conviction. However, if a deferred adjudicated probationer violates the conditions of probation and probation is revoked by the court, appeal of the revocation is not permitted.[14]

Standard Probation

Most probationers are supervised under standard or straight probation. Probationers are evaluated and classified according to needs and risk and placed under the supervision of a probation officer. They are expected to follow all of the standard conditions of probation as well as special conditions. Unlike deferred probation, criminal records will indicate that the defendant was sentenced to a probation term and how that term ended. The probationer will have a record of a conviction upon completion of the probation term.

Shock Probation

Shock probation allows the judge to impose short-term imprisonment upon the offender prior to being released into the community for probation supervision. The judge sentences the offender to prison with a review of the sentence to take place after a specified period of time (30, 60, 90, or 120 days). Following the time served, the judge suspends the sentence and places the individual on probation.[15] While shock probation may be a strategy to save money, reduce prison overcrowding, and permit community supervision of the offender, there is little evidence to suggest that the strategy works.[16] Some have suggested that the short stay in prison actually decreases the chances for successful rehabilitation.[17]

Shock probation differs from shock incarceration. Shock incarceration is an intermediate sanction that serves as an alternative to incarceration for offenders who are prison bound. It is a short stay at a military-style boot camp that attempts to teach the offender discipline.

---

14. Fred Dahr. *Understanding Deferred Adjudication and Straight Probation,* http://www.texasdefenselaw.com/texas-criminal-law-guide/deferred-adjudication/deferred-adjudication-vs-straight-probation.

15. Edward Latessa (2002). "Split Sentence," *Encyclopedia of Crime and Punishment,* Volume I, Edited by David Levinson. Thousand Oaks, CA: Sage Publications, p. 1559.

16. T. C. Sims (1979, September/October). "Shock Probation: Background, Issues, and Trends," *Texas Journal of Corrections* 5(5):10–13.

17. Ibid.

Intensive Probation Supervision

Intensive supervision probation is an intermediate punishment that was first implemented in Georgia in 1982. Its features include small caseload sizes, intensive supervision and surveillance, community service, and strict enforcement of the conditions of probation.

Split Sentence

The **split sentence** requires the convicted offender to serve part of the sentence in jail/prison and part in the community under probation supervision. The split sentence may also be referred to as a combination sentence or mixed sentence, where a portion of the sentence may include incarceration or jail time and a portion may include probation.[18]

Length of Probation Supervision

The length of the probation term varies from state to state. Probation terms are set by the court; the actual probation term may not be related to the sentence recommended by the criminal code of the state. In Illinois, the maximum is four years for more serious felonies and 30 months for all other felonies. In Texas, the maximum is 10 years. In recent years, the trend has been towards shorter sentences, with most not exceeding five years. Research has shown that the likelihood of failure increases after five years of supervision.[19] Sometimes, a probationer may request early termination of the probation sentence. Prior to being considered for early termination, probationers must demonstrate exemplary conduct, complete at least one half of the probation sentence, pay all fines and restitution, complete mandated counseling and drug/alcohol treatment, and comply with all of the conditions of probation.

Violation of Probation

Probation Violations

A probation violation occurs when the probationer violates court-ordered conditions of supervision. There are two types of probation violations: technical violations and new arrest violations. **Technical violations** occur when the

---

18. Dean Champion (2008). *Probation, Parole and Community Corrections*. 6th Edition. Upper Saddle, NJ: Pearson/Prentice Hall, 227.
19. Kathryn Morgan (1994). "Factors Influencing Probation Outcome," *Journal of Criminal Justice 22*: 341–353.

supervised probationer violates one of the administrative rules of probation. Failure to pay fees, report to the probation office as directed, and participate in court-ordered treatment programs are technical violations of probation. **New arrest violations** occur when the probationer is arrested and charged with a new crime.

> **A technical violation** is the violation of the administrative conditions of probation.

Process of Revocation

The **revocation** process begins with probation officers who have a quasi-judicial role in that they decide whether or not to seek revocation. A decision to pursue revocation may be influenced by the officer's attitude towards the probation violation and the probationer's performance under probation supervision. If the violation is serious enough, the probation officer will file a motion to request revocation of probation or a delinquency report to the court. The report details the alleged violations, the probationer's progress under supervision and a recommendation from the officer. The officer may recommend a return to probation with amended conditions, jail time, or revocation of the probation term. The officer may also decline to make a recommendation.

Once the report is filed, the probationer is arrested or given a copy of the alleged violations with a date to appear in court. In most states, there is a probable cause or preliminary hearing. If not in custody, the probationer may waive the right to a preliminary hearing. If the probationer is in custody, there must be a preliminary hearing. At the preliminary hearing, the probationer may plead guilty or deny the charges of probation violation. Probationers who plead guilty may be restored to probation or have their probation sentences revoked. If the probationer denies the charges and if there is sufficient evidence of probation violations, the date for a probation revocation hearing is set.

During the revocation hearing, probationers are entitled to due process rights, including (1) written notice of alleged probation violations, (2) disclosure of the evidence against the probationer, (3) an opportunity to be heard and present witnesses and evidence, (4) the right to confront and cross-examine witnesses unless the courts finds a good reason for not allowing the confrontation, (5) a neutral and detached hearing body, and (6) a written statement of the evidence used and the reasons for revoking probation.

Unlike a criminal trial, the standard of proof in the revocation hearing is **preponderance of the evidence**, a lower standard also used in civil trials. Secondly, evidence which would not be allowed in a criminal trial, such as hearsay, is permitted during the revocation hearing. If the probationer is found guilty of probation violations, the judge has several options, including:

- Reprimand of the probationer and restoration to probation.
- Returning the probationer to probation supervision with an amended probation order. The probationer may be ordered to serve jail time, receive additional drug/alcohol treatment, and pay additional fees or other conditions.
- Revocation of probation and imposing a prison term. Revocation of probation indicates that the court has rescinded conditional release. Revoked probationers may be given credit for "street time."

Critical Thinking Box 4.3

Probation is considered a privilege to the probationer or an act of mercy by the court. When a probationer violates the conditions of probation, he violates the terms of his contract with the court and the original sentence should be imposed. Probationers might argue that imposing the original sentence is a violation of their rights. Imposing the original sentence without regard for the time spent on probation supervision makes them serve more time than originally assessed. How would you respond to that claim?

Profile of Felony Probationers: Who Is on Probation Supervision?

What are the characteristics of those who are under probation supervision? The majority of those under supervision are males. According to the 2009 Bureau of Justice Statistics, males comprised 76% of the total adult probation population and females constituted 24% of the adult probation population.[20] The number of females under probation supervision has been increasing over the past decade. In 2000, female probationers comprised 22% of the populations, but by the 2008 and 2009 statistical years, the percentage of women had increased to 24%.[21] This increase may reflect the increase in the number of fe-

---

20. Lauren Glaze and Thomas Bonczar (2010, December). *Probation and Parole in the United States, 2009.* Washington, DC: U.S. Department of Justice, Office of Justice Programs, Bureau of Justice Statistics.

21. Linda Sydney (2005, October). *Gender-Responsive Strategies for Women Offenders.* Washington, DC: U.S. Department of Justice, National Institute of Corrections.

males arrested and the extent of female poverty and substance abuse. Women are more likely to be sentenced to probation for property and drug offenses. Whites are more likely to be supervised under probation; 55% of adult probationers are white. Black probationers comprise 30% and the Hispanic probation population has remained stable since 2000 at 13%.[22] Statistics also indicate that the majority of probationers are felons (51%) who are on active supervision (72%). The adult probation population consists mainly of property offenders (26%) and drug offenders (26%).[23] Offender characteristics of probationers under supervision include being young (under age 30), single, unemployed with no job skills, and not having completed high school or obtained a GED.[24]

Critical Thinking Box 4.4

Studies have revealed that the race is a major factor at every level of decision-making in the criminal justice system, suggesting that there is racial discrimination in the criminal justice system. Current statistics indicate that 55% of probationers are white. There are those who disagree and point out that minorities have more severe criminal histories and commit more serious crimes and are therefore subjected to more severe punishment. Which position do you accept and why?

Issues Related to Probation Supervision

Probation Recidivism

As the use of probation increases, concerns about outcomes and effectiveness of probation as a correctional alternative also increase. The issue of **recidivism** has been prominent in corrections literature since Martinson's study of correctional rehabilitation programs. In his analysis of 230 rehabilitation programs, Martinson concluded that all had the same outcome:

> **Recidivism** is reoffending or repeating criminal behavior.

---

22. Lauren Glaze and Thomas Bonczar (2010). *Probation and Parole in the United States, 2009.* Bureau of Justice Statistics. U.S. Department of Justice: Office of Justice Programs (NCJ231674). December, p. 26.

23. Ibid., p. 26.

24. Kathryn Morgan. (1994). "Factors Influencing Probation Outcome," *Journal of Criminal Justice,* Volume 22 (4), 341–353.

"this program shows no appreciable effect on recidivism."[25] In the 1970s, probation was closely scrutinized and criticized by a community who believed that it is too lenient and does not rehabilitate, deter criminal behavior, or protect society. Studies reporting high probation failure rates support the public's belief. It is estimated that about 50% of felony probationers fail to comply with court-ordered conditions but 50% of those never go to jail or prison for non-compliance.[26] Joan Petersilia and her colleagues found that 65% of all probationers had been rearrested, reconvicted, and sent to prison after being on probation.[27] A Kentucky study found that probation recidivism rates are about 18% and not the high rates as reported by most researchers studying probation outcomes.[28]

Measuring Recidivism

When discussing probation outcome and failure, you must be aware of the difficulty in defining failure. In most instances, failure is defined as contact with the criminal justice system through rearrests, reconviction, and reincarceration after the individual had been placed under supervision. Using rearrests and reincarceration to measure failure has been somewhat misleading if you attempt to show, as the Rand study did, that felony probationers continue to commit serious crimes even while under supervision. Often, rearrests of probationers may occur if the police suspect involvement in a crime or if the probationer lives within close proximity to where a crime has been committed. In many of these cases, probationers are never officially charged with any crime. The probationer may be reincarcerated if there is a new offense; but reincarceration may also occur if the probationer has repeated technical violations. Failure to pay assessed fees or failure to report as ordered could possibly result in revocation and reincarceration. Reconviction more accurately reflects failure because it indicates that a crime has been committed by a probationer and evidence is sufficient enough to prove guilt beyond a reasonable doubt. However, when referring to probationers, revocation as measure of failure cannot be ignored. With revocation, the court which grants the pro-

---

25. Robert Martinson (1974). "What Works?: Questions and Answers about Prison Reform," *The Public Interest* 35: 22–34.

26. John Whitehead (1991). "The Effectiveness of Felony Probation: Results from an Eastern State," *Justice Quarterly* 8(4): 525–543.

27. Joan Petersilia (1985). *Granting Felons Probation: Public Risks and Alternatives*. Santa Monica, CA: The Rand Corporation, pp. 45–46.

28. Gennaro Vito (1987). "Felony Probation and Recidivism," *Federal Probation* 50(4): 17–25.

bation privilege to the offender makes a statement that this individual has failed under probation supervision either by committing a crime serious enough to warrant taking away conditional freedom or has consistently violated technical rules. Seldom does the court rescind the privilege of probation for a single violation of probation rules.[29] More recent statements about probation recidivism suggest that the use of evidence-based strategies, practices that have been proven effective by scientific research, can reduce recidivism rates significantly.[30]

Characteristics of Probation Failures

Investigations of probation outcomes consistently reveal probation failures have common characteristics. Variables associated with probation failure include:

- Gender: Males are more likely to fail under supervision
- Type of Offense: Property offenders fail more
- Employment status: Unemployed or in low-paying jobs
- Marriage Status: Single or divorced
- Age: Younger are more likely to fail
- Those given more than five years
- Those who have a prior criminal record with two or more felony convictions
- Educational status: those who did not finish high school

Factors that are consistently found to be unrelated to failure are:

- Type of Supervision
- Race
- Conditions of probation[31]

Absconding

Absconding is major concern for probation departments. **Absconding** occurs when a probationer fails to report as required and the probation department loses contact with that probationer. The probationer may be labeled an absconder after about six months of failure to report or no contact with the

Absconding refers to leaving the known address and failing to maintain contact with the probation or parole department for six months or more.

---

29. Kathryn Morgan. (1994). "Factors Influencing Probation Outcome," *Journal of Criminal Justice*, Volume 22 (4), p. 343.

30. Frank Schmallenger and John Smykla (2013). *Corrections in the 21st Century*. New 6th Edition. New York, NY: McGraw Hill, 107.

31. Ibid., Morgan, Factors Influencing Probation Outcome, p. 351.

supervising officer. The probation officer loses contact and the ability to monitor the behavior of the probationer. It is estimated that about 4–10% of all probationers abscond each year and account for 37% of the technical violations of probation.[32]

Absconders undermine the rehabilitation and deterrent purposes of punishment and put the community at risk of becoming victims of offenders who are no longer monitored by the courts or following court-ordered conditions. When probationers abscond, court-ordered fees are not being paid and victims are not receiving restitution for the harm caused by the crime.[33]

Characteristics of Absconders

Who are the absconders who discontinue contact and communication with the probation department? In comparing absconders with active probationers, studies have shown that they have different characteristics. Absconders:

1. Are felony offenders with an average sentence of 18 months;
2. Have more serious criminal histories and may have as many as seven prior felony convictions;
3. May have a prior probation and/or parole revocation;
4. Are younger than most probationers;
5. Are often minority males;
6. Are usually on probation for a drug offense;
7. Have a history of alcohol and drug problems;
8. Have a history of unemployment; and
9. Have fewer academic and vocational skills.[34]

Absconders are more likely to have more technical violations and commit more crimes while they are active probationers. One study showed that probationers who eventually become absconders demonstrate a pattern of violating the administrative conditions including failure to report, pay assessed fees, perform community service, or participate in court-ordered drug/alcohol programs. There are also more arrests for new crimes while under probation supervision, and crimes are committed early in the probation term than those of successful probationers.[35]

---

32. Roni Mayzer, Kevin Gray, and Sheila Maxwell (2004). "Probation Absconders: A Unique Risk Group?" *Journal of Criminal Justice 32*: 137–150.

33. Ibid.

34. Faye Taxman and James Byrne (1994, March). "Locating Absconders: Results from a Randomized Field Experiment," *Federal Probation 53*: 13–23.

35. Mayzer, Gray, and Maxwell. "Probation Absconders: A Unique Risk Group?" p. 147.

Although absconding is a major problem, there is often little effort to apprehend probationers who abscond from supervision. Given limited resources in many probation departments, probation management must decide if resources should be used to locate absconders. Often, they are "hiding in plain view" with nothing being done to apprehend them. This sends a message to other probationers—"You can stop reporting to probation officials and nothing will be done."[36]

It has been suggested that more intensive field monitoring can reduce absconding and facilitate the location and apprehension of absconders. Identifying potential absconding probationers and taking a proactive approach to supervision also reduces the number of probationers who abscond.

> ### Critical Thinking Box 4.5
>
> Looking at the characteristics of failures and absconders, it has been said that they have no "stake in conformity" and that leads to nonconformity. Most of these probation violators feel that they have nothing to lose by violating the rules. As a probation officer, how do you help probationers have a reason to comply with the rules of probation?

Probation Fee Collection

Probationers under supervision are required to pay a number of fees including fines, courts costs, and restitution. They are also required to pay probation supervision fees. In most states, criminal justice agencies, just as other social and educational programs, have been greatly affected by the fiscal crisis. Corrections programs are being called upon to "do more with less" as more offenders are being supervised but less money is being allocated. As the number of probationers under supervision has increased the demand for services, supervision fees have become much more necessary. In states that authorize probation fee collection, all probationers are charged a supervision fee. Where probation fee collection is authorized, regular probationers pay a minimum monthly fee of $20.00; intensive supervision offenders pay $15.00 per week. Some states limit the imposition of fees to those who are gainfully employed, those serving a split sentence (jail/probation), and those serving sentences either in a residential facility

---

36. Ibid., p. 138.

or in home confinement. Although 11 states do not place limits on fee amounts collected, in most of the 26 states, fee amounts range from $10 to $30 for regular probation and up to $40 for probationers and parolees on intensive supervision. These fees are used for operational expenses and the supervision of probationers and offenders in community residential and work release programs.[37]

Several arguments support and advocate the use of fee collection for probationers. Those who support fee collection contend that fees are important to the operation of the probation agency because fee collection provides a cost-effective source of revenue that helps corrections departments improve and maintain correctional services to clients.[38] Fees provide and expand social services that are presently unavailable to many probationers. Most departments need social services such as counseling, drug and alcohol treatment, and job training that can ultimately produce more correctional successes than failures. Finally, supporters of fee collection practices point out that those who are indigent and cannot pay will have their fees waived so that probationers are not punished for inability to pay.[39]

Those opposed to the charging of supervision fees point out that convicted offenders are "involuntary consumers" of correctional services. Thus, it is unfair to impose a fee for services that the offenders may not refuse, decide how much to take, or receive elsewhere.[40] Secondly, opponents argue that making a probation department dependent on collection of supervision fees shifts the mission of the agency from supervision and treatment to fee collection.[41] Harlow and Nelson (1982) emphasize that the weight placed on fee collection in the supervision process could result in "net-widening." Those who might have been diverted out of the criminal justice system will be given probation, increasing the number of offenders subject to control and payment of fees.[42] Given the limited resources available for the criminal justice system and corrections, stressing fee collection could affect the funding to probation departments by state legislatures. Finally, opponents highlight that probation supervision fees represent an unstable source of revenue because probationers are poor payment risks; collection costs will exceed the actual amount of money collected.[43]

---

37. Dale Parent (1990). "Recovering Correctional Costs Through Offender Fees," Washington, DC: National Institute of Justice.

38. Ibid.

39. Ibid.

40. Charles Ring (1989). "Probation Supervision Fees: Shifting the Costs to the Offender," *Federal Probation* 42(1): 43–49.

41. Ibid.

42. N. Harlow and K. Nelson (1982). *Management Strategies for Probation in an Era of Limits*. Washington, DC: National Institute of Corrections.

43. Dale Parent (1990). "Recovering Correctional Costs Through Offender Fees," p. 2.

Probation officers recognize the importance of fee collection for their department. Studies have revealed that most probation officers generally support the practice of collecting supervision fees and even believe that collection of fees has some positive effects for the offender and the department. The major difficulty involves the process. Officers think that the fee collection process consumes too much of the time that they need to devote to other duties (field contacts, report writing, court work) and often makes them feel more like "bill collectors" than criminal justice professionals.[44]

Critical Thinking Box 4.6

As probation caseloads have increased, probation agencies are called upon to do more with less — to provide more services and manage more probationers but with fewer resources. The collection of probation supervision fees allows probation departments to improve operations and provide social services and other programs that may not be possible without the collection of those fees. Those who oppose fee collection argue that probationers are "involuntary consumers" of correctional services. Therefore, they should not be required to pay for services that they did not request but cannot refuse. Which of these arguments do you agree with and why?

Recap and Review

- Offenders are granted probation by judges who consider many factors, including the attitudes of the geographic location in which the court is located, overcrowding in the jails and prisons, and whether or not the offender has a family to support or restitution to pay.
- Judges must consider the severity of the offense, the criminal history of the offender, sentencing guidelines, the rehabilitation potential of the offender, the attitude of the community towards the offender and the offense, and whether or not the offender expresses remorse.
- The judge's decision to grant probation is largely influenced by the seriousness of the offense and the offender's criminal history. Some studies have concluded that the judge may also be influenced by extrale-

---

44. Kathryn Morgan (1995). "A Study of Probation and Parole Supervision Fee Collection in Alabama," *Criminal Justice Review* 20(1): 44–55.

gal factors (e.g., age, race/ethnicity, gender, class) and the type of attorney representing the offender.

- Probationers are given probation conditions to follow while under supervision. Standard conditions are punitive conditions that reflect the seriousness of the offense and are designed to punish the probationer and monitor behavior. Treatment conditions address the needs of the probationer as indicated by the presentence investigation report.
- Although judges have discretion in setting probations conditions, probation conditions must be reasonably related to rehabilitation and protection of the community and must not violate the U.S. Constitution.
- Technical violations are violations of administrative rules. New arrest violations occur when probationers have been arrested and charged with a new offense.
- In revocation hearings, the standard of proof is preponderance of the evidence not proof beyond a reasonable doubt as in criminal trials.
- When the court revokes probation, it indicates that there is enough evidence to show that the person did violate the conditions of probation. The probation contract between the court and the probationer has become void, the privilege is rescinded, and the original sentence is imposed.
- Those supervised under probation are more likely to be male, white, young, unemployed, and a property or drug offender.
- Those most likely to fail under supervision are younger males who are unemployed, single, and property offenders. Other variables related to failure are lack of educational attainments, two or more felony convictions, and a sentence length of five or more years.
- Race, type/level of supervision, and conditions of probation are not related to failure.
- Absconders are probationers who repeatedly fail to report to the probation department or cease contact.
- Although warrants are issued for absconders, many probation departments do not have the resources to actively search for these missing probationers, who may go undetected. This may send a message to other probationers that "if you stop reporting, no one will come looking for you."
- Absconding undermines the goals and integrity of the court and the probation department. The public is not protected from convicted felons who are not monitored or supervised, and victims may not be receiving restitution.
- Absconders are more likely to be minority males with serious criminal histories, drug and alcohol problems, and employment problems.

- Probationers under active supervision are required to pay a supervision fee to the probation department ranging from $20–$40 per month. Probationers under intensive supervision are required to pay as much as $60 each month.
- Probation fees are used to cover operational expenses and provide needed services to probationers.
- Supporters of fee collections point out that those fees are cost effective and provide services to probationers that can produce correctional successes.
- Opponents of fee collection argue that forcing involuntary consumers of correctional services to pay supervision fees can lead to net-widening, diversion from supervision responsibilities, and withdrawal of funding by state legislatures.
- Probation officers generally support fee collection but feel that it is time consuming.

Questions for Review

1. What are some of the factors that the judge must consider before placing an offender under probation supervision?
2. Identify the types of probation supervision and briefly describe each.
3. Distinguish between a technical and new arrest violation.
4. Discuss the preliminary and revocation hearings in the revocation process.
5. Although judges have discretion when setting probation conditions, what are two principles that control their decisions?
6. What is intensive probation supervision? What are some of the features of this type of supervision?
7. Distinguish between standards conditions and treatment conditions of probation. Provide examples of each type.
8. Although men outnumber women on probation, the number of women on probation are increasing. Explain why those numbers are rising.
9. Shock probation has been both praised and criticized. Identify the advantages and disadvantages of using shock probation.
10. Discuss the length of probation supervision. What has begun to happen in recent years regarding probation sentences?
11. What due process protections are available to the probationer during the revocation process?
12. Identify the characteristics of those most likely to under probation supervision.

13. Discuss the failure rates of probationers. Identify the characteristics of probation failures.
14. When trying to measure recidivism, what are some of the problems specifically with probationers?
15. What are absconders and how do they affect the supervision process?
16. What are some of the characteristics of absconders?
17. How do most probation agencies respond to absconders?
18. According to supporters of the fee collection practice, what are some of the benefits of fee collection for probation departments?
19. What are some of the reasons given by opponents for not using fee collection?

Questions for Discussion

Please use these questions for discussion. Choose the response that you think is most appropriate and explain your reasoning. Why are the other responses not appropriate?

1. You receive the presentence investigation report of a probationer who has been assigned to your caseload. In reading the criminal history, you discover that there are at least three arrests for aggressive behavior. Further reading of the marital history indicates some domestic violence. Yet, the conditions of probation do not address these apparent aggressive tendencies. How do you respond?
   A. You do nothing. Your responsibility is to enforce the conditions of probation as ordered by the court.
   B. You plan to discuss this information with the probationer on the first visit and decide what to do from that point.
   C. You refer the case back to the court for further processing and reprimand the judge for failure to address this behavior.
   D. You use this information to show that the probationer poses a danger and request revocation of probation.

2. Robert is on probation for felony DUI. As conditions of probation, he is prohibited from having a driver's license or operating a motor vehicle. You discover that he has been driving to and from work each day. He informs you that he has no other alternative since he works 10–15 miles from home. As his probation officer, you should:
   A. Suggest that he find new employment in walking distance.
   B. Suggest that he should quit his job.

    C. Suggest that he should try to get an occupational driver's license.

    D. Charge him with a new crime in violation of criminal law.

3. Probation conditions may be of two kinds: standard or special. Standard conditions are those that apply to all offenders placed on probation. Special conditions are those given to a probationer because of a particular need: they are tailor-made for a probationer situation. Which of the following conditions would be a special condition?

    A. Obey all laws and commit no other crime.

    B. Maintain suitable employment.

    C. Do not leave the jurisdiction without permission.

    D. Attend anger management classes.

4. Brandon, who is on probation for burglary, has been unemployed for the past eight months. Each time you approach the subject of his unemployment, he starts to talk about general unemployment problems and the "bad economy." Realizing that his situation is not getting any better, you decide to:

    A. Encourage him to develop a plan that focuses on reasons for his unemployment and how he plans to seek employment.

    B. Prepare a delinquency report citing failure to maintain employment — prison would be a solution to his unemployment issues.

    C. Allow him to continue to talk; it is healthy for him to express himself.

    D. Request an amended probation order that waives the employment condition.

5. During curfew checks, you find that an 18-year-old on your caseload has repeatedly violated his court-ordered curfew. After warning him several times, he ignores your warning and continues to stay out past his 11:00 PM curfew. You decide to:

    A. Notify his employer and ask that he threaten to fire him if he continues the violation.

    B. Take no action because an 11:00 PM curfew for an 18-year-old is unreasonable.

    C. File a violation report to the judge recommending some jail time to be served on weekends.

    D. File a violation report requesting revocation of probation and imposing the prison sentence.

6. If you were making an argument that there are many advantages of probation, which of the following statements would *not* be included?

   A. Probation and parole supervision is less expensive than incarceration.
   B. Releasing dangerous offenders in the community increases the risk of harm to the community.
   C. It allows offenders under supervision to be employed.
   D. It helps to avoid further criminalization of the offender.

7. Daniel has been convicted of "indecency with a child," which he committed during his employment with a children's program of the Department of Human Resources. He was given a 10-year probation term and ordered to register as a sex offender and refrain from employment involving children. Six months into the probation term, you discover that he has not registered and has taken a job with an agency, Children First, which provides services to the children of incarcerated parents. You:

   A. File a request to have probation revoked because he has violated probation conditions.
   B. Advise him that if he quits his job and registers as a sex offender, you will not inform the court of his violations.
   C. Allow him to remain on probation and keep his job if he will independently seek mental health counseling.
   D. Do nothing because he needs the job to stay compliant with probation conditions.

8. A probationer that you have supervised for two years approaches you with a request to have his curfew modified—moved from 10:00 PM to 12:00 AM. You check his record and find that he has paid his fine and court costs and is up-to-date on his probation supervision fees. He reports consistently and follows all of the rules. You decide to:

   A. Inform the probationer that conditions can never be amended for the duration of the sentence.
   B. Inform the probationer that conditions can only be amended if there are repeated technical violations or a new arrest.
   C. Request that the judge amend the probation order to drop the curfew.
   D. Request that the judge amend the probation order to move the curfew from 10:00 PM to 8:00 PM.

9. Which of the following would be most likely to result in revocation by the court?

   A. Failure to pay probation fees for two months.
   B. A new arrest for robbery.

    C. Missing the last curfew check.

    D. Requesting travel out of the jurisdiction to a concert.

10. When probationers are required to pay the victim for the expenses of the crime, this payment back to the victim is called:

    A. restitution

    B. retribution

    C. probation supervision fees

    D. fine

11. A woman comes to your office and says that she thinks that her neighbor is on probation and wonders if you as the probation department supervisor could confirm that for her. You respond by:

    A. Checking out the probationers supervised by your office and providing her with the information about his case.

    B. Informing her that you cannot confirm or deny that kind of information because of confidentiality issues.

    C. Having her arrested for invasion of privacy.

    D. Having security remove her from the office after lecturing her about prying into others' business.

12. Sheila, who is on your probation caseload, informs you that her son's fourth-grade class will be taking an overnight field trip to the 4-H camp 200 miles away. His teacher, explaining that they don't have enough parents going on the trip, has asked her to serve as one of the chaperones. The school and her son are not aware that she is on probation with limitations on her travel, so she does not know what to do. When you are approached, you respond by:

    A. Informing her that she will have to explain to her son and the school that she will have to decline.

    B. Encouraging her to make up an excuse to give the teacher.

    C. Requesting an amended probation order form to allow her to travel for the specified period of time.

    D. Calling the teacher to explain the mother's legal problems.

13. An alternative to incarceration that allows an offender to remain under supervision in the community with court-ordered conditions, violation of which may result in revocation and the imposing of the sentence. This describes:

    A. parole

    B. commutation

    C. probation

    D. pardon

14. Which of the following defendants is more likely to be granted probation?

    A. A repeat violent offender

    B. A first-time offender convicted of forgery

    C. A property offender facing his third incarceration for burglary

    D. A parolee who commits another violent offense

15. Which of the following probationers would be most likely to be success-ful under probation supervision?

    A. A drug-addicted probationer with a history of repeat property offenses

    B. A probationer with a family and steady employment

    C. An unemployed probationer who lives at home with his parents

    D. A probationer who has frequent problems with drug abuse

16. Joyce is a single mother of five children who has been given a five-year probation term for forgery. She has been ordered to pay fines, court costs, and probation supervision fees. She is presently 12 months behind on all of her fees. You know that she is working two jobs and an additional part-time job on weekends just to make ends meet. As the supervising officer, you decide to:

    A. Prepare a delinquency report requesting revocation of probation for a technical violation — failure to pay fees.

    B. Recommend a 30-day jail term to scare her into paying the delin-quent fees.

    C. Report the delinquency to your supervising officer and let her make decisions about case.

    D. Request an amended probation order to waive fees until she can pay.

17. You have 10 probationers on your caseload who have been classified as "absconders." What does that mean?

    A. It means that the probationers have been revoked.

    B. It means that there has been no contact with the probation officer, who has no information about the probationers' location.

    C. It means that these probationers have been classified for special treat-ment.

    D. It means that the probationers have fulfilled their financial obligations and can be terminated early.

18. As a probation officer, you are required to collect supervision fees for probation/parole services to clients. If you were *opposed* to the collection of fees, which of the following arguments would you use?

    A. Collection of fees takes too much time away from important probation and parole responsibilities to clients.

    B. It is appropriate to collect fees from correctional clients who are granted the privilege of probation or parole.

    C. Collection of probation and parole fees for supervision allows departments to provide more services to clients.

    D. Fee collection makes correctional clients responsible some of the costs of supervision.

Case Studies

Case Study 1

Questions 1–3 are based on the following case.

Diane is a 21-year-old female serving a 10-year probation term for theft (six counts), and receiving stolen property. She has two juvenile arrests for possession of marijuana and burglary of her mother's home. As an adult, she has six arrests and five convictions for retail theft, receiving stolen property, burglary, and possession of drugs. Three of her sentences were concurrent for three years. On these charges, she was granted parole after six months on the condition that she enters a residential drug treatment program. Her participation was unsuccessful and she refused to comply with other conditions of her parole. She was sent back to prison to serve the remainder of her sentence.

Diane is the younger of two children. Her parents were divorced when she was a year old. She lived with her mother until her mother remarried and she did not fit into her mother's new lifestyle. Therefore, her grandmother and her aunt raised her. When her grandmother and aunt could no longer take care of her, she was turned over to the Department of Child Welfare which placed her in and out of foster care. She lived on the street for a while, making her living mostly through prostitution. When she was 16, she had a child that was given up for adoption. She has very little contact with any of her family members. She last saw her real father about five years ago.

Diane got married four years ago because she was pregnant. Her husband was an addict and got her addicted. They separated after a year because he was physically abusive and she realized that she could not "kick the habit" as long as he was around. She began keeping company with another man, got pregnant, and had another child. The child was abandoned in a parking lot when she was trying to avoid an arrest. Although her husband is in prison, she is still legally married and her child is in the care of the Department of Welfare.

Diane dropped out of school in the ninth grade. She confessed that she did not really want to go to school anyway. Diane has never held a full-time job or developed any kind of work history. The defendant has been hospitalized for drug overdoses and has had hepatitis four times. She is presently in good health. She has an extensive drug history beginning at age 12. She was addicted to heroin by age 16. She has been clean of drugs for about 11 months.

1. Diane has informed you that she wants to get a job, find suitable living arrangements, and regain custody of her children. She admits that she does not know how or where to start since she does not have any skills or education that would help her secure employment. She admits that her family refuses to help her since they gave up on her a long time ago. As her probation officer, you are the only person that she has to provide some guidance. You should:
   A. Inform her that providing this kind of advice is not a part of your job but wish her luck with her goals.
   B. Encourage and assist Diane in developing realistic goals as well as a plan for reaching those goals.
   C. Express your doubts about the seriousness of her desire for a better life.
   D. Tell her that she is still too young and that the state would never return her children.

2. Diane confides that she ran into some old friends who convinced her to have one last "high" with them. She admits that she was feeling a bit "depressed" and decided to get high. She feels guilty and says that she doesn't want the drug life anymore. You respond by:
   A. Notifying the judge that Diane has violated probation.
   B. Demeaning her for her lack of self-control.
   C. Being a broker and referring her to a drug treatment program or someone who can help her at this time.
   D. Suggesting that she try to get arrested and revoked; prison would solve her job and housing problems.

3. Diane calls you to tell you that her husband is being released from prison. She heard through his family members that he plans to "get her" when he gets out because it was her fault that he got busted. As her probation officer, you:

A. Inform her that domestic issues are not your responsibility.
B. Inform her that since this is only hearsay, she should ignore it.
C. Call his family and threaten to have them arrested for frightening your client.
D. Refer her to the domestic violence program that may be able to provide safe shelter since there is some history of abuse.

Case Study 2

Questions 4–7 are based on the following case.

Johnny is a 28-year-old male who is on probation for burglary, theft, and receiving stolen property. He has been given a 10-year probation term, restitution of $5,000, and fine and court costs totaling $2,000. He is in his second year of this 10-year term. His criminal record indicates five juvenile arrests and convictions, all for property crimes. He was also on juvenile probation. As an adult, he has three felony arrests and two convictions for burglary, auto theft, and receiving stolen property. He also has two misdemeanor convictions for simple assault and theft. He previously served a probation term of five years after pleading guilty to two charges of burglary. His only incarceration has been two years in county jail on a burglary charge.

Johnny is the second of four brothers and two sisters born to his mother and father who never married but lived together for over 20 years. He had a close relationship with both parents but was closest to his father. His father was a strong disciplinarian who kept the house in order. After he died, his mother was not a strong disciplinarian and often let the children do what they wanted. When his father died, his mother remarried a man who took the family savings and left after a year. One of Johnny's brothers was killed in the process of a robbery. His youngest brother is wanted in several states and is characterized as a thief.

Johnny married at 20, but the marriage lasted one year and produced one child. He married again at 23 and had three more children. The marriage has been shaky because of his drinking and his irresponsible behavior in other areas.

Johnny dropped out of school in the tenth grade. Therefore, he has only had unskilled laboring jobs. In the last two years, since being on probation, he has quit three jobs and been fired from two. He receives state public assistance to take care of his living expenses. He was in the army and was discharged after going AWOL three times. He is emotionally immature and seems to constantly stress about something. The defendant has no assets or debts. Some form of public assistance covers most of his living expenses.

4. As you read Johnny's case history, how would you characterize him?
    A. Johnny is a decent guy who has just had a few bad breaks.
    B. Johnny's history shows a pattern of irresponsible behavior and immaturity.
    C. Johnny has been unfairly labeled, which has left him trying to prove himself.
    D. Johnny's dysfunctional relationship with his father has left deep scars.

5. How would you characterize Johnny's criminal history?
    A. There is a strong pattern of aggressive and violent behavior.
    B. Johnny is heavily into the economic side of drugs—he sells.
    C. Johnny's criminal history shows patterns of petty, victimless crimes that should not have been prosecuted.
    D. Johnny's juvenile and adult criminal history shows a pattern of property offending.

6. How would you characterize Johnny's home and family life as he was growing up?
    A. It was dysfunctional from the day that he was born.
    B. It was a home where children saw and experienced violence on a regular basis.
    C. It was a home that appeared to be stable but became dysfunctional after his father died and his mother remarried.
    D. It was a home that appeared to tolerate and encourage criminal activity to survive.

7. On his most recent monthly visit to your office, Johnny informs you that he would like to enroll at the local junior college to pursue an associate's degree in a trade. You respond by:
    A. Laughing in his face at his latest project that he will never finish.
    B. Encouraging him but allowing him to take the initiative to explore the programs, start the application process, and talk to advisors at the college.
    C. Threatening to request probation revocation if he doesn't get a job.
    D. Questioning why he would want to get a trade and a job since he is receiving financial assistance from the state.

Case Study 3

Questions 8–11 are based on the following case.

Carolyn is a 34-year-old female who is on probation for robbery. She took $50 from a cab driver who picked her up along the interstate. She and her husband called the police; Carolyn turned herself in and repaid the cab driver. She was given probation because the victim didn't think that she should be incarcerated, she never showed a gun, and she returned the $50.

She has one juvenile arrest for shoplifting, for which she served a six-month juvenile probation term. This is her first offense as an adult.

Her childhood was basically uneventful. She came from a stable family where both parents worked and took care of the family. She has an older brother and sister whom she sees frequently. There is no history of criminal activity in the family; they all support her and are willing to help in any way they can.

Carolyn married when she was 17 because she was pregnant. She admitted during the presentence investigation that she was mentally, physically, and sexually abused during this two-year marriage. The child's paternal grandmother has legal custody of her son and she is allowed to see him once every two months. At age 23, she married her present husband who is also on probation for possession of a gun without a license. Although the marriage has had rough spots, it has lasted for over 10 years and appears to be stable.

Carolyn graduated from high school even though her grades were very poor. Before being placed on probation, she had started to take a course in medical assisting but had to drop for financial reasons. She states that she would like to become a nurse's aide or medical assistant. She has had only one job, at a meat packing plant. She was laid off because of a knee injury. She started to drink when she was 16 and admits that she is an alcoholic. She has been hospitalized for depression and alcoholism.

8. You receive Carolyn's file prior to her initial visit. Your overall assessment of this case is that:

   A. This woman has no business on probation; she should be in prison.
   B. Prison would have been more harmful to her because it is obvious that she is more in need of treatment than punishment.
   C. She has an extensive criminal history which the judge didn't consider before sentencing her to probation.
   D. Carolyn appears to be a danger to her and society and should be locked up in prison or a mental hospital.

9. Which of the following would be an important advantage in Carolyn's rehabilitation?

    A. Having a supportive husband and family that are willing to help in whatever way they can.
    B. Being 34 years old and having no children and no plans to have any.
    C. Being unemployed and having no skills.
    D. Being a white female.

10. Carolyn tells you that she drinks mostly during the day when she is home alone and bored. She would like to go back to her medical assistant's course and get a job. You respond by:

    A. Encouraging her to explore the amount of time that she has left to complete the course and then helping her to explore ways to pay for her study.
    B. Advising her to get any job because she is in violation of probation conditions.
    C. Advising her to stay at home and try to be the best wife that she can be.
    D. Advising her that since she started this before she was placed on probation, helping her or advising her about this is inappropriate.

11. After supervising Carolyn for a month, you observe that she is depressed. She expresses fear that she will start to drink again. She is unwilling to seek counseling, therefore, you respond by:

    A. Doing nothing. You hope that the problem will get better on its own.
    B. Requesting that the probation order be amended to include counseling as a condition.
    C. Attempting to counsel her during monthly visits.
    D. Waiting for her to violate probation conditions so you can request revocation of probation.

Case Study 4

Questions 12–14 are based on the following case.

Billy is a 26-year-old male is serving a 15-year probation term for burglary and retail theft. The defendant was convicted of burglary (eight counts), and one count of retail theft. He has five prior arrests as a juvenile but no convictions. As an adult, he has had seven felony arrests and convictions. Offenses included larceny, receiving stolen property, and failure to stop at the scene of an accident. He was sentenced to 10 years for these convictions but was paroled after three years.

Billy grew up in a dysfunctional family where family life was chaotic. His father has been married and divorced seven times. There was no financial stability because the father was a truck driver. His mother left the family when Billy was four years old and took two of the five children with her when she left. A neighboring family adopted one child while his paternal grandparents raised Billy and his sister.

He married two years ago but the marriage is unstable because he stays in jail so much. He has only worked unskilled laboring jobs and has no real employment history. While serving in Vietnam, he developed a heroin addiction and has used as much as $400–$500 of heroin a day. Much of his criminal behavior is related to his drug addictions. Drug treatment has failed in the past and he believes that there is little hope of him ever kicking the drug habit.

12. As you read Johnny's case file, you conclude that:
    A. Billy's drug addiction is probably a major factor in his criminal behavior.
    B. Billy is violent and should be incarcerated.
    C. Billy is probably better off in prison because of his unemployment and lack of skills.
    D. Billy's wife should get a divorce.

13. After you have read the case file, you conclude that Billy has many problems that need attention. Which of the following would not be one of Billy's major problems?
    A. Lack of job skills and unemployment
    B. Drug addiction
    C. Violent and aggressive tendencies
    D. Irresponsible behavior and a hopeless attitude

14. Just from the information contained in Billy's case file, how would you characterize his chances for probation success?
    A. Excellent: he knows what prison is like and doesn't want to return.
    B. Good: the support from his family, especially his father and wife, will help him through.
    C. Good: he understands that he will lose his family, job, and conditional freedom by returning to prison
    D. Poor: he has no job, no job history, no skills, little family support, and a drug addiction that he admits will never improve.

Case Study 5

Questions 15–18 are based on the following case.

Today is your first day to see your new probationer, John. John has been placed on probation for aggravated assault with a deadly weapon. You notice in his PSI that this is not the first violent offense on his criminal record. Excluding the present charge, he has three previous offenses for simple assault. He was convicted for only one of the assault charges. He was placed on misdemeanor probation and completed the two-year term without incident. He also has one prior conviction for burglary. He has never been sent to prison, although he did spend nine months in jail on the burglary charge. He had been granted probation but was revoked after he was arrested for simple assault. He is now on probation for a new assault charge. He shot a "friend" after the friend accused him of cheating in a crap game. His criminal history indicates that he was first arrested and taken to juvenile court at the age of 14 for cutting a student with a razor after school. He was given probation and sent to counseling for his behavior.

This is his first visit to see you since leaving court and getting his probation conditions. His appointment was scheduled for 9:00 A.M., but he fails to show up. Then, at about 10:30, the receptionist announces that John is in the waiting area. When he comes into your office, he slumps into the chair. He hands you the report form that has been completed incorrectly and in a handwriting that is not legible.

He starts to explain his tardiness. "Well, my friends came by last night to see if I wanted to go drinking. I really did not want to go because I always seem to get into trouble when I am with them, but they are my friends. My wife has been annoying me about a job. I have not worked since being laid off from the tire plant about a year and a half ago. So to get a little quiet (at least from her), I thought that I would get out of the house for a while. We stayed out drinking until 3:00 A.M. because none of us had to get up to go to work. By the time that I got home, I was really out of it—I drank way too much. My wife and I started fighting again, and after I pushed her down, I crashed into the bed. I guess I intended to be on time, but when the alarm went off, my wife started again. So here I am, and I'm late. So what are you going to do to me—put me in jail? Big deal! I don't really care."

15. As the supervising probation officer, how would you characterize John as indicated by the pattern in his criminal history?

   A. John is aggressive with violent tendencies.
   B. John is a petty thief.

C. John is a repeat property offender.

D. John has a tendency to commit victimless crimes.

16. During this initial visit, you realize that it will be almost impossible to communicate with your new probationer. Therefore, you decide to:

A. Advise him to leave and come back when he gets his attitude together.

B. Review the conditions of probation and stress the importance of obeying those conditions.

C. Write a note to the judge informing him that John should have his probation revoked.

D. Get hostile to let him know that you can be just as tough and hard.

17. You recognize that this will be a difficult case to supervise because there are so many problems and issues. You do an assessment of his needs and risk of returning to crime. You discover that John is has a high need level and is at a high risk for returning to crime. You:

A. Do nothing and hope that he violates probation quickly so you can get him off of your caseload.

B. Conclude that he is hopeless and nothing can be done to help him.

C. Change his supervision level from maximum to medium so that you only see him once monthly instead of biweekly.

D. Prioritize his needs and develop a plan for helping him address the most serious needs first.

18. Six months into supervision, John informs you that his uncle has hired him as a plumber's helper and plans to teach him the trade. John confides to you something that you had already figured out—that he cannot read. You advise him to:

A. Find another job that will not require reading.

B. Enroll in the night literacy program at the local high school.

C. Tell his uncle that he is not interested in learning plumbing.

D. Fake it.

Case Study 6

Questions 19–22 are based on the following case.

Sheila Brown is a 19-year-old female who was convicted and given 10 years' probation for five counts of possession of a controlled substance. She and her boyfriend sold cocaine, speed, and heroin to an undercover police officer. She denies that she sold anything but says that her boyfriend might have had drugs.

He is now serving a 10-year prison term for his conviction. She has no juvenile or adult criminal record.

Sheila grew up with her mother and two younger sisters but never knew her father. Her mother married when Sheila was six years old. She got along well with her stepfather until he became overly protective and harsh on Sheila and her two sisters. When she turned 17, she moved in with her boyfriend and lived with him for two years before he was arrested. She was pregnant when she was arrested but had a miscarriage soon after. She was an average student but quit school in the tenth grade. She plans to get her GED soon. Sheila has no employment history and no desire or plans to work. She wants to be a homemaker with a large family. Presently, there seems to be no visible means of income.

She has used many different kinds of drugs and is now addicted to speed. One of her conditions of probation is that she must spend 60 days in Bradford Clinic for drug treatment. She denies having a drug problem and believes that going to Bradford for drug treatment is a waste of time.

In addition to receiving drug treatment, Sheila has been ordered to get her GED, find suitable employment, and move from the neighborhood where she lived with her boyfriend. Crime rates are high and it is known as an area where a person can get any kind of drug that he or she wants. She has refused to go to treatment and still lives in the same neighborhood.

19. During her initial visit into your office, she again denies being involved in any sale or use of drugs. She further denies any addictions even though she admits to experimenting with some different drugs. In the supervision of this case, what is likely to be the major obstacle to Sheila's rehabilitation?

    A. She is too young to understand the seriousness of her crime.
    B. She refuses to take responsibility for her actions.
    C. She grew up in a dysfunctional home.
    D. She has a past criminal history.

20. Sheila has no high school diploma, no GED, no skills, no employment, and no desire to get and maintain employment. Her goal is to be a homemaker with a large family. How can you motivate her to get her GED, find employment, and change her present living arrangements?

    A. Remind her that she is in violation of probation conditions but also encourage her to develop a plan to get her GED as well as a job.
    B. Recognize that you cannot motivate her and request that her probation be revoked.

    C. Do nothing, wait for her to mess up, and then request revocation.

    D. Notify her landlord that she is on probation and request that he evict her from her apartment.

21. Sheila continues to live in her apartment, paying bills and even purchasing new furnishings despite no visible source of income. You become even more concerned when another probationer told his officer that Sheila sells drugs and engages in prostitution. You:

    A. Ignore the rumors and conclude that her mother and stepfather are helping her financially.

    B. Hope that she gets arrested so that she can be revoked and off your caseload.

    C. Submit a violation report to the judge requesting a 30-day shock probation period based on her refusal to abide by any of the conditions of probation.

    D. Ask police officers to spy on Sheila and arrest her at the first sign of criminal behavior.

22. A week before she goes to court on the probation violations, Sheila informs you that she has a job offer at a local restaurant but she needs to get her GED. She asks you for help. You respond by:

    A. Referring her to the adult literacy program by giving her all of the information and waiting for her to follow up on the information.

    B. Dismissing her actions as an attempt to stay out of prison.

    C. Telling her that she should wait until she gets to prison to get her GED.

    D. Leave it up to her to find out the information and follow through.

Case Study 7

Questions 23–25 are based on the following case.

    Michael is a 19-year-old male who is serving a 15-year sentence for burglary, receiving stolen property, and theft. Michael was hooked on cocaine and heroin. Because he could not afford it but couldn't stop, he resorted to stealing to keep up with his habit. He is still addicted to drugs but says that he has been drug free for the last two months. Michael has had six arrests and three convictions as a juvenile. He was on probation for six months but has had no incarcerations. His adult criminal history has consisted largely of property offenses to get money for drugs.

Michael, the oldest of five children, grew up in a home where his father was gone much of the time because he was in the military. The family spent two years overseas. After his father returned from Vietnam, he was seriously addicted to drugs. Michael has no contact with his father but has a close relationship with his mother. He has never been married mainly because of his drug addiction.

He dropped out of school in the eighth grade. In school, he was a poor student who was disruptive and suspended often. He got his GED but has never had any job. Michael went into the Navy but got kicked after only one week because of drugs.

23. Reading Michael's case file information, it is apparent that his criminal behavior is the result of:
    A. A home where the father was absent much of the time.
    B. His addiction to drugs.
    C. Rebellion because he was kicked out of the Navy.
    D. His rebellion against his father for being addicted to drugs.

24. As Michael's institutional counselor, what would be your priority in developing his treatment plan?
    A. Intense drug therapy
    B. Employment counseling
    C. Rebuilding the relationship with his family
    D. Finding the right prison job

25. After a year and a half in prison, Michael presents you his plan for getting vocational training in prison, starting a drug support group called Boys Against Drugs (BAD) and reestablishing a relationship with his family, especially his father. You respond by:
    A. Informing him that you think that he is trying to "con" the warden and the parole board with his change in behavior.
    B. Encouraging him to continue these positive efforts and assuring him that you will do whatever you can to assist him.
    C. Telling him that you don't believe that he will follow through on his plans.
    D. Telling the other counselors and correctional officers to watch him because he must be "up to something."

Chapter 5

Parole Process and Supervision

Key Terms

Case review date	Presumptive parole date
Commutation	Salient factor score
Discretionary parole release	Shock parole
Executive clemency	Supervised release
Furlough	Truth-in-sentencing laws
Mandatory release	Unconditional release
Pardon	Work release
Parole plan	

Learning Objectives
1. Summarize the administration of parole and other types of prison release.
2. Outline the parole process.
3. Discuss issues related to parole supervision.

Parole Process and Supervision

Getting Out of Prison

At the end of 2009, state and federal correctional authorities reported that there were approximately 1.6 million people incarcerated in federal and state prisons.[1] While the U.S. incarcerates more people than any nation, 95% of all of those prisoners will be released from incarceration to reenter society at some point in time. It is estimated that prisoners are released at a rate of 600,000

---

1. Heather C. West and William J. Sabol (2010). *Prisoners in 2009*. Washington, DC: U.S. Department of Justice, Office of Justice Programs, Bureau of Justice Statistics. (NCJ 231675). Revised 10/27/2011. December.

per year or 1,600 per day.[2] The average length of stay before parole is about 30 months.[3] Discretionary parole is the mechanism by which most inmates are released. Discretionary parole refers to the release of an offender from prison prior to the expiration of his or her term. The remainder of the time is served in the community under the supervision of parole authorities. Although released from confinement, the parolee remains under the legal custody of the state.

Overview and Administration of Parole

Release from Prison

There are three mechanisms of release from prison: discretionary parole release, mandatory release, and unconditional release.

Discretionary parole release is conditional release granted by a state's parole board after the inmate has served at least one-third of the sentence. Until the mid-1970s, all states and the federal government had systems of discretionary release by which the parole board determined how much time the person actually spent in prison and the time of return to the community.[4] Discretionary release is linked to the indeterminate sentencing structure where the judge sets a minimum and maximum term of incarceration and the parole board determines the release time within these limits. Discretionary parole is closely related to the rehabilitation model that advocates the release of an inmate at a time that would be most beneficial. Lengthy incarceration periods may result in greater social harm for the individual and society.

Mandatory release is a method of release related to determinate sentencing that allows the inmate to be released after serving the entire sentence minus the good time.

Mandatory release is the result of a legislative shift to a determinate sentencing structure. Mandatory release is granted after an inmate has served the full sentence minus good time. Determinate sentencing abolished parole in about 20 states and the federal government. Maine was the first state to abolish discretionary parole. In states where parole has been abolished, mandatory release becomes the primary method for releasing inmates back into the community. It is presently used by the federal government and states operating under a determinate sentencing structure.[5] It

---

2. Joan Petersilia (2004). "What Works in Prisoner Reentry? Reviewing and Questioning the Evidence," *Federal Probation* 68(2): 4–8.

3. Ibid., 4.

4. Todd Clear and George Cole (2000). *American Corrections*. Belmont, CA: Wadsworth Publishing, 348.

5. Ibid.

is the date on which the inmate must be released. Upon arriving in prison, classification personnel calculate a "mandatory release date," which includes good time and other credits. When the mandatory release date arrives, the person must be released. The person cannot be held longer than the actual sentence. Recent statistics indicate that approximately 41% of the inmates released annually are granted a mandatory release.[6] This number indicates that mandatory releases are now surpassing discretionary releases.

Unconditional release is granted to offenders who are released with no further correctional supervision because they have completed their sentences, received a pardon, or had their sentences commuted.[7]

Historically, discretionary parole[8] has been the most popular form of release from U.S. prisons. Despite the increase in mandatory releases and recent attempts to abolish parole, parole populations have continued to increase annually. Since 2007, there has been a decline in the number of adults under community supervision. While much of the decline has been in the number of adults under probation supervision, parole has also seen declining numbers. By the end of 2012, the national parole population was 851,000, a decline of 9% from the previous year.[9] Despite parole being one of corrections' key components, there is little known about parole board decisions, parole supervision, and parole revocation processes.[10]

The emergence of parole is associated with the emphasis on rehabilitation and the development of the indeterminate sentence. The sentencing judge imposes a minimum and maximum sentence, leaving it up to the parole board to determine the actual length of the sentence. Parole was subsequently used to assist in the rehabilitation and reintegration of the offender back into society. It helped to avoid further criminalization and the increased likelihood of recidivism.

Although used mainly as a rehabilitation technique for the offender, parole has also served other functions. As early as 1893, California used parole for

---

6. Bureau of Justice Statistics (2001). "Trends in State Parole, 1990–2000." Washington, DC: U.S. Department of Justice, Office of Justice Programs.

7. Clear and Cole (2000). *American Corrections*. Belmont, CA: Wadsworth Publishing Company. 349.

8. Howard Abadinsky (2003). *Probation and Parole*. Englewood Cliffs, NJ: Prentice-Hall. 282.

9. Laura M. Maruschak and Thomas P. Bonczar (2013, December). *Probation and Parole in the United States, 2012*. Washington, DC: U.S. Department of Justice, Office of Justice Programs, Bureau of Justice Statistics.

10. Jeremy Travis and Sarah Lawrence (2002). *Beyond the Prison Gates: The State of Parole in America*. Washington, DC: Urban Institute Press. 2.

non-rehabilitative functions, such as minimizing the use of clemency and correcting for sentences that were considered excessive (Messinger, 1985).[11] Many agree that parole and parole release are more closely related to parole board characteristics and the economic and political environment than to goals of rehabilitation.[12] In his study of the changing parole process, Simon (1993) notes that the transformation of the parole process has been related to the political and economic changes of society; thus rehabilitation concerns have been replaced by management concerns.[13] Institutional and political matters, including efforts to control prison overcrowding and correct sentencing disparities for inmates who have been sentenced unfairly because of race/ethnicity, gender, and social class, have taken priority over rehabilitation issues.[14]

Other Types of Prison Release

There are other types of release from prison, including the furlough, work release, and shock parole.

The **furlough** grants the inmate a short leave from prison for the purpose of searching for employment opportunities or visiting community residential centers prior to release. Inmates may also be furloughed in order to attend funerals or visit family members who are ill.[15] A prerelease furlough program implemented by the U.S. Bureau of Prisons requires placement in a community residential center for every inmate nearing release in order to facilitate the transition back into society.[16] The use of the inmate furlough received a great deal of media attention in the 1988 presidential election when the case of Willie Horton derailed the presidential hopes of Massachusetts Governor Michael Dukakis.

---

11. Sheldon Messinger (1985). "The Foundations of Parole in California," *Law and Society Review 19*: 69–106.

12. Betty Luther (1995). *The Politics of Criminal Justice: A Study of the Impact of Executive Influence on Parole Decisions between 1985 and 1992.* Unpublished doctoral dissertation, Northeastern University; Antonio Fabelo (1984). *System Responses to Correctional Reforms: The New Function of Parole and Its Effect on Decision Making.* Unpublished dissertation, University of Texas at Austin; Don Gottfredson and Kelly Ballard (1966). "Differences in Parole /Decisions Associated with Decision-Makers," *Journal of Research in Crime and Delinquency 3*(2): 112–119.

13. Jonathan Simon (1993). *Poor Discipline: Parole and the Social Control of the Underclass, 1980–1990.* Chicago: University of Chicago Press.

14. Paul Hofer (1999). "The Effect of the Federal Sentencing Guidelines on Inter-Judge Disparity," *Journal of Criminal Law and Criminology 90*: 239–321.

15. Todd Clear and Harry Dammer (2000). *The Offender in the Community.* Belmont, CA: Wadsworth.

16. Ibid.

In 1986, Horton, serving a "life in prison without the possibility of parole" sentence for robbery and murder, was released on a weekend furlough, a prison program supported by Governor Dukakis. While on furlough, Horton raped and assaulted a woman in the presence of her husband. The furlough of a violent offender who committed a violent crime while on a temporary leave from prison was the target of negative media attention that cost Governor Dukakis the presidency. In 1976, during his first term as the 65th governor of Massachusetts, Governor Dukakis initially vetoed the bill enacting the furlough for convicted murderers.[17]

Work release grants temporary release to inmates to allow them to take jobs in the community. Work release had its beginnings in Wisconsin in 1913 as a way to release inmates to work in the community during the day but return to the prison at night while still serving their prison sentences.[18] It serves two purposes: (a) it aids the inmate's transition back into society and (b) it helps the inmate gain employment prior to release. Of the 600,000 inmates released from prison each year, approximately 66% will be returned within three years of release. Work release can reduce recidivism by facilitating the transition back into the community. Through the work release program, inmates obtain employment, reestablish relationships with family members and the community, and adjust to community life while still under supervision.[19]

Shock parole occurs when the state parole board makes a decision to release someone from prison after a short period of incarceration. It is used for first-time offenders who will not need further confinement for rehabilitation. Prison and paroling authorities hope that the short stay will "shock" the offenders enough for them to change their behavior for the better. Inmates barred from shock parole include violent offenders, offenders with a previous commitment to state or federal prison, and inmates diagnosed as psychopaths.[20]

Executive Clemency

Executive clemency refers to the power given to the president in federal cases or the governor of a state to show the convicted offender mercy by modifying the sentence, forgiving the offense, or granting a temporary suspension in the

---

17. Jack Germond and Jules Witcover (1989). *Whose Broad Stripes and Bright Stars: The Trivial Pursuit of the Presidency.* New York: Warner Books.

18. Howard Abadinsky (2003). *Probation and Parole.* 8th Edition. Upper Saddle, NJ: Pearson.

19. Todd Clear and Harry Dammer (2000). *The Offender in the Community,* 196.

20. Ibid., 197.

execution of a sentence.[21] The Constitution of the United States and state constitutions grant the president and state governors powers to modify inmate sentences and grant pardons and reprieves.[22] Originating in English common law, the exercise of executive clemency powers may be motivated by three things:

1. Questions regarding the innocence of the convicted offender or the punishment that might be viewed as excessive or unequal to others convicted of similar offenses. It may provide relief in cases where there is undue harshness or concerns about the circumstances of the conviction.
2. Compassion or mercy. Concerns about the health or age of an inmate may prompt the president or governor to show mercy. An offender who is aged and ailing may receive a pardon or commutation of a sentence as a humanitarian act of compassion.
3. The belief that the offender has been rehabilitated and will never again commit a crime. Religious conversions or charity work may be evidence of a change.[23]

Three acts commonly classified as acts of executive clemency are commutation, pardon, and judicial reprieve.

1. *Commutation.* **Commutation** represents a modification of the sentence to benefit the offender. A sentence may be commuted if the inmate has a terminal illness, has assisted prison staff, or cooperated with prison officials during an investigation into a criminal act. Some states (i.e., Georgia) will allow a sentence to be commuted if it is viewed as too harsh. In 1989, Evangelist Jim Baker, founder of PTL Ministries in Charlotte, North Carolina, was sentenced to 45 years in prison for fraud and attempting to defraud his followers. His sentence was later commuted to 18 years; he was released after serving five years. Sometimes, there is no apparent reason why governors will commute a sentence.

Critical Thinking Box 5.1

As the leader of the victims' rights group in your state, you have been asked to respond to the governor's decision to commute the death sentence of a death row inmate who raped and murdered a child. How would you respond?

---

21. Peter Ruckman, Jr. (1997, Spring). "Executive Clemency in the United States: Origins, Development and Analysis (1900–1993)," *Presidential Studies Quarterly 27*: 251–71.
22. Ibid.
23. Ibid.

2. *Pardon.* **Pardon** is granting relief from the disabilities of a conviction and restoring certain civil and political rights, such as the right to vote and obtain certain licenses. In most states, the parole board reviews the case, conducts the hearing, and makes the recommendation to the governor, who makes the final decision. To be considered for a pardon, a person who has been discharged from prison without parole must wait two years; parolees must wait two years after discharge from parole supervision; probationers must wait two years after discharge from supervision.[24] Granting a pardon is not automatic. The convicted felon must demonstrate the need for a pardon and show evidence of good citizenship.

3. *Reprieve.* The **reprieve** is a temporary suspension of the execution of a sentence. It is used in capital punishment cases where there is a temporary suspension in the execution of the death sentence. Although reprieves are rare, inmates' executions may be delayed because a pregnant woman needs to give birth or there is new evidence that impacts the case. More recently, reprieves have been granted because of problems associated with the administration of lethal injections.

Abuse of Executive Clemency Power

There is always the possibility that abuse of executive clemency powers will occur. Abuse of clemency powers may transpire when the president or governor accepts bribes to grant clemency, uses clemency powers for personal reasons such as opposing the death penalty or to benefit a family member or friend, or uses clemency powers for political reasons.[25] In the 1980s, Governor Ray Blanton of Tennessee was indicted for "selling pardons" and accepting bribes to commute sentences for 52 convicted offenders, including 24 convicted murderers. He was later convicted of federal mail fraud and sentenced to prison.[26] Although recent cases do not represent the same level of abuse of power as seen in the Blanton case, critics maintain that there is abuse of the unlimited discretion given to executives in clemency cases.

---

24. Howard Abadinsky (2003). *Probation and Parole.* 8th Edition, p. 265.

25. Joseph N. Rupcich (2003). "Abusing a Limitless Power: Executive Clemency in Illinois," *Southern Illinois University Law Journal 28*: 131–156.

26. Carlton Smith (2000). *Hunting Evil.* New York: St. Martin's Press.

Critical Thinking Box 5.2

Concerns about the exercise of executive clemency power surfaced again in the 1990s in Alabama when the outgoing governor, Fob James, commuted the death sentence of death row inmate Judith Ann Neely. In 1992, Judith Ann Neely and her husband Alvin abducted Lisa Ann Millican, a 13-year-old Georgia teen, from a Rome, Georgia, shopping mall parking lot. After several days of rape and torture, Judith and her husband took the teen to a cliff and shot her several times before Judith pushed her lifeless body over the cliff. Several days later, they kidnapped another couple and shot both. The girlfriend died; the boyfriend survived the attack. When caught, Judith was put on trial in Alabama, where she was convicted and sentenced to die. In 1999, on the day that she was scheduled to be executed, Governor James commuted her sentence to life in prison. This executive directive infuriated many who called it a horrible injustice because of the heinous nature of the crime. When her death sentence was commuted from death to life imprisonment with the possibility of parole, she attempted for the next several years to be released from prison, claiming that she had served 25 years. In 2005, the state legislature passed a law stating that when a death sentence is modified, it can only be commuted from death to life in prison without the possibility of parole. Judith Neely appeared before the Alabama Board of Pardons and Parole in 2014. She was again denied parole release. Can this be viewed as an example of the misuse of a governor's power of executive clemency? Why?

The Parole Process

Parole Eligibility

In states using an indeterminate sentencing structure, the offender is given a minimum and maximum term; consideration for parole is determined by the parole board in that state. Some states give incoming inmates a **presumptive parole date.** All offenders who are not excluded by law from getting parole are given advance notice of parole. The inmate will be released, unless there are major problems.[27] In states still using discretionary parole, the law stipu-

---

27. Clear and Dammer (2000). *The Offender in the Community.* Belmont, CA: Wadsworth Publishing, p. 199.

lates that a person may be considered for parole release after serving at least one third of the sentence. Most states prohibit parole consideration for:

- Offenders given a sentence of "life in prison with possibility of parole."
- Offenders who have been sentenced under a definite/determinate sentencing structure.
- Former death row inmates whose sentences have been commuted from death to life in prison. Some states allow an inmate to be considered for parole after serving 25 years of the sentence.[28]

One of the provisions of the Comprehensive Crime Control Act of 1984 (Public Law 98-473, October 12, 1984) was the elimination of parole at the federal level by 1992. The new legislation specified that:

- Offenders sentenced to a determinate sentence would get about 15% sentence reductions for good time.
- Post-release supervision would be called **supervised release** rather than parole.
- Decisions regarding the conditions of supervised release and revocation would be made by the courts rather than by the U.S. Parole Commission.[29]

Parole Board

Although there is variation, in most states members of the parole board are appointed by the governor; the exception is Utah, where parole board members are appointed by the Department of Corrections.[30] The number of board members and the terms of membership vary from state to state. In Alabama, the Board of Pardons and Parole consists of three members who serve six-year terms; in Georgia there are seven members who serve five-year terms. Parole boards exercise a great deal of discretion and make a number of decisions including:

1. setting the date for the first parole consideration;
2. setting dates for subsequent parole hearings;
3. granting or denying parole;

---

28. Dean Champion (2008). *Probation, Parole and Community Corrections*, pp. 376–377.

29. United States Parole Commission (2003). *History of the Federal Parole System*. Washington, DC: U.S. Department of Justice.

30. Howard Abadinsky (2003). *Probation and Parole 8th Edition*, p. 235.

4. awarding good time;
5. determining the length of the sentence for prison and/or parole, and assessing special conditions for parole. The sentencing judge may set the minimum and the maximum term of the sentence but the parole board may decide how much time the inmate actually spends in prison. Sometimes the parole board may even waive the minimum term.[31]

Parole boards have been criticized for several reasons: (1) there is a lack of knowledge about how parole boards make decisions, (2) many parole board members do not have adequate background and education (in many states, the only requirement is that the members be politically responsive to the appointing power), and (3) low pay and the extensive travel requirements make parole board membership less attractive than other political appointments.[32]

Parole Plan and Investigation

The parole process begins when the inmate's name appears on a computer-generated list indicating eligibility. Victims and trial officials are notified and a list is sent to the institutional parole officer. In most states, a person will become eligible for parole after serving one third of the term. It simply means that the inmate has fulfilled the legal requirement for time served; approval for release must be granted by the board. The institutional officer interviews the inmate to get a statement and assists with the preparation of the inmate's parole plan. The parole plan details what the inmate will do if granted release. The plan contains information about living arrangements, employment prospects, and treatment plans. A recent study showed that in at least 40 states, the parole board requires a very detailed parole plan, including information about a place to live, a job, plans for transportation, plans for assuming family responsibilities, and plans for spending leisure time.[33] A copy of the pre-parole plan is sent to field services for investigation and verification. The pre-parole investigation is done by a field parole officer. The

> The parole plan provides information about the inmates' life if released. It covers three areas that the parole board expects to see: employment prospects, prospective living arrangements, and plans for treatment.

---

31. Michael Gottfredson and Don Gottfredson (1988). *Decision-Making in Criminal Justice: Towards the Rational Exercise of Discretion.* New York: Plenum Press.

32. Gene Bonham (1986). "Predicting Parole Decisions in Kansas via Discriminant Analysis," *Journal of Criminal Justice* 14(2): 123–133; Don Gottfredson and Kelly Ballard (1976). "Differences in Parole/Decisions Associated with Decision-Makers," *Journal of Research in Crime and Delinquency* 3(2): 112–119.

33. Dean Champion, *Probation, Parole and Community Corrections*, pp. 376–377.

pre-parole investigation has the same function for the parole board that the PSI report has for the judge. It provides the decision-makers with information to make informed decisions regarding parole release. Most parole boards will oppose release if the inmate does not have employment or other "satisfactory" resources. Even if the parole plan is acceptable and checks out, the board may choose to deny parole based on time served, seriousness of the offense, or some other reason.

Institutional parole officers place the plan in the inmate's case file along with the PSI, institutional records relating to education, training, physical and psychological exams, and misconduct. A hearing is scheduled where the inmate, the inmate's family and supporters, the victim, the victim's family, and others who may oppose or support parole release request will speak to the parole board. When interviewing the inmate, parole board members will ask such questions as: "If you are paroled, what do you think will happen? Do you think that something about the way you were before entering prison could be changed? How have you changed since being here? What are your plans if you are released?" These hearings are not adversarial nor does the inmate have interests that must be protected by the presence of an attorney. Therefore, it is not required that an attorney is present to represent the inmate; most jurisdictions do not permit legal counsel. After reviewing the file, each board member votes to approve or deny parole.

The U.S. Board Commission established administrative guidelines that identify the three variables that should take precedence in parole decisions: time served, offense seriousness, and risk of recidivism.[34]

According to paroling guidelines, the amount of time served is an important legislative guideline for parole decisions. Although parole boards may exercise discretion in unusual cases, laws require that an inmate serve at least one-third of the minimum sentence before being considered for parole release. In some instances, the parole board may refuse to consider the inmate even after the one third has been served. In others, the board may consider an inmate prior to the completion of the one-third requirement.

Seriousness of the offense is also a major factor for parole consideration. Parole boards rate offense seriousness from low seriousness (simple theft) to higher seriousness (planned and deliberate killing). Although parole boards may have some discretion, the usual policy is that those offenses that range in

---

34. Michael Gottfredson and Don Gottfredson (1988). *Decision-Making in Criminal Justice: Towards the Rational Exercise of Discretion.* New York: Plenum Press.

the high seriousness range are likely to be treated more severely and inmates will serve more time.[35]

The salient factor score is an actuarial device used by the United States Parole Commission as an aid in assessing a federal prisoner's likelihood of recidivism after release.

Parole guidelines also call for some prediction of parole success or risk of recidivism. The **salient factor score** predicts the likelihood of the inmate's success on parole. This prediction is based on the inmate's criminal history, prior imprisonment, prior probation, prior parole, previous drug use, and pre-prison unemployment. The lower scores will result in longer periods of incarceration.[36]

Parole board members consider several things, such as the seriousness of the crime, the length of time served, inmate's age, prior criminal history, alcohol and drug use, and the institutional record. They also consider opposition from police, the district attorney, and the victim or victim's family. If the parole board grants parole, a parole release date is set. Victims are notified and a release certificate is prepared and sent to the prison system. Prison officials prepare for release and the inmate is released. The parolee is released under supervision and subject to revocation for a new conviction of violation of release conditions. If parole is denied, the inmate is notified in writing within two weeks of the decision. No reason is given for the denial. Besides having an unacceptable parole release plan, there are four reasons why parole may be denied:

1. The offender gives indication that he or she will not conform to conditions of release.
2. The offender's release may decrease the seriousness of the offense. The parole may be viewed as promoting disrespect for the law.
3. The offender needs to continue to participate in a correctional program.
4. The person's release will have a negative effect on prison discipline. An inmate who has been disruptive or troublesome in prison should not be rewarded.[37]

CRD refers to the new date for the next parole review, which is usually scheduled for one to three years from the date that parole was denied.

If parole is denied, the inmate is given a **case review date** (CRD). The inmate's case may be given the designation "serve-all," which means that the inmate will remain in prison until the end of sentence (EOS). Inmates given an end of sentence date will not be considered again for parole but will serve the remainder of the sentence and be released without supervision upon the completion of the sentence.

---

35. Ibid.
36. Howard Abadinsky (2003). *Probation and Parole 8th Edition*, p. 246.
37. Ibid.

If individuals are granted parole, they are released under the supervision of parole field services or the Adult Parole Department. The parolee is released with conditions of parole. Violations of parole conditions may result in the revocation of parole and a return to prison to serve the remainder of the sentence.

Critical Thinking Box 5.3

Despite parole being an important correctional program, there remains a lack of knowledge about the parole release process and how parole decisions are made. How can the process be made more transparent? Why is it important that we have more knowledge about the parole release process?

Parole Process in Alabama

In the state of Alabama, three politically appointed board members, who serve six-year terms, are responsible for making parole decisions. Approximately 18% of those who leave Alabama prisons do so as the result of discretionary parole release decisions made by the parole board. Unlike the parole process in many states, the Alabama parole process is a two-stage process consisting of preliminary screening and the parole release hearing.

Preliminary Screening

When inmates become eligible for parole release consideration, there is a preliminary screening process by parole board members who determine if inmates are ready to be considered for parole release. There is no legal requirement for a preliminary screening, but it assists the board in deciding who may be the best candidates for parole. Despite serving the required one-third of the sentence, Alabama board members may not select an inmate for a parole hearing after conducting the preliminary screening. In this process, board members rely heavily on recommendations from the warden and other institutional parole personnel to make these preliminary decisions.

If the decision by the board during the preliminary screening process is not to proceed, the process stops. If the parole board concludes that the inmate is a good candidate for parole and should be considered for release, the parole process continues. The parole release hearing is set and victims and the victim's family are notified of the parole release hearing. Notifications are sent to the victim or victim's family, prosecuting district attorney, and other groups that might have an interest in the outcome of the parole process. Those who receive notices have 30 days to indicate plans to attend or send letters of protest. Protest letters are "red-tagged" and placed in the inmate's file. In one of the few studies conducted of the effects of victim participation on parole release decisions, Morgan and Smith found that when victims participate in the parole release hearing, through either letters or attendance at parole release hearings, inmates are less likely to receive parole.[38]

At the parole release hearing, the board members review the inmate's file and hear statements from supporters and opponents regarding the inmate's release. At the conclusion of the hearing, board members vote to grant or deny parole. If the inmate has not served at least one third of the sentence, the vote must be unanimous; all three members must vote for release. If parole review comes after the one third has been served, only two of three votes are needed. If the decision is made to grant parole, the inmate is released within two weeks. If the inmate is denied parole, the board sets a new case review date.

In Alabama, an inmate may waive parole and remain in prison until the end of sentence date, thus choosing to be released without parole supervision.

If granted parole, the inmate may leave the facility two weeks after the parole release authorization has been signed; if problems arise with the inmate's behavior during those two weeks, the board may void the parole release decision. When granted parole, the parolee remains under the supervision of the parole board until end of sentence date. Upon release to field services, parolees may be classified into one of five levels for supervision:

Levels of Supervision upon Release
a. Level 1: House arrest with electronic monitoring. $15/week.
b. Level 2: House arrest without electronic monitoring. $15/week.
c. Level 3: Report once a month. $20/month.
d. Level 4: Report once a year. $20/month.
e. Level 5: Unsupervised status.

Conditions of Parole

Every parolee or conditionally released offender is required to sign an agreement to abide by conditions of parole. The parole board imposes standard conditions and special conditions that are viewed as acceptable for conditional release. Standard conditions require the parolee to maintain suitable employ-

---

38. Brent Smith and Kathryn Morgan (1997). "The Effect of Victim Participation on Parole Decisions: Results from a Southeastern State," *Criminal Justice Policy Review* 8(1): 57–74.

ment and acceptable living arrangements, refrain from associating with other felons, remain in the jurisdiction of supervision, obey all laws, visit the parole officer as ordered, and notify the officer of any change in status (e.g., address, employment, marital). Special conditions are customized to the needs and characteristics of the individual offender. The parole board may impose special conditions such as enrolling in drug treatment programs, seeking mental health counseling, avoiding certain areas (bars, schools, playgrounds, etc.), or participating in other programs that are necessary for the control and rehabilitation of the parolee.

Length of Supervision

There are two things that govern the length of the parole term:

1. Length of the original sentence
2. Laws of the state where he/she was convicted

The length of supervision varies from state to state. For example, in the state of Oregon a person is released from parole supervision after serving six months; in Illinois, a parolee may serve a parole period of one to three years depending on the offense. In Alabama, however, a person may be released from parole only after serving five years. After serving five years successfully, the person is granted a pardon by the Board of Pardons and Paroles. Most states follow the general rule that a person's supervision may be terminated as long as that final release from supervision is not harmful to the welfare of society.[39]

Violation of Parole Conditions

There are two types of parole violations. Technical violations occur when the parolee fails to comply with the conditions of parole, such as failure to:

• maintain employment,
• seek ordered substance abuse treatment,
• remain in the jurisdiction, or
• meet with the parole officer as ordered.

New offense violations occur when the parolee is arrested and prosecuted for committing a new crime.

The violation process begins when the parole officer becomes aware of a violation. If the decision is made to pursue the violation, a warrant is issued to have the parolee arrested. In some states, parole officers carry an order to de-

---

39. Dean Champion, *Probation, Parole and Community Corrections*, pp. 426–427.

tain that can temporarily hold a parolee until an official warrant can be secured (usually within 48 hours). After arrest as a parole violator, the parolee is taken before a judge for bail decisions. Since the parolee has little to lose and may pose a flight risk, it is unlikely that release on bail will be granted. If there was the commission of a new crime, the parolee may already be in custody and will be detained until the hearing. If the violations are not serious, the parole officer will issue a citation requiring the parolee to appear in the parole department for an informal case review.[40]

The revocation process includes two hearings: a preliminary hearing and a revocation hearing. The preliminary hearing is scheduled within 14 days after the arrest and after the parolee has received a written notice of the alleged violations and the delinquency report has been submitted to the parole board.

> The hearing officer is a person hired by the board to serve as an objective fact finder who hears the facts of the case, summarizes those facts, and makes the information available to the board.

A hearing officer presides over the preliminary hearing, which is a probable cause hearing. The objective of the preliminary hearing is to determine if there is enough evidence to show that the parolee violated parole conditions. The parolee is entitled to legal counsel, but the state is not required to provide an attorney. During the preliminary hearing, the parolee's attorney has the right to confront and cross-examine witnesses, challenge the charges, and present evidence. The parolee's adjustment while under parole supervision may be considered during this time. It is also an opportunity to show that the parolee did or did not comply with the rules, such as reporting, participating in treatment programs as ordered, or maintaining suitable employment. After all the witnesses have been interviewed and evidence presented, the hearing officer decides if there is enough evidence to support a finding of probable cause.

If there is a finding of probable cause, the hearing officer prepares a report for the board and the revocation hearing is scheduled. The objective of the revocation hearing is for the board to decide if the violations are serious enough to revoke parole and return the parolee to prison. In making a decision, the parole board will consider adjustment under supervision, other problems, mitigating circumstances surrounding the violations, and the recommendation from the hearing officer. The board members vote for or against revocation. At the end of the revocation hearing, the board may decide to:

---

40. Howard Abadinsky, *Probation and Parole*, p. 254.

- Restore the parolee to supervision.
- Restore the parolee to supervision with an amended order that requires participation in a treatment program, jail time, or transfer to a halfway house or treatment facility.
- Revoke parole and return the parolee to prison.

In some states, if the decision is made to revoke parole, the parole board must provide the parolee a copy of the hearing officer's report.

Critical Thinking Box 5.4

Parolees are not entitled to counsel at parole release hearings and in some states are not allowed to have an attorney present. Being represented by counsel at the revocation becomes a right of the parolee. How do you explain the difference?

Issues Related to Parole Supervision

Parole and Truth-in-Sentencing

As policies became tough on crime and criminals, more and more offenders were being sent to prison. Many prisons found themselves faced with an increased population of offenders serving longer terms. Severe crowding required the release of prisoners to reduce population pressures. Many states started early release programs to reduce crowding. Data compiled by the Bureau of Justice Statistics revealed that in 1996, prisoners were serving 30 months or approximately 44% of their sentences.[41] The system was locking up more people who were spending less time in prison. The efforts to toughen criminal penalties were being undermined by prison release policies, with the consequence that inmates were serving less time.

As a part of the Federal Sentencing Reform Act of 1984, the federal government abolished parole and implemented truth-in-sentencing for federal offenders that required convicted federal offenders to serve 85% of their court imposed sentences. Prisoners would be required to serve 85% of the sentence imposed

---

41. Paula Ditton and Doris James Wilson (1999, January). *Truth in Sentencing in State Prisons*. Washington, DC: U.S. Department of Justice.

by the court before being considered for release, clemency, or good time.[42] Washington State was the first state to implement truth-in-sentencing in 1984. By 1999, 14 states had completely abolished discretionary parole board release for all offenders (Arizona, Delaware, Maryland, Florida, Illinois, Indiana, Kansas, Maine, Minnesota, Mississippi, North Carolina, Ohio, Oregon, Washington, and Wisconsin).[43] **Truth-in-sentencing laws** reduce the power and discretion of the parole board because of the mandate that inmates serve all of their sentences or a substantial portion of the sentence. Most states following the lead of the federal government set 85% as the target for time served. Critics of truth-in-sentencing point out that this mandate for tougher sentencing increases the prison population, escalates already high prison costs, and removes the incentive of early release. Michigan and Wisconsin witnessed excessive increases in prison costs after ending early release programs. Since implementation in 1998, the plan has cost Michigan taxpayers hundreds of millions of dollars for increasing health costs and additional prison beds in overcrowded prisons.[44] Wisconsin enacted truth-in-sentencing laws in 1999, and prison costs increased from $700 million in 1999 to $1.2 billion in 2009.[45] Judges and correctional administrators argue that this approach leaves the judge little or no discretion and shifts sentencing decisions from the judge to the legislature.

> **Truth-in-sentencing laws** reduce the possibility of early release and require prison inmates to serve all of their sentences minus good time.

Victim Participation in Parole Release Hearings

A major goal of many victims groups has been to influence offender sanctioning. Victims potentially may have an effect on the severity of punishment at two points in the judicial process: sentencing and parole release hearings. Victim impact statements (VIS), designed to influence case outcomes, allow victims the opportunity to speak directly to the court regarding the consequences of the crime on their lives. Research has indicated that the victim impact statement has had little effect on sentence severity and disposition. These statements do not influence decisions to sentence defendants to probation or prison.[46]

42. Ibid.
43. Ibid.
44. Michigan Policy Network (2011, January 27). *Truth in Sentencing Plan*, http://www.michiganpolicy.com/index.php?option=com_content&view=article&id=1005:truth-in-sentencing-plan&catid=237:employment-current-issues&Itemid=353.
45. Joshua Curtiss. *Truth in Sentencing Laws*, http://www.ehow.com/about_5449420_truth-sentencing-laws.html#ixzz1PSlhrDtx.
46. Edna Erez and Pamela Tontodonato (1992). "Victim Participation in Sentencing and Satisfaction with Justice," *Justice Quarterly*, 9(3): 393–417; Robert Davis and Brent

Victims may also influence outcomes at parole release hearings. Although the research into victim impact on parole release decisions has been minimal, there is evidence that victims may have more influence on parole release outcomes. Victims may participate by protesting the release at the parole release hearing or they might choose to write letters of protest that will be read by board members considering the inmate's release. McLeod (1989) found that when "where no victim impact statements are available for board review, 40 to 50 percent of parole applications are denied; when statements are submitted, the rate of parole denial rises sharply to approximately 80 percent."[47] Smith and Morgan (2005) found that when victims write letters, it is unlikely that inmates will receive parole. When victims attend hearings, it is almost certain that parole will be denied because victims' oral participation has great impact on decisions made by parole board members.[48] The extent to which parole boards will consider victim input and not inmate rehabilitation as the most important variable is a concern and policy issue. How far are decision-makers willing to go to appease victims of crime? Are prison officials and parole boards willing to keep offenders locked up even when they present a low risk of recidivism simply because victims oppose the release? Parole grew out of the rehabilitative ideal and has been used to assist in the rehabilitation and reintegration of the offender back into society. Ideally, an inmate is released at a time when he or she could benefit most from conditional release, thus allowing the inmate to avoid further internalization of the prison subculture and subsequently reducing the likelihood of a return to a life of crime. An incipient and disturbing pattern suggests that victim influence, not institutional behavior or participation in rehabilitation programs, is the important factor in the decision to grant or deny parole. The question is, to what extent will parole boards allow victim influence to override concerns for the inmate? Is it fair to further punish an inmate who presents a low risk of recidivism for future criminal behavior because victims show up at hearings to protest the release? Should victim input and participation become the most significant consideration or simply one of many variables to be considered in these decisions?[49]

Smith (1994). "Victim Impact Statements and Victim Satisfaction: An Unfulfilled Promise?" *Journal of Criminal Justice* 22(1): 1–12.

47. Maureen McLeod (1989). "Getting Free: Victim Participation in Parole Board Decisions," *Criminal Justice* 4(1): 12–15, 41–43.

48. Kathryn Morgan and Brent Smith (2005, May). "Victims, Punishment, and Parole: The Effects of Victim Participation on Parole Hearings," *Criminology and Public Policy* 4(2): 901–929.

49. Ibid.

Parole Effectiveness: Success or Failure

It is commonly accepted knowledge that parole failure rates are high. In 1983, the Bureau of Justice Statistics reported that 63% of released offenders were rearrested within three years.[50] Data reported by the Bureau of Justice Statistics in 1994 revealed that 68% of released prisoners were rearrested within three years.[51] It is estimated that about 46% of parolees complete parole supervision without absconding or committing a new offense.[52] In 2004, 187,000 parolees were revoked and returned to prison as the result of violation of parole rules or commission of a new offense.[53] The number of parolees returning to prison each year continues to rise. Recent statistics indicate that nationally parolees constitute 35% of all prison admissions.[54]

Recap and Review

- Approximately 95% of those who go to prison will eventually be released back into the community.
- Mandatory release grew out of the determinate sentencing structure and requires the offender to serve the entire sentence. Recent statistics indicate that the number of mandatory releases have surpassed discretionary releases.
- Discretionary release comes with decisions made by the parole board. It is related to indeterminate sentencing and rehabilitation.
- The president and governors of the United States exercise executive clemency powers that allow them to modify the sentence to benefit

---

50. Allen Beck and Bernard Shipley (1989). *Recidivism of Prisoners Released in 1988.* Washington, DC: U.S. Department of Justice, Office of Justice Programs, Bureau of Justice Statistics.

51. Patrick Lanagan and David Levin (2005). *Recidivism of Prisoners Released in 1994.* Washington, DC: U.S. Department of Justice, Office of Justice Programs, Bureau of Justice Statistics.

52. Lauren Glaze and Seri Palla (2005). *Probation and Parole in the United States, 2004.* Washington, DC: U.S. Department of Justice, Office of Justice Programs, Bureau of Justice Statistics.

53. Ibid.

54. Allen Beck and Christopher Mumola (1999). *Prisoners in 1998.* Washington, DC: U.S. Department of Justice, Office of Justice Programs, Bureau of Justice Statistics.

the offender. The pardon, commutation, and reprieve are three acts of executive clemency.

- There are some inmates prohibited from parole consideration. They include those given a sentence of "life without the possibility of parole" and those sentenced under a determinate sentencing structure.
- Although parole was phased out at the federal level by the Comprehensive Crime Control Act of 1984, federal inmates still get a 15% reduction of their sentence and are on supervised release upon leaving prison.
- State parole boards are mainly responsible for conducting parole release and revocation hearings. Membership and terms of appointment vary from state to state.
- The pre-parole plan is prepared by institutional parole services and provides information about the plans of the inmate if released. The parole plan should include information about prospective employment, living arrangements, and entry into a treatment program.
- Time served, seriousness of the offense, and risk of recidivism are important variables in parole release consideration.
- Alabama's parole process consists of a two-stage process. In the preliminary stage, inmates are screened for their suitability for parole. Those who are determined as suitable continue to the parole release stage.
- Parolees may violate the conditions of parole by being arrested for a new crime or violating administrative rules.
- The parole revocation process consists of two hearings: the preliminary hearing and the revocation hearing. The preliminary hearing is a probable cause hearing where evidence is presented and witnesses are called. The revocation hearing is used to determine if the charges are serious enough to revoke the conditional release and send the parolee back to prison.
- Following the lead of the federal government, many states passed truth-in-sentencing laws that reduced the possibility of early release and required inmates to serve the entire sentence.
- Critics point out that truth-in-sentencing has increased prison overcrowding and prison costs, removed the incentive of early release, and shifted the sentencing decision from the judge to the legislature.
- Approximately 68% of inmates return to prison within three years of being released. Forty-six percent complete parole without absconding or committing a new offense.

Questions for Review

1. What is mandatory release? How does it differ from discretionary release?
2. Identify and define the three acts of executive clemency.
3. Under what circumstances might the governor of a state commute a sentence?
4. What is the furlough? How did the furlough impact the presidential election of 1988?
5. How did the passage of the Comprehensive Crime Control Act of 1984 affect parole at the federal level?
6. What are the responsibilities of the members of the parole board?
7. What is the pre-parole plan and what are the three components of the parole plan?
8. What are four reasons that parole may be denied?
9. What does it mean when a parolee receives a CRD or EOS at the end of the parole release process?
10. How does the parole process in Alabama differ from that of most states?
11. What are the two factors that determine the length of parole?
12. Describe the preliminary and revocation hearings in the parole revocation process.
13. What is role/function of the hearing officer in the revocation process?
14. What does it mean that "probable cause" has been established in the preliminary hearing?
15. What is truth-in-sentencing? What was the purpose of the legislation?
16. What were some of the disadvantages of truth-in-sentencing?
17. How has victim participation in parole release hearing affected the process?

Questions for Discussion

Please use these questions for discussion. Choose the response that you think is most appropriate and explain your reasoning. Why are the other responses not appropriate?

1. In the last few years, there have been several attempts to abolish parole. Which of the following would be a good reason for not abolishing parole?
   A. It allows the parole board to maintain complete power and autonomy within the corrections system.
   B. Parole takes much of the burden off of the court system.

C. Parole provides important post-custody supervision for the released inmate.

D. Most states have abolished parole because there have been no good reasons for keeping it.

2. Which of the following is *not* likely to be a condition of parole?

   A. Report to your parole officer as instructed.

   B. Associate with known felons and ex-cons to help with reentry.

   C. Maintain suitable employment.

   D. Notify the parole officer of any change of address or employment.

3. The wife of a parolee calls you to inform you that since her husband was released from prison, he has been drinking and staying out late at night. You respond by:

   A. Calling the parolee in to talk with him about the accusations made by his wife.

   B. Having a warrant issued for his arrest.

   C. Informing the parole board that you will be submitting a delinquency report requesting a hearing.

   D. Doing nothing.

4. As a field parole officer, you have been asked to verify employment and living arrangements information given by the inmate in his pre-parole plan. In your investigation, you discover that the inmate has not been truthful. Family members are opposed to him living at home and the prospective employer knows nothing about a promise to hire him. You should:

   A. Recommend to the sentencing court that additional time to be added to the original sentence.

   B. Report the facts of your investigation back to the institutional parole officer.

   C. Inform the parole board of the discrepancies and recommend denial of parole.

   D. Not report the discrepancies; the inmate has spent enough time in prison and deserves release.

5. An inmate has been denied parole for the third time in six years. He tells you, as his institutional parole officer, that he plans to appeal because he was denied an attorney at all three parole release hearings. As his parole officer, you:

   A. Inform him that since he is incarcerated, he has no present private interest to be protected and does not have the right to an attorney.

B. Encourage the appeal because inmates have a right to counsel at parole release hearings.

C. Approach parole board members about the unfair treatment of the inmate.

D. Assist the inmate in finding an attorney to represent him for the appeal.

6. A female inmate who has previous charges of prostitution has indicated in her parole release plan that she has a job at a restaurant called the Lion's Den. When field officers attempt to verify employment, they discover that the "restaurant" is really a topless bar that is under investigation for prostitution. You decide:

A. To tell her that you know about her prospective employer, but you will keep quiet.

B. That this is not suitable employment but will work with her to find a more appropriate place to work.

C. To tell the inmate that you know about her place of employment but will keep quiet for a little "hush money."

D. That you would not speak to the inmate but go directly to the parole board with the information.

7. Revocation of parole means:

A. The probationer has been placed on shock probation.

B. The courts have taken away conditional freedom for the parolee.

C. The parole board decides to send the parolee back to prison to complete his or her prison term.

D. The courts give the parolee additional years to serve in prison.

8. Which of the following may not be considered in the assessment for parole release?

A. Length of time served

B. Institutional record

C. Prior criminal record

D. Number of dependents

9. A parolee has been under parole supervision for one year; he commits a new burglary and is arrested and detained. Within a week, he is sent back to prison to serve the remainder of the sentence. Six months later, he appeals the revocation on the grounds that he was not given a revocation hearing nor provided an attorney. Does he have a legitimate case?

A. No, parole is a privilege and he was not entitled to a hearing or counsel since he violated the terms of that privilege.

B. Yes, since he was losing conditional freedom, he was entitled to a hearing and representation by counsel.

C. He was entitled to a hearing but not representation by an attorney since he had no interest to be protected.

D. No, since parole is administrative, due process does not apply.

10. You have been informed that your parolee has been denied access to a state-operated drug treatment program because he is an ex-con even though he was ordered to participate as a condition of parole. As the supervising officer, you respond by:

A. Seeking revocation since the parolee cannot fulfill the requirements of the parole order.

B. Doing nothing; as the parole officer, you are law enforcement and not a social worker.

C. Investigating to determine why the parolee was denied access and find another program if necessary.

D. Filing a lawsuit against the drug treatment program for discrimination.

11. After looking for a job for the past year, your parolee finally found employment as a construction laborer. You receive a call from the city jail informing you that he has been arrested for stealing from the local grocery store. You investigate and discover that he had shoplifted ham, cheese, crackers, and cookies totaling $12.00. He informs you that he had not eaten in three days and was trying to get food to eat for lunch. Even though the store does not press charges, he violated parole conditions. You are facing a dilemma. What should you do?

A. File a motion to have parole revoked because he violated the conditions.

B. Talk with the parolee about the incident but file it away for future reference, with punishment if there is another violation of parole conditions.

C. Pretend that you never received information about the violation.

D. Approach the store manager and request that he file charges so that you can have grounds for revocation.

12. You have been supervising John, a parolee, for the last year. For most of his visits, he has come to your office dressed in women's clothing and complaining about his inability to get job. He informs you that whenever he applies for a job and interviews, no one wants to hire him although he has a college degree. You handle the situation by:

A. Doing nothing because you have heard that John can be violent.

B. Talking with John about possible concerns of employers and making suggestions for future job searches.

    C. Doing a role play with John where you tell him that he looks foolish applying for a job in women's clothing.

    D. Hoping that he never gets a job so that you can have him revoked and get him off of your caseload.

13. A parolee has been released from prison after serving time for felony drug possession. As a condition of parole, he is ordered to wear a pink shirt with "I am a convicted drug dealer" written in large black letters. He complains that this condition of parole is humiliating, stigmatizing, and interferes with rehabilitation. You respond by:

    A. Telling him that parole is a privilege, so "suck it up."

    B. Sending a request to the judge to amend the parole order.

    C. Requesting that the parole board rescind this condition.

    D. Doing nothing.

14. As Mary's parole officer, you have received information that she has violated parole conditions by working at the Top Hat Lounge as a "dancer" and violating curfew. This information has come from Mary's estranged husband, from whom she recently separated because of verbal and physical abuse. You decide to handle this by:

    A. Filing a motion have Mary appear before a hearing officer.

    B. Filing a request for a motion to detain.

    C. Ignoring the report; his word can't be trusted.

    D. Calling Mary to come in and discussing the matter with her, reminding her of the conditions of parole.

15. A new parole officer in your unit has informed you that a parolee under his supervision violated parole conditions by purchasing a car under an assumed name and giving police false information after having a minor accident. The officer has made arrangements to have him arrested and sent back to prison. The officer asks for your advice after the parolee tells him that he is violating his due process rights. You respond by:

    A. Informing the supervisor that the new officer needs to be fired.

    B. Informing the officer that he has taken the correct actions in sending the parolee back to prison.

    C. Contacting the parolee to inform him to file a lawsuit against the parole officer for violation of due process.

    D. Informing the new officer that he will violate the parolee's due process rights and explaining to him the right procedure.

16. If you were a member of the parole board considering release of an inmate, which of the following would you look for in the parole plan?
    A. Prospective employment, treatment plans, and suitable living arrangements
    B. Age of parents, family history, and remorse by the inmate
    C. Treatment plans, restitution payments, and suitable living arrangements
    D. Prospective employment, hobbies, and age

17. When a parolee is arrested for a new offense or other violation of parole conditions, there is an order to detain and no bail to keep the parolee in custody. Why is this important?
    A. The parolee has nothing to lose and may disappear.
    B. The parolee should sit in jail and think about the crime that he or she has committed.
    C. Time in jail will make the parolee plead guilty to avoid the time and expense of court.
    D. The parole board operates with complete autonomy and can do whatever it desires.

18. An inmate will be going before the parole board in two weeks for a parole release hearing. You discover from the victim service officer that the inmate has made contact with his victim and threatens harm if she appears before the parole board. As the supervising institutional parole officer for the past five years, what do you do with the information?
    A. Nothing, since he has been a model prisoner.
    B. Contact the parole board directly so that they may stop the parole process.
    C. Accuse the victim service officer and victim of being vindictive and dismiss the claims.
    D. Discuss the matter with the senior officer and warden to determine how to proceed.

Case Studies

Case Study 1

Questions 1–6 are based on the following case.

Joyce, age 20, has been serving a five-year sentence for forgery. She found some social security checks that she signed and cashed. The victims were two elderly residents who lived in the same housing project as Joyce.

Joyce has had several arrests and convictions for drugs and property offenses but this is her first prison term. She has been on probation twice, had it revoked, and spent time in the county jail. She has served 18 months and is presently up for parole. For the first six months of her prison stay there were some adjustment problems; she had a number of fights to get a reputation for being "bad." She has been working in the prison laundry and seems to get along well with other inmates.

As she prepares to go before the parole board, there are a number of concerns with her release. She denies having a drug problem. Although Joyce completed high school with above average grades, she has no marketable skills and has been unemployed most of the time since graduating from high school. She stated that she lives with friends because she and her mother do not get along; her mother was always harassing her about going to college. It should be noted that these friends are suspected drug dealers and users; this house is currently under surveillance even though it has not been raided or entered with a search warrant.

The probation officer conducting the presentence investigation was somewhat concerned that Joyce was always extremely well-dressed even though she has been unemployed with no visible source of income. All through her prison stay, she has always received money and supplies from "friends." Although unconfirmed, there has been a rumor that Joyce is selling drugs in prison for those "friends."

1. As her institutional parole officer, you assist Joyce in preparing her parole plan. How would you view Joyce's chances of success if released on parole?
    A. Good, she has friends that are supportive and who will help her make the adjustment once released.
    B. Excellent, although she had problems initially, she has made satisfactory adjustment while in prison.
    C. Fair, although she has a drug problem, she has made progress in other areas of her life.
    D. Poor, she has no employment, unknown living arrangements, a possible drug problem, and friends who are suspected drug dealers.

2. How would you characterize her adjustment to prison life over the last 18 months?
    A. Overall, her adjustment to prison has been satisfactory but there are some questions about her continued associations with people on the outside who may be involved with drugs.
    B. Joyce has learned the "con" game and uses it to her advantage.

    C. Joyce has constantly gotten in fights throughout her 18-month prison stay.

    D. Her overall adjustment to prison has been very poor; she is a bad influence on the other prisoners.

3. Joyce has informed you that she would like to enroll in the prison cosmetology course because she realized that she has no job skills for employment when released. You respond by:

    A. Discouraging her from applying because you don't feel that she is serious.

    B. Dismissing this as an attempt to impress the parole board.

    C. Encouraging and then helping her to get enrolled for the course.

    D. Recommending to the parole board that Joyce be denied parole because she has violated prison rules.

4. You overhear inmates discussing Joyce's suspected criminal activity and you decide to:

    A. Report this information to the parole board to support your recommendation for denial.

    B. Use snitches to spy and report on her illegal activity.

    C. Do nothing, as you would not want to jeopardize her chance for parole.

    D. Talk to Joyce about her alleged criminal activity and warn her of the consequences.

5. If Joyce is granted parole release, what recommendations would you make about her living arrangements?

    A. I would recommend that Joyce live with her mother for no less than one year.

    B. I would allow her to live anywhere people are willing to let her move in.

    C. I would recommend that Joyce live with her friends because they stuck by her even when she was in prison.

    D. Suggest that Joyce secure her own apartment before leaving prison.

6. If Joyce is released, which of the following conditions should the parole board *not* give as a condition of parole?

    A. Get drug treatment.

    B. Work with the police department to catch her suspected friends, who are drug dealers and users.

    C. Do not associate with criminals or those suspected of criminal activity.

    D. Maintain suitable employment.

Case Study 2

Questions 7–10 are based on the following case.

For the past two years, you have been the institutional parole officer for Debra, a 35-year-old female who is serving a 20-year sentence for two counts of attempted murder and two counts of aggravated assault. She shot her boyfriend after she accused him during an argument of having an affair. She also shot another man who attempted to break up the fight. When police got there, she told them that she had done this. Later, she expressed her remorse to the victims' families. She has two juvenile arrests for prostitution. As an adult, Debra has 10 arrests and six convictions. Four of those convictions were for assault and assault and battery. She had two convictions for receiving stolen property and forgery. She has also been arrested several times for prostitution and disorderly conduct. She has served seven years of her 20-year sentence. This is her first prison commitment. She will be eligible for parole release next year.

Debra was an only child who grew up very poor. Her father worked at a shipyard in North Carolina and made decent money. Because of his excessive gambling, he did little to take care of his family. Her mother died when she was four, and her father remarried and sent Debra to live with her grandmother. By the time she was 14, her grandmother had put her out of the house for incorrigible behavior. At age 14, Debra was homeless, living on the streets, and prostituting to survive. At age 17, Debra married a cocaine addict who got her addicted shortly after they were married. He left her for another woman who later killed him. Then Debra met Harry, who became the victim of her crime. They lived together for two years before the incident occurred. They had a good relationship up until about six months before she shot him. Debra says that he started drinking, gambling, and having affairs with other women.

Debra dropped out of school in the eighth grade. She was a poor student who was absent from school a lot. She says that she hated school and saw no value in it when you could make money on the streets. Since she has been incarcerated, she has gotten her GED and received training and a license in cosmetology. She has had mostly unskilled jobs with her longest being a housekeeper for a family for five years before she was incarcerated.

She started to drink heavily by age 13 and use drugs at age 15. She was addicted to crack cocaine by the time she was 19. Since she has been incarcerated, she has received counseling for her drug use. She says that she has been drug free since she has been incarcerated.

7. Although she has been ordered to have no contact with the victims, she confides to you that her ex-boyfriend has been calling and writing her for the past year. She also tells you that he has asked her to come and live with him once she is released from prison. She asks you for your advice. How do you respond?

   A. Report to the prison authorities that she has been contacting the victim of her crime and recommend that she be punished.
   B. Suggest that she find other living arrangements; this would not be acceptable to the parole board.
   C. Recommend to the parole board that parole should be denied because she has violated prison rules by contacting the victim.
   D. Say nothing; keep quiet about her contact with her ex-boyfriend and proposed living arrangements.

8. Although Debra has gotten a GED, a cosmetology license, and has become drug free, she expresses fear of being released. She fears that she will drift back into her old lifestyle. What recommendation would you make to Debra?

   A. Debra should commit another crime to lengthen her sentence.
   B. Debra should approach the parole board and ask if she could max out or serve all of her sentence.
   C. Debra should request to go to work release or a halfway house before being released.
   D. Debra should not bother you with this; there are other inmates with more serious concerns.

9. As you read Debra's case file information, you notice that she has had drug treatment while incarcerated, vocational training, and educational classes to obtain her GED. You are concerned that she has never had counseling to focus on her violent tendencies. You recommend that she should receive additional counseling. How do you justify your recommendation?

   A. Debra grew up as the victim of her father and grandmother's abuse.
   B. Debra was abused by her husband and ex-boyfriend.
   C. Additional counseling will likely impress the parole board.
   D. Debra's criminal history, including the offenses for which she is serving time, shows a pattern of violent behavior.

10. How would you evaluate Debra's chances of success if she is released on parole?

    A. Debra would not succeed because she has no GED and no marketable skills.

    B. Debra would fail because she has not shown remorse for her behavior.

    C. Debra would likely succeed because she has been productive in prison, getting a GED and a cosmetology license.

    D. Debra does better in prison than in community so she should stay in prison.

Case Study 3

Questions 11–16 are based on the following case.

John White, former attorney, is a smart lawyer and a successful and ambitious person. He owns stock in a farm equipment company and owns a thriving automobile company and a large motel. Prior to his conviction, he was a prominent member of the community and considered to be a model citizen. He had close associations with public officials and was always a friend of law enforcement. He would give an annual party for public officials and law enforcement officers. He was convicted of receiving stolen property and disposing this property through a convicted felon who was the fence. He was given probation.

While on probation, John had a problem with reporting or allowing the officer to visit him in the field. He did not see himself as a criminal and thought that contact with the probation officer was beneath him.

After being on probation for a year, he was arrested for receiving stolen property. Although the probation officer recommended continued probation with amended conditions, John White's probation was revoked and he was sentenced to five years in prison. The presiding judge stated that by revoking John's probation, he wanted to send a clear message to the public: "If you do the crime over and over again with no regard for the law or legal system, you *will* pay, regardless of who you are and who you know." John, his family, and his friends in the legal community were clearly shocked by the judge's decision. John has served one and a half years of the five-year term. He has become eligible for parole. When John arrived at the Correctional Classification Center, he was hostile and angry that he was being treated as a "common criminal." He argued that he no was no threat but a supporter of the community. He stated that he was not a criminal but a "shrewd businessman"; his business practices were no different than those of other people that he knew.

John was finally sent to Brown Correctional Center where he was given a job in the prison library. He has updated the library holdings and has even gotten two extra computers for inmates to take their high school equivalency tests. There have been no documented disciplinary problems.

When he first arrived at the prison, he refused to have anything to do with the other inmates, constantly reminding them that they were "criminals" and he was not. Later, he made friends with some of the inmates. Six months ago, it was discovered that John had continued his "property" business from within the prison. However, this time, it was noted that John now had a flourishing drug trade in the prison and outside using prison guards and inmates that he had befriended. This drug and property business resulted in five inmates receiving additional prison time and the firings of three guards. Even though the investigators know that John is the leader, they need more proof. Although there are hints, no one will state that John White is the leader. One inmate, who told investigators that he was willing to identify the main leader, suddenly "committed suicide."

Now, John is being considered for parole and in your mind this issue is still unresolved. The parole release hearing is here and John is demanding that the state provide an attorney to represent him at the hearing.

11. How would you characterize Mr. John White?
    A. Mr. White is an upstanding citizen who made a mistake and received a cruel and unusual punishment.
    B. Mr. White is a repeat offender who uses his money and associations to manipulate people and the criminal justice process.
    C. Mr. White is a shrewd businessman who sometimes bends the rule of law to make a profit.
    D. Mr. White is an innocent man who is the victim of jealous competitors and vindictive judges and police officers.

12. As you review Mr. White's case, what do you see as the major obstacle to his rehabilitation?
    A. Police who will continue to harass him and accuse him of illegal activities.
    B. The stigma attached to the criminal label.
    C. Refusal to accept responsibility or show remorse for his behavior.
    D. Lack of family and community support.

13. Mr. White has demanded to have an attorney present to represent him at the parole release hearing because it is his due process right. How do you respond?
    A. Since he knows people in high places, I will make sure that he has counsel.

B. Remind him that inmates are not entitled to counsel at release hearings but can have an advocate.

C. Report directly to the parole board that Mr. White is being difficult and should remain in prison.

D. Give him names of attorneys that could file a lawsuit against the prison for violation of his due process rights.

14. You were informed that one of the neighbors in the gated community where John and his family have lived for the past 15 years was concerned about John moving back into the community and the danger that he might pose to the residents. How do you respond?

A. You inform her that John is dangerous and could be a threat to the community.

B. You inform her that John's crimes have been property offenses and he has shown no indication of being a threat to the community.

C. You inform her that he is a threat to the community and to their children.

D. You point out the pattern of violence in his criminal history.

15. The parole board voted to deny John's parole and has given him a new case review date. Which of the following statements best reflects the reason for that denial?

A. There is a pattern of violent offenses in John's background.

B. The judge ruled that he should denied parole.

C. There were concerns about some alleged criminal conduct in prison that needed further investigation.

D. There were concerns about John being a flight risk and that he would likely leave.

16. If John had been released on parole, what were his chances for success?

A. His prospects are excellent because he has businesses, family, and friends to support him.

B. His prospects are not good because he has never viewed his behavior as criminal and there are allegations that his criminal behavior has not stopped in prison.

C. His prospects are good because he has the connections to keep him out of the court system.

D. His prospects are very good for success; he has been innocent from the beginning.

Chapter 6

Intermediate Sanctions

Key Terms

Collateral contacts	Home incarceration
Continuous signaling transmitter device	Intensive Supervision Probation (ISP)
Direct contacts	Shock incarceration
Electronic monitoring (EM)	Simple curfew
Home confinement	Voice identification system

Learning Objectives

1. Provide an overview of intermediate sanctions and their role in the criminal justice system.
2. Identify the controversies associated with intermediate sanctions.
3. Discuss intermediate sanctions and their characteristic features.

Overview of Intermediate Sanctions

Between 1965 and the mid-1970s, American society experienced escalating crime rates and the public's increasing fear of crime and victimization. There was also disillusionment with rehabilitation and its promise to reduce recidivism and crime rates. This discontent intensified when Robert Martinson published the results of his review of 231 evaluations of rehabilitations programs. Martinson concluded that all had the same bottom line: "this program shows no appreciable effect on recidivism." As a result, Martinson concluded, "Nothing works."[1] Although these conclusions were criticized, it was enough to fuel a major attack on rehabilitation. The rehabilitation ideology that had dominated correctional policy for 70 years was now being replaced by an ideology that emphasized public safety and punishment of

---

1. Robert Martinson (1974). "What Works?: Questions and Answers about Prison Reform," *Public Interest* 35: 22–54.

rational offenders who choose crime because of the perceived benefits over costs. Many lost faith in rehabilitation programs and their promise to provide treatment to the offender and reduce crime rates. Many of these programs were criticized for failure to address the problems of offenders or benefit society. Rehabilitation was replaced by a desire to punish, incapacitate, and deter the offender while protecting society from the potential criminal activities of these offenders.

Rising crime rates, the war on drugs, increased public fear of crime, more emphasis on punishment, and a desire to protect the community resulted in tougher penalties and more people going to prison. Prison populations swelled, causing overcrowding and escalating prison costs. Incapacitating the offender in prison might have reduced crime, but the prison costs were overwhelming. In the late 1970s, some states passed community corrections acts, which was legislation that provided for the creation of halfway houses for inmates who were leaving prisons.[2] In the 1980s, when prisons began to experience overcrowding, intermediate sanctions became a cost-effective way to punish offenders while saving money.[3] **Intermediate sanctions** are a variety of punishments that are more restrictive than traditional probation but less severe and less costly than incarceration. While addressing prison overcrowding in a cost-effective way is the primary reason for the development of alternative community sanctions, historically, the community has been the best place to deal with offenders. The community provides the most humane environment for meeting the needs of offenders.[4] Clear, Cole, and Reisig point out additional benefits of using intermediate sanctions:

Intermediate punishments refer to a variety of sentencing alternatives between traditional probation and incarceration designed to alleviate prison overcrowding, reduce prison costs, and provide more punishment than standard probation.

1. In many cases, prison is unnecessary and ineffective. Intermediate sanctions provide an alternative to prison.
2. Intermediate sanctions provide the intensive supervision and specialized programs for serious offenders that are not available through regular probation.
3. Intermediate sanctions provide more sentencing alternatives to judges.[5]

---

2. Marcus Nieto (1996). *Community Corrections Punishments: An Alternative to Incarceration for Nonviolent Offenders.* California Research Bureau.

3. Ibid.

4. T. Clear, G. Cole, and M. Reisig (2011). *American Corrections.* 10th Edition. Belmont, CA: Wadsworth Publishing.

5. Ibid.

Many offenders do not need the expensive and severe treatment of prison, yet regular probation is ineffective in managing offenders with serious criminal histories that require more intense surveillance and supervision. Often, regular probation caseloads are large and do not allow probation officers to provide the intensive supervision that these offenders need.[6]

Intermediate sanctions fall in severity between prison and probation; these programs are more restrictive than probation but less severe and less expensive than prison and include a variety of sentencing options, including intensive supervision probation, electronic monitoring, community service, and home confinement programs. Generally, these programs include features of increased surveillance and supervision, community service, restitution, and curfews.[7]

Intermediate Sanctions Strategies

There are a number of strategies that are classified as intermediate sanctions for supervising offenders in the community. These strategies include intensive supervision probation, home confinement, day reporting centers, electronic monitoring, drug courts, boot camp, and community service. This chapter focuses on four of those strategies: intensive supervision probation, home confinement, electronic monitoring, and boot camp or shock incarceration.

Intensive Supervision Probation

History of Intensive Supervision Probation

Intensive supervision probation (ISP) is an intermediate sanction that emphasizes punishment and the intensive supervision and surveillance of probationers.

Intensive supervision probation is an intermediate sanction that emphasizes constant supervision and surveillance of probationers.

Although intensive supervision probation has become one of the most popular programs in corrections, the idea of intensive supervision is not new. The concept first appeared in California over 30 years ago with the establishment of a Special Intensive Parole Unit. It was first introduced in probation in 1981 in Texas with the Texas Intensive Probation Program. In-

---

6. Ibid.

7. Marcus Nieto (1996). *Community Corrections Punishments: An Alternative to Incarceration for Nonviolent Offenders.* California Research Bureau.

tensive supervision was a condition of probation and probation officers supervised regular probationers and a caseload of intensive probationers.[8] In 1982, Georgia implemented the first Intensive Supervision Probation Program for the purposes of reducing prison overcrowding, punishing offenders, and diverting offenders from prison.[9] ISP programs target probation and parole violators, non-violent offenders, and offenders with chronic criminal histories that may disqualify them from regular probation supervision.[10]

There are two important goals of ISP programs:

1. Reducing prison population and relieving prison overcrowding.
   The first goal of ISP programs is to reduce prison populations and reduce prison costs. ISP offenders are able to maintain employment, sustain family and community relationships, and take advantage of community treatment resources.[11]
2. Promoting public safety and protection.
   The second goal of ISP programs is to promote public safety and protection. Because ISP offenders are high-risk offenders, there is more emphasis placed on surveillance, supervision, and higher accountability. Under supervision, ISP offenders may have five mandatory officer contacts each week, mandatory community service, and required curfews.[12]

Three Intensive Supervision Probation Models

Although there are many variations of ISP programs, three models are currently used in corrections.

Front-end release mechanism for prison-bound offenders

This model, used in Georgia, was developed to prevent offenders from entering prison. After offenders are sentenced to prison, ISP program officers

---

8. Howard Abadinsky (2008). *Probation and Parole: Theory and Practice*. 8th Edition. Upper Saddle, NJ: Prentice-Hall.

9. Arthur Lurigio and Joan Petersilia (1992). "The Emergence of Intensive Probation Supervision Programs in the United States," in *Smart Sentencing: The Emergence of Intermediate Sanctions*. Newbury Park, CA: Sage Publications.

10. Ibid.

11. Lurigio and Petersilia, The Emergence of Intensive Probation Supervision Programs in the United States, p. 9.

12. A. Lurigio and J. Petersilia (1992). "The Emergence of Intensive Probation Supervision Programs in the United States," in *Smart Sentencing: The Emergence of Intermediate Sanctions*. Newbury Park, CA: Sage Publications.

conduct eligibility interviews. If the offender is suitable for the program, a request is made to the sentencing judge to rescind the prison sentence and consider ISP.[13] This method reduces prison overcrowding and saves money while protecting the public through strict surveillance and supervision of offenders.

Back-end early release mechanism for prisoners[14]

The goal of this program is to reduce prison costs and relieve prison overcrowding; this model is used in New Jersey. After inmates have served a minimum time of incarceration, they may be considered for release. After a lengthy intake process to determine eligibility, selected inmates are released prior to their anticipated parole release date.[15] Similar to the front-end release mechanism, this model reduces incarceration costs by granting prisoners early release into the community where they will be closely monitored and supervised.[16]

Intensive supervision for felony probationers on regular probation[17]

The third model, used in Massachusetts, improves case management for felony probationers under regular probation supervision. Regular probationers may be assigned to the ISP program based on the assessment of risk for future criminal behavior. Reducing prison costs is not the major goal of this model. The emphasis is placed more heavily on strict surveillance and monitoring to prevent future crime and protect the community.[18]

ISP Program Features

Although program features may vary from state to state, there are common characteristics of the majority of ISP programs. Program aspects include:

- increased supervision and surveillance
- increased contacts: most program require a minimum of five face-to-face contacts per week with the supervising officer
- unannounced field visits

---

13. B. Erwin (1987). *Evaluation of Intensive Probation Supervision in Georgia.* Atlanta: Georgia Department of Corrections.

14. Lurigio and Petersilia (1992). The Emergence of Intensive Probation Supervision Programs in the United States, p. 10.

15. Frank Pearson and Alice Harper (1990). "Contingent Intermediate Sentences: New Jersey's Intensive Supervision Program," *Crime and Delinquency 36*: 75–86.

16. Ibid.

17. Lurigio and Petersilia, The Emergence of Intensive Probation Supervision Programs in the United States, pp. 10–11.

18. Ibid.

- mandatory community service
- mandatory employment
- unannounced drug and alcohol testing
- mandatory curfew
- small caseloads (not to exceed 40 offenders)
- referrals to community resources for special services needed by the offenders (i.e., drug and alcohol treatment)

In addition to required contacts between the offender and the supervising officer, there are also collateral contacts made with family members, neighbors, or employers.

Direct contacts are those made with the offender under supervision to monitor and supervise the offender. Collateral contacts are made by the supervising officer with family members, employers, and others who might have regular contact with the offender.

Although most ISP programs share common features, there may be two critical areas of difference: (1) definitions of "intensive" and (2) target populations.

There are differences in how states may define "intensive." In some states, "intensive" is defined as several face-to-face contacts with probation officers during a single week, while in other states, "intensive" refers to increased surveillance, periods of imprisonment, curfew checks, collateral contacts with family members and employers, and restitution to victims.[19] Other programs define "intensive" by the level of surveillance, caseload size, and the length of the sentence.[20]

ISP programs vary in their target populations. Petersilia (1990) points out that some programs may exclude drug and alcohol offenders and others target those same offenders. The ISP program in Montgomery County, Maryland, targets offenders that have drug, alcohol, and mental health problems. An ISP program in Suffolk County, New York, targets unemployed and underemployed probationers.[21] In some states, violent offenders are excluded from participation in ISP programs, while in other states, they are the target population. In several states, the target population includes probation and parole violators and other repeat offenders.[22] In California, ISP caseloads are specialized caseloads that target drug and alcohol

---

19. Lurigio and Petersilia, The Emergence of Intensive Probation Supervision Programs in the United States, p. 11. Dean Champion (2008). *Probation, Parole and Community Corrections*. 6th Edition. Upper Saddle, NJ: Pearson, p. 217.

20. James Byrne and April Pattavina (1992). Assessing What Works in the Adult Community Corrections System. in *Smart Sentencing: The Emergence of Intermediate Sanctions*. Newbury Park, CA: Sage Publications, 281–303.

21. Joan Petersilia and Susan Turner (1990). *Intensive Probation for High Risk Offenders: Findings from Three California Experiments*. Santa Monica, CA: RAND Corporation.

22. Byrne (1986). "The Control Controversy: A Preliminary Investigation of Intensive Supervision Programs in the United States," *Federal Probation 50*: 4–16.

offenders, domestic violence offenders, sex offenders, and violent gang offenders.[23] The New Jersey ISP program targets offenders who have served at least three months in prison; they are released from prison into the program.[24] Massachusetts targets high-risk probationers who are identified through risk and needs assessment strategies. Probation conditions are more rigorously enforced and include mandatory referrals to community agencies for offenders' high-risk problem areas. There are also strict revocation procedures for probation violations.[25]

Evaluation of Intensive Supervision Programs

Most evaluations of ISP programs have focused on the effect of intensive supervision on recidivism, prison costs and prison populations. These evaluations of ISP programs have yielded mixed results. RAND Corporation's studies of ISP Programs in Texas, Oregon, and Georgia report that ISP programs fail to reduce costs, prison overcrowding, and recidivism. Results showed no significant difference between ISP program participants and those supervised under regular probation.[26] A study of the Georgia ISP program revealed that program participants resembled the prison population more than regular probationers, proving that they were prison-bound offenders who had been diverted from prison. Further results indicated that new offense arrests for the ISP participants were much lower than arrests for regular probationers.[27] In the results from a nationwide evaluation of intensive supervision probation programs, Petersilia and Turner (1993) concluded that intensive supervision probation programs were more effective and successful as intermediate sanctions. These programs have high number of face-to-face contacts, more collateral contacts, increased surveillance, law enforcement checks, and employment monitoring. There is also increased drug and alcohol testing. These features increase the punitive value of the program. In some instances, offenders may view the intensive supervision programs as more punitive and restrictive than prison.[28]

---

23. Joan Petersilia and Susan Turner (1990). *Intensive Probation for High Risk Offenders: Findings from Three California Experiments*, pp. 50–53.

24. Marcus Nieto (1996). "Community Corrections Punishments: An Alternative to Incarceration for Nonviolent Offenders," *Criminology 30*(1): 21–45.

25. Ibid.

26. Joan Petersilia (1999). "A Decade of Experimenting with Intermediate Sanctions: What Have We Learned?" *Justice, Research and Policy 1*: 9–23.

27. B. Erwin and L. Bennett (1987). *New Dimensions in Probation: Georgia's Experience with Intensive Probation Supervision.* Washington, DC: National Institute of Justice.

28. Joan Petersilia and Susan Turner (1993). *Evaluating Intensive Supervision Probation/Parole:Results of a nationwide Experiment. Washington, DC:* U.S Department of Justice, Office of Justice Programs, National Institute of Justice, pp. 1–11.

> **Critical Thinking Box 6.1**
>
> You are trying to initiate an ISP program in your jurisdiction for probation and parole violators. As you present arguments to support the creation of the program, you are confronted with the mixed results regarding effectiveness of ISP programs, especially those that suggest that these programs do not divert offenders, alleviate prison crowding, or save money. How do you address these issues in order to gain support for your program?

Home Confinement

Home confinement, also known as house arrest, allows selected prison-bound offenders to serve their sentences confined to their homes under house arrest instead of in prison. It is considered the most punitive of the intermediate sanctions. Home confinement permits the offender to continue employment and support dependents, reduces prison crowding and supervision costs, maximizes public safety through intense supervision of the offender, and promotes offender reintegration into society.[29]

Three versions home confinement include:

Home confinement is a community-based alternative to imprisonment that requires offenders to be confined to their homes for a mandatory period of time except for court approved absences, including employment, counseling sessions, medical appointments, and treatment.

a. *Home incarceration* (most restrictive) requires the offender must be at home at all times unless a situation arises such as a medical or legal appointment.

b. *Home confinement* (more restrictive) requires offenders must be home at all times except for work, counseling, school, religious activity, or doing public service work.

c. *Simple curfew* (least restrictive) requires offenders to be home by a certain hour.

There are advantages and disadvantages associated with home confinement. Advantages include that: (1) it is cost effective because it reduces the cost of offender supervision, (2) it is responsive to both community and offender needs, (3) it is easily implemented, and (4) it addresses prison overcrowding.[30] Among the disadvantages are that: (1) it may widen the net of social control, (2) it

---

29. Dean Champion (2007). *Probation, Parole and Community Corrections*. 6th Edition. Upper Saddle, NJ: Pearson.

30. J. Petersilia (1999). "A Decade of Experimenting with Intermediate Sanctions: What Have We Learned?" *Justice, Research and Policy 1*: 9–23.

may not be severe enough as a sentence, (3) it is intrusive, (4) it may promote a race and class bias in the selection of offenders, and (5) it may compromise public safety.[31]

The home confinement program targets probation violators, parole violators, and offenders guilty of noncapital offenses who are not suitable for regular probation due to serious criminal histories. Program features include: (a) minimum of seven direct and collateral contacts weekly; (b) random urine testing; (c) at least 16 phone calls per week by officers to make sure that the offender is at home; (d) mandatory employment, mandatory community service and restitution; and (e) supervision by specially trained officers with a caseload of only 20 offenders.

Early Home Confinement Programs

The Florida Community Control Program (1983) and the Oklahoma House Arrest Program (1984) represent the earliest home confinement programs implemented in the United States. The Florida program serves as an alternative to incarceration; the Oklahoma House Arrest Program serves as a back-door early release program.

Florida Community Control Program

Home confinement began in Florida in 1983 as the Florida Community Control Program. Florida was the first state to address the problem of prison overcrowding and the need for intermediate sanctions to be used as alternatives to incarceration.[32] As a front-end program, it is an alternative to incarceration to divert offenders from prison. Offenders are required be confined to their approved residences except for work, community service, and medical needs. All other absences require pre-approval by the supervising officer. Offenders are supervised by senior correctional officers who make 28 direct and collateral contacts with the offender each month.[33] The Florida Program targets three types of offenders:

- Offenders convicted of nonviolent offenses,
- Probation and parole violators who have technical or misdemeanor violations, and

---

31. Ibid.

32. Deborah K. Padgett, William Bales, and Thomas Blomberg (2006). "Under Surveillance: An Empirical Test of the Effectiveness and Consequences of Electronic Monitoring," *Criminology and Public Policy* 5(1). 61–92.

33. The Florida Senate (2009, September). *The Effectiveness of the Departments of Corrections' Community Control Program.*

- Other offenders deemed appropriate by the judge.[34]

Offenders must support families, perform community service, pay restitution, pay supervision fees of $30–$60 per month, and comply with all of the conditions, especially those that restrict movement.[35] Recent evaluation of the Florida program indicates that 50% of the program participants would have gone to prison; the other 50% would have been placed on regular probation.[36]

Oklahoma House Arrest Program

Unlike the Florida program, the Oklahoma House Arrest Program is a backdoor program to grant early release from prison to high-risk offenders. Inmates eligible for the program include:

- Inmates who have served 15% of their maximum sentence.
- Nonviolent offenders who are within 27 months of release.
- Violent inmates who are within 11 months of release.

Sex offenders and those denied parole within the last six months are not eligible for consideration.[37] House arrestees are supervised by a two-member team consisting of a correctional case manager and a community control officer. Program participants are required to have regular office visits and field contacts with the supervising team, be subject to random drug testing, and pay a $45 monthly supervision fee. From 1984–1985, 2,400 offenders were supervised in the Oklahoma program. Sixty-seven percent (67%) completed the program successfully. Five percent (5%) committed new crimes while under supervision.[38]

Home Confinement at the Federal Level

The Federal Bureau of Prisons uses intermediate sanctions to manage offenders in custody at the federal level. The Community Control Program, a home confinement program with electronic monitoring, has gained the most attention and support.[39] The program has two main goals: (a) to make sure that program participants comply with the requirements of conditional release, and

---

34. M. Nieto (1996, May). *Community Correction Punishments: An Alternative to Incarceration for Nonviolent Offenders.*
35. Ibid.
36. Ibid.
37. Ibid.
38. Ibid.
39. Ibid.

(b) to develop a supervision plan that will reduce the risk of future criminal behavior while implementing a plan of correctional treatment to address problems of the offender.[40]

To be eligible for the Community Control Program, offenders must meet eligibility criteria including: (1) having been previously considered for parole release by the Parole Commission; (2) being referred to the program; (3) planning to live in a judicial district where the program operates; (4) undergoing an assessment of health, mental stability, substance abuse history, and prior criminal record; and (5) having a residence and plan to live with someone who is supportive of the program requirements and the sacrifices that must be made.[41]

Program participants include probation violators, parole violators, prison-bound offenders who are given home confinement as an alternative to incarceration, and probationers and parolees who are given home confinement as a condition of release. Offenders may be denied selection for the program if they have no residence, lack employment prospects, have less than 60 days before parole release, and have a history of violence and severe drug use.[42]

Issues in Home Confinement

Several issues have emerged concerning the use of home confinement. First, many people do not view home confinement as punishment. Although those sentenced to home confinement see it as real punishment, most people argue that being confined to home is more luxury than punishment. Court decisions have established that time confined in homes, as punishment, cannot be compared to incarceration in jail or prison. In addition, when home-confined offenders leave home without permission, they are not charged with escape but a technical violation of program conditions.[43]

40. J. Klein-Saffran (1991, May/June). "Electronically Monitored Home Confinement — Not a Panacea for Corrections, But a Useful Tool," *International Association of Residential and Community Alternatives Journal.*

41. Ibid.

42. Ibid.

43. Dean Champion (2002). *Probation, Parole and Community Corrections.* Upper Saddle River, NJ: Prentice-Hall.

> **Critical Thinking Box 6.2**
>
> The perception by many is that being confined to home is not a punishment but a luxury, and court decisions have upheld the fact that home confinement cannot be equated to prison time. How is it possible to argue that home confinement is an alternative to incarceration that is more punitive than regular probation?

Second, concerns about public safety arise when a convicted offender is allowed to remain at home in the community without constant surveillance. Although home confinement permits the offender to remain in the community and avoid the stigma of incarceration, it can only be safe for the community if strict selection criteria are implemented and enforced.[44]

A third issue focuses on the deterrent effect of home confinement. Although there are no specific claims that home confinement deters crime, supervising officers can exercise strict supervisory control to make sure that offenders comply with program conditions. Further, research results are mixed regarding the effectiveness of home confinement programs. Some researchers conclude that participation in home confinement programs produces low rearrest rates. Other research results suggest that the effectiveness of the program wears off after about six months. After this time, it becomes more difficult to enforce detention conditions. Therefore, the program is more suitable for low-risk offenders who already have stable residences.[45]

> **Critical Thinking Box 6.3**
>
> Critics question whether home confinement promotes a race and class bias in the selection process. How would you address this charge?

Electronic Monitoring

Electronic monitoring (EM) became a popular method of supervision in the 1980s. This strategy relies on electronic devices to supervise and monitor the movement of offenders and verify that they are at specific locations dur-

---

44. Ibid.
45. D. Anderson (1998). *Sensible Justice: Alternatives to Prison.* New York: New Press.

ing particular times. The use of electronic monitors expands the surveillance capacity of supervision. Its current use in correctional supervision can be traced to 1983 in New Mexico when a judge placed a probation violator on electronic monitoring for one month. Following the lead of New Mexico, other states (Florida, California, and Kentucky) began to experiment with electronic monitoring as a cost-effective solution to prison overcrowding for non-violent offenders. Because electronic monitoring is cheaper than prison costs, its use will likely increase as incarceration becomes more expensive. Prison costs are six times higher than costs of electronic monitoring.[46]

> **Electronic monitoring** is a supervision technique often used with home confinement or intensive supervision probation that requires the use of an electronic device to assist in monitoring the offender.

Home Confinement with Electronic Monitoring

Electronic monitoring has been used most often with home confinement to monitor high-risk offenders who remain in the community. In 1984, Florida was the first state to electronically monitor offenders confined to their homes for punishment. Since then, the use of electronic monitors has become important to the success of home confinement programs because it reduces the likelihood of technical violations, revocations, and absconding for monitored offenders.[47]

Two monitoring systems used in correctional supervision are:

a. *Continuous signaling device.* A transmitter bracelet is strapped on to the wrist or ankle. The transmitter emits a signal that is monitored by a receiver connected to the telephone in the house. A central computer receives calls from this receiver. Whenever an offender goes outside of the range of the signal, the receiver automatically dials the computer that indicates that the offender is outside of the residence.

b. *Voice identification system.* Telephone and computerized voice identification. The computer records the offender's voice and stores it. At random times, the computer is programmed to call the offender. During the call, the offender is asked to repeat some phrases which the computer then matches the repeated words to the earlier recording.[48]

---

46. Dean Champion (2008). *Probation, Parole and Community Corrections*, p. 96.

47. William Bales, Karen Mann, Thomas Blomberg, et al. (2010, January). "A Quantitative and Qualitative Assessment of Electronic Monitoring." Final Report submitted to NIJ.

48. K. Padgett, W. Bales, and T. Blomberg (2006). "Under Surveillance: An Empirical Test of the Effectiveness and Consequences of Electronic Monitoring," *Criminology and Public Policy* 5(1): 61–92.

Those who favor electronic monitoring suggest that EM:

a. facilitates offender reintegration back into the community while avoiding incarceration,
b. assists in monitoring and supervision of offenders,
c. reduces prison overcrowding and the costs of incarceration,
d. permits the offender to keep a job and support dependents, and
e. reduces possible recidivism.[49]

Those opposing the use of electronic monitoring point out that:

a. By making offenders pay for expensive equipment, there is the potential of promoting a race and class bias.
b. EM is intrusive; offenders being electronically monitored cannot have any additional features on the telephone. Therefore, family members are required to make sacrifices in order for the offender to participate in the program.
c. EM may be too coercive and increase the likelihood that offenders will not comply with such a rigid system.
d. It compromises public safety.
e. It raises concerns about privacy and protection from search and seizure.
f. The use of EM raises constitutional concerns about whether or not it discriminates against offenders who do not have permanent housing or telephones.
g. Findings regarding the effectiveness of EM are inconsistent.[50]

Is Electronic Monitoring Effective?

Empirical studies yield mixed results about the success of electronic monitoring in reducing recidivism.

a. Petersilia (1987) found that recidivism rates decline to five percent when offenders are electronically monitored.[51]
b. Home confinement in combination with electronic monitoring is successful with DWI/DUI offenders.[52]

---

49. Dean Champion, (2008). *Probation, Parole and Community Corrections*, p. 103.
50. Ibid., Champion, p. 103.
51. Joan Petersilia (1987). *Expanding Options for Criminal Sentencing*. Santa Monica, CA: The Rand Corporation.
52. Robert Lily et al. (1992). "The Pride, Inc.: An Evaluation of 5 Years of Electronic Monitoring," *Federal Probation* 55(4): 42–47.

c. In their study of electronic monitored offenders in Florida, Bales, Mann, Blomberg, et al. (2010) found that electric monitors reduce an offender's risk of failure by 31%.[53]

d. Electronic monitoring is less effective for violent offenders and more effective in controlling property, sex, and drug offenders.[54]

e. Electronic monitoring reduces the likelihood of reoffending and absconding for offenders on home confinement.[55]

Electronic Monitoring as a Cost-Effective Option

Is electronic monitoring more cost effective than prison? The consensus seems to be that electronic monitoring has both direct and indirect savings benefits. Although the initial costs of electronic monitoring might be more expensive, it saves money in the long term. It is estimated that EM costs between $5 and $25 per day compared to approximately $50 per day for incarceration. In Florida, electronically monitored offenders are ordered to pay $64 per month even though fees are often waived. Using electronic monitoring reduces the annual costs of housing and caring for offenders as well as costs associated with new prison construction.[56]

In interviews with electronically home-confined offenders in Florida, Bales, Mann, Blomberg, et al. (2010) reveal that there are other costs of electronic monitoring. First, there are negative costs associated with relationships. Relationships with spouses and significant others suffer and offenders feel shamed and stigmatized. Children try to imitate the monitored parent or have a constant fear that a probation officer is coming to take the parent away if the monitor beeps. Second, offenders report that getting and keeping a job is difficult because of the visibility of the monitor or the beeping alarm that indicates a signal has been lost. Third, others reported that being monitored affects relationships with friends indicating that it is difficult to make new friends or maintain the relationships that you had.[57]

---

53. William Bales, Karen Mann, Thomas. Blomberg, et al. (2010, January). "A Quantitative and Qualitative Assessment of Electronic Monitoring." Final report submitted to NIJ.

54. Ibid., p. 64.

55. Kathy Padgett, William Bales, and Thomas Blomberg (2006). "Under Surveillance: An Empirical Test of the Effectiveness and Consequences of Electronic Monitoring," *Criminology and Public Policy* 5(1): 61–92.

56. Bales, Mann, Blomberg et al. A Quantitative and Qualitative Assessment of Electronic Monitoring." Final report submitted to NIJ. (2010) pp. 31–32.

57. Bales, Mann, Blomberg et al. A Quantitative and Qualitative Assessment of Electronic Monitoring." Final report submitted to NIJ. (2010) pp. 90–91.

Shock Incarceration

Shock incarceration is a short period of incarceration in a military-style boot camp setting. Its emphasis is on punishment and discipline.

Shock incarceration, also known as "boot camp," was established by the Georgia Department of Corrections in 1983 as a community-based alternative to incarceration. Unlike shock probation, which sentences an offender to a short period of incarceration in a prison before probation, **shock incarceration** sentences the offender to short-term, highly structured, military-style confinement characterized by military-style training and discipline.

The goals of boot camp are to (1) punish offenders; (2) ease prison overcrowding and costs; (3) provide discipline for youthful offenders; (4) discourage future crime and delinquency by the offender; and (5) provide rehabilitation services such as educational and vocational services, counseling, and drug intervention to offenders.

Program Participants

Participants in boot camps are youthful offenders, usually between the ages of 17 and 25. They have been convicted of nonviolent crimes and are serving their first prison sentence. Often boot camp participants may be probation violators. Participants are referred by the Department of Corrections or judges, or they may volunteer for the program. A short stay in boot camp is usually followed by intensive probation supervision or electronic monitoring.

Critical Thinking Box 6.4

Many argue that shock incarceration cannot be effective because offenders stay in the program for such a short period before being released back into the same communities. Given the fact that these programs are not likely to be successful and have high costs, many believe that they should be abolished. What is your position?

Program Features

Although boot camps may have similar features, there is much variation in features across programs. Most programs are punitive in an effort to deter future criminal behavior and integrate a disciplined environment to teach self-control, designed to strip them of their street identity. Stays in the boot camp are usually short, lasting from three to six months. Other common features include military-style training that includes marching; drills; long days; harassment by drill officers; and no television, radio, or telephone privileges.

Critical Thinking Box 6.5

Since boot camps are based on military-style discipline and rule violators may be punished immediately, there might be some concern for due process. Rule violators may be punished without proper protections. Should this be a concern since offenders are already being punished?

Critical Thinking Box 6.6

The selection process for admission into intermediate sanction programs has been criticized for being biased against racial and ethnic minorities, women, and the poor. Yet the goal of these programs is to select offenders that have the best chances of succeeding. If you were an administrator of one of these programs, how would you address the bias issue?

Recap and Review

- Intermediate sanctions are a variety of punishments that are more restrictive than traditional probation but less severe and less costly than prison.
- Intermediate sanctions provide more sentencing alternatives to judges and may be more desirable when prison may be unnecessary and probation cannot provide the intensive supervision that serious offenders need.
- Characteristics of intermediate sanction programs include increased surveillance and supervision, community service, restitution, and curfews.
- Goals of intermediate sanctions include providing alternatives to prison to reserve prison for the most serious offenders, giving judges more sentencing alternatives, protecting the public by providing more control over offenders than regular probation, and reducing prison costs by keeping the offender in the community.

- The concept of intensive supervision first appeared in parole in California with the establishment of a Special Intensive Parole Unit. In 1982, Georgia established the first Intensive Supervised Probation program for the purposes of relieving prison overcrowding, punishing offenders, and diverting offenders from prison.
- Common features of intensive supervision probation programs include increased supervision and surveillance; increased face-to-face and collateral contacts; unannounced field visits; mandatory community service, curfews, and employment; small caseloads; and random drug and alcohol testing with subsequent referrals for treatment.
- Programs vary in the target population. Some states target violent offenders and others target probation and parole violators, drug and alcohol offenders, or felony probationers already under regular supervision.
- Results have been mixed regarding the effectiveness of ISP programs. Some results indicate that ISP participants have lower arrest numbers for new offenses than regular probationers and that programs divert offenders from prison.
- Home confinement allows the offender to remain at home rather than serve a sentence of incarceration. It is an alternative to incarceration. The three versions of home confinement include home incarceration, home confinement, and a simple curfew.
- Home confinement began in Florida in 1983 as the Florida Community Control program. The Florida program is a front-end program that serves as an alternative to incarceration. The Oklahoma House Arrest Program is a back-door program that recruits high-risk offenders from jails and prisons before their parole release.
- The Federal Bureau of Prisons has implemented a home confinement program known as The Community Control Program. The goals of the program include the reduction of the risk of future criminal behavior and correctional treatment to address the offender's problems.
- Electronic monitoring was first used in New Mexico in the early 1980s when a judge placed a probation violator on electronic monitoring for one month.
- Prison costs are six times higher than the costs of electronic monitoring, and therefore use of electronic monitors to save prison costs and relieve prison overcrowding is likely to increase.
- Electronic monitors are important to the success of home confinement. Used for high-risk offenders, EM can reduce the likelihood of failure or absconding.

- Supporters of electronic monitoring suggest that EM facilitates rehabilitation, eases prison-overcrowding, assists in supervision of offenders, and saves prison costs.
- Opponents argue that EM is intrusive, may violate the constitutional rights of the offender, compromises public safety, promotes a race and class bias, and increases the likelihood of recidivism.
- Research shows that electronic monitoring can be effective in reducing recidivism for property, drug, and sex offenders but is less effective for violent offenders. Electronic monitoring may have negative impacts on relationships with spouses and children as well as making it difficult for offenders to get and keep jobs.
- Shock incarceration, also known as boot camp, was implemented in Georgia in 1983 as a highly structured short-term period of incarceration. The primary objectives include reducing prison costs and crowding, promoting discipline and rehabilitation, and discouraging criminal behavior.
- The target groups for participation in boot camp programs are younger offenders who have been convicted of nonviolent offenses and are bound for prison.
- The program features military-style discipline and intensive physical training, harassment by drill officers, and an attempt by the program to "break" the offender's street identity.

Questions for Review

1. What was the Martinson study and how did it affect rehabilitation?
2. Increasing disappointment with rehabilitation and incarceration in the 1970s and 1980s led to the search for alternatives that would save on costs of incarceration and compensate for the limitations of regular probation. How do intermediate sanctions save money and improve on regular probation?
3. What are intermediate sanctions and why were these programs introduced as correctional alternatives?
4. How do intermediate sanctions differ from regular probation?
5. What are the benefits of intermediate sanctions to corrections?
6. What are some of the problems associated with intermediate sanctions?
7. What are the three types of bias that might exist in the selection process for intermediate sanction programs?
8. How does shock incarceration differ from shock probation?

9. Define electronic monitoring and identify why the use of electronic monitors has increased.
10. Identify five reasons to oppose the use of electronic monitors.
11. How might EM negatively affect the offender's family and employment opportunities?
12. Identify the three versions of home confinement. Which of the three is most punitive?
13. What are the advantages and disadvantages of home confinement?
14. Compare and contrast the Florida Community Control Program and the Oklahoma House Arrest Program.
15. Identify some of the major issues related to the use of home confinement.
16. What is intensive supervised probation? Identify the three ISP program models.

Questions for Discussion

Please use these questions for discussion. Choose the response that you think is most appropriate and explain your reasoning. Why are the other responses not appropriate?

1. As a part of his requirements for intensive probation supervision, Robert, an 18-year-old repeat property offender, is required to wear an ankle bracelet and perform community service at his former high school. You recently discovered that he has not been performing the service and has attempted to remove the bracelet. When questioned, he admits that he is embarrassed because most of the students know him and tease him about "working for the state." You respond by:
   A. Telling him that you have no sympathy for him because he really should be in prison.
   B. Informing him that he is in violation of his court-ordered conditions and that you will attempt to find him a different placement.
   C. Filing a request to have his probation revoked and the sentence imposed.
   D. Doing nothing and hoping that he will commit a crime so he can be sent to prison.

2. Jonathan has been in boot camp for the past six months. When he returns home, he will be placed on intensive supervision probation for three years. He wants to move in with his brother in a neighborhood known for its gang violence and drug trafficking. The judge refuses to order Jonathan to live with his parents even though you have told him that this young man

will be back in jail in less than a month. When the judge does not take your advice, you decide to:

A. Increase surveillance and remind Jonathan that if he gets into more trouble, he will go to prison.
B. Lie to him and tell him that the judge changed his mind, ordering him to move home.
C. Make an appeal to the judge to change the probation order.
D. Report the judge to the bar association for negligence.

3. The wife of an offender on home confinement comes to your office to complain that because her husband is under home confinement and monitored with the voice identification system, the entire family has to suffer. She states that it is unfair that phones in the home cannot be equipped with modern technology and conveniences. According to her, "this whole supervision thing is intrusive and expensive, and it is unfair to the family." You respond by:

A. Suggesting that she should get a divorce and put him out of the house.
B. Telling her that she could remove him from home confinement and have him sent to prison.
C. Reminding her that prior to placing him on home confinement, she understood the intrusive nature of the supervision and agreed to the conditions of home confinement with electronic monitoring.
D. Inform the judge that there is a major problem with this case that should be addressed by the court.

4. Those who support a labeling perspective might argue that being required to wear a monitoring bracelet further stigmatizes the offender, making it difficult to reintegrate into society. This has the effect of leading to more criminal behavior. How would you address this charge?

A. Labeling theory is just that—a theory with no real world application.
B. Offenders given an intermediate sanction have already failed at probation or parole supervision and have chronic criminal histories or drug and alcohol problems that have brought them into contact with the criminal justice system more than once.
C. The alternative is to go to prison and come out with an even greater stigma.
D. Criminologists who develop theories have no understanding of real world policies and practices.

5. One of the recurring criticisms of intermediate sanctions is that they promote race and gender bias, often rejecting minorities and females in favor of men who are viewed as more suitable for these programs. How would you address this issue?

    A. Judges and decision-makers must use discretion and select offenders who are more likely to be successful in these specialized programs.

    B. The programs are privileges—these offenders deserve prison. They have no right to complain.

    C. Recognize that there is bias or the potential for bias and find ways to alleviate it.

    D. Design special programs for minorities and women.

Case Study

Questions 1–4 are based on this case.

Richard was given a six-year probation term after pleading guilty to several burglaries. During the first six months of supervision, you notice that his behavior is changing. He is becoming more angry and aggressive. When you attempt to talk with him, he becomes even more hostile and angry. You talk with your supervisor in the probation department about his increasingly aggressive attitude. One night Richard assaults a friend after they argue over a football game. In your delinquency report to the courts, you recommend that the court would either revoke his probation and give him prison time or give him jail time with mandatory psychiatric evaluation and treatment. The court decides to revoke his probation but place him on home confinement for one year followed by two years of intensive probation supervision. You reiterate that Richard is not a candidate for an intermediate sanction since he poses a threat to himself and the community. Your recommendation for mandatory counseling and electronic monitoring was ignored. Six months later, Richard kills a state trooper during a routine traffic stop and is charged with capital murder.

1. During the investigation into the case, you are asked why this offender who posed a threat to community was not locked up. You respond by:

    A. Saying that you could not comment since he was no longer under your supervision.

    B. Writing a letter reporting judicial misconduct.

C. Providing your delinquency report and a copy of your recommendations to the court.

D. Quitting your job because of guilt that you didn't do more.

2. Opponents of intermediate sanctions use this case to show that prison-bound offenders should be sent to prison and not given an alternative that allows them to stay in the community. How would you address these critics?

A. You point out that intermediate sanctions such as home confinement provide an alternative to incarceration that has shown some success; violent acts are usually rare.

B. You admit that you agree and decide to join protesters in their efforts to abolish intermediate sanctions.

C. You do nothing because you don't want to lose your job.

D. You refer them to your supervisor, who has a prepared statement.

3. Because of the attention brought about by this case, you are asked to serve on a panel to make recommendations for improving the supervision of home-confined offenders. Which of the following statements would represent one of your recommendations and why?

A. You would recommend that the use of intermediate sanctions be abolished in your jurisdiction because you know very little about these sanctions and their effectiveness.

B. You recommend that there should be more extensive investigation of offenders and tighter restrictions on who would be eligible.

C. Since fewer resources are being allocated to probation departments, you recommend that resources could be better utilized in other areas.

D. You recommend closer scrutiny of judges and their decisions.

4. Which of the following actions would you have recommended in this case and why?

A. Revocation and incarceration

B. Home confinement with electronic monitoring

C. Incarceration with mandatory psychiatric treatment

D. Restoration to probation

Chapter 7

Probation and Parole Officer Roles and Responsibilities

Key Terms

Advocate	Risk control
Broker	Risk reduction
Burnout	Role conflict
Caseworker/Treatment model	Role overload
Law enforcement model	Structured enforcement
Risk	

Learning Objectives
1. Discuss the major probation and parole officer functions and responsibilities.
2. Identify supervision styles of probation and parole officers.
3. Outline the challenges to probation and parole officers in the performance of their duties and responsibilities.

Probation and Parole Officer Roles and Responsibilities

Probation and parole officers are key players in the supervision process for probationers and parolees. Although officer roles, orientations, and challenges have changed over the years, probation and parole officers are still important to successful outcomes for offenders under supervision. This chapter focuses on the roles and responsibilities of parole officers. Additionally, there is an important discussion about the challenges that probation and parole officers face in their job responsibilities.

Although probation and parole officers have many responsibilities, their primary function is to supervise court-sentenced or parole-released offenders in the community.

The primary duty of probation and parole officers is to supervise offenders that are in the community because they have been given probation as an alternative to incarceration or they have been incarcerated but have been released from prison prior to the expiration of their term. As the supervising officer, the probation or parole officer is charged with a number of responsibilities. Offender classification is an important supervision responsibility. Probation and parole officers assess offender risk and offender needs to assist in monitoring behavior, the identification of needs, and determination of appropriate supervision level and program placement.[1]

> Offender classification is categorizing offenders into levels of supervision such as "intensive," "high risk," or "low risk" to manage offenders' needs and risks.

Assessment of risk and needs is crucial to probation and parole supervision because it helps officers to identify offenders who require intensive supervision and the interventions that are needed to address behavior. It also assists officers in the development of a supervision plan to reduce recidivism.[2] According to Lowencamp, Pealer, Smith, and Latessa (2006):

> Offenders with a high risk of recidivism must be intensely supervised and receive comprehensive treatment services. Conversely, offenders with a low risk of recidivism should receive minimal services. Recent research indicates that the failure to follow the risk principle leads to higher recidivism rates.[3]

Risk Assessment

Risk is the degree to which an offender presents a risk of committing a new crime.

> Risk is the degree to which an offender is likely to commit a new crime. It refers to something that might happen and *not* something that will happen.

Through risk assessment, officers identify criminogenic factors that could lead to future criminal behavior. These risk factors help to predict the likelihood of a person committing a new offense and may include long criminal histories, several convictions for property offenses, chronic unemployment, unstable living arrangements, and drug use.[4]

---

1. Clear and Dammer (2000). *The Offender in the Community*. Belmont, CA: Wadsworth Publishing, 70.

2. Scott VanBenschoten (2008, September). "Risk/Needs Assessment: Is This the Best We Can Do?" Federal Probation 72(2): 39–42.

3. Christopher Lowenkamp, Jennifer Pealer, Paula Smith, and Edward Latessa (2006, December). "Adhering to the Risk and Need Principles: Does It Matter for Supervision-Based Programs?" Federal Probation 70(3): 3–8.

4. Clear and Dammer, *The Offender in the Community*, 72.

Needs Assessment

Probation and parole officers must also manage offender needs. Officers must identify "needs factors" that include drug and alcohol problems, money management problems, unstable or undesirable living arrangements, and marital difficulties. Needs include anything that might be an obstacle to re-habilitation and law-abiding behavior.[5] Officers must identify the crimino-genic as well as the non-criminogenic needs of the offender. According to Andrews and Dowden (2006), criminogenic needs may focus on academic and vocational education, anger management, family, management of anti-social peers, and employment, while non-criminogenic needs include in-creasing self-esteem, improving living conditions, and enhancing conventional goals and ambition.[6]

After identifying offender risk and needs, a plan of supervision is imple-mented to address needs, control risk, and reduce risk.[7] **Risk control** restricts the offender's freedom of movement so there is less opportunity to engage in criminal behavior. Risk control strategies include electronic monitoring, cur-fews, restricting associations, and a person's access to places that sell alcohol.[8] The goal of **risk reduction** is to reduce the motivation to commit crimes. Suit-able treatment strategies and appropriate placement of offenders into these programs can reduce both the motivation and the risk of offenders commit-ting new crimes.[9]

Probation and Parole Officer Responsibilities

Probation and parole officers are important to the probation and parole process. They play a major role in the day-to-day routines of probation and pa-role activities. They are charged with performing three major tasks within their offices: intake, investigation, and supervision.

---

5. Dean Champion (2008). *Probation, Parole and Community Corrections*. Upper Sad-dle, NJ: Prentice Hall/Pearson.

6. D. A. Andrews and Craig Bowden (2006, February). "Risk Principle of Case Classi-fication in Correctional Treatment: A Meta-Analytic Investigation," *International Journal of Offender Therapy and Comparative Criminology* 50(1): 88–100.

7. Abadinsky, 2003, *Probation and Parole*, p. 210.

8. Ibid.

9. Clear and Dammer, *The Offender in the Community*, 220.

Intake and Screening

Intake and screening are used most often for juvenile offenders who have been referred to juvenile court. As intake officers, juvenile probation officers review cases and interview the juvenile, his or her parents, and the complainant. The officer exercises discretion in making decisions about the case at this stage of processing. If the decision is to treat the case informally, the juvenile may be unconditionally released to parents, required to get counseling, or placed on unsupervised probation without further involvement in the court. If cases are treated formally, the juvenile may be detained and held for adjudication through juvenile court.[10]

Investigative Function

The probation/parole officer role has an investigative function. Probation officers will conduct investigations to determine if defendants should be released on their own recognizance or released on bail. They also conduct investigations and prepare reports that the courts use in making sentencing and treatment decisions.

Presentence Investigations

Presentence investigation (PSI) reports are requested by the courts to assist in the sentencing and correctional programming of the offender. In order for the judge to make an intelligent and well-informed decision, the probation department conducts a thorough investigation into the person's background. The officer conducting the investigation interviews the defendant and others relevant to the case and reviews criminal, school, employment, and health records. Petersilia (1997) points out that this investigation and the report are important to the court because it provides the judge with knowledge of the defendant that is often limited to what is contained in the PSI. Judges often follow the recommendations for sentencing and treatment made by the probation officer.[11]

---

10. Melissa Sickmund (2003, June). *Juveniles in Court.* Washington, DC: Office of Juvenile Justice and Delinquency Prevention, 5.

11. J. Petersilia (1997, September). "Probation in the United States," *National Institute of Justice Journal*, 2–7.

Pre-Parole Investigations

When inmates are eligible to be considered for parole, they must prepare a parole plan that provides information about employment prospects, living arrangements, and treatment plans once they leave the institution. Institutional parole officers assist in the preparation of this plan that will considered by the parole board. Once the plan has been completed, field parole officers conduct investigations to verify the information in the pre-parole plan.

In Georgia, the parole officer conducts two investigations and writes reports for the parole board. As a part of the parole process, the parole officer writes a legal investigation report after reviewing the inmate's arrest and court records and interviewing arresting officers, court officials, victims, and witnesses. The report provides details of the inmate's current offense and a summary of any prior offenses in the same county. The second investigation is the pre-parole investigation. The parole officer interviews the inmate and completes a personal history statement questionnaire. The inmate is asked to provide information about: (a) his version of the crime, (b) where he has resided and worked, (c) family members are and where they live, and (d) where he plans to live and work. The parole review summary is provided to members before they make a final decision. The parole officer also conducts a social history investigation and writes a personal history statement that presents a revealing picture of the inmate's life from birth to current imprisonment. Furthermore, the reports include discussion of the offender's behavior, attitude, mental and physical health, work performance, and participation in rehabilitation and self-improvement activities.[12]

Supervisory Function

The most important duty performed by probation and parole officers is the supervision of offenders who are serving a probation or parole sentence. As supervisors, probation and parole officers (a) assist offenders in making an adjustment to the community and (b) protecting society. There are four models of probation and parole supervision: the advocate/broker model, the case worker/treatment model, the law enforcement model, and a blended or mixed model. In addition to the other major roles, Czajkoski (1973) states that the probation officers exercise quasi-judicial roles in the performance of their du-

---

12. State Board of Pardons and Parole. *The Parole Process in Georgia.* http://pap.georgia .gov/parole-process-georgia.

ties. At the intake level for juveniles, probation officers exercise discretion and decide whether to treat the case informally or formally. Parole and parole officers set conditions of probation and decide which conditions of probation to enforce. If offenders violate conditions, officers make decisions about whether to initiate the revocation process. They recommend appropriate sanctions for those violations.[13]

Supervision Models

Advocate/Broker Model

The advocate/broker model of supervision endeavors to assist the probationer or parolee in gaining access to services and programs. Under this model, the officer takes advantage of community agencies or services that will assist in meeting needs and refers clients to those services. The probation/parole officer makes sure that the offender is not denied rights to services or fair treatment. There are times when regulations and practices will not allow probationers and parolees to obtain services or get needed help.[14]

As a **broker**, the probation or parole officer focuses on the referral of the correctional client to those community agencies or services that will assist in meeting needs.

Caseworker/Treatment Model

The caseworker/treatment model focuses on assisting the client with problems by using treatment strategies to guide the offender towards rehabilitation and a law-abiding lifestyle. The emphasis of this supervisor role is the improved welfare of the probationer or parolee. In this model, the officer assumes the role of counselor and caseworker, who develops a relationship with the offender and emphasizes treatment and counseling to promote rehabilitation and change in the offender.

The Law Enforcement Model

This supervisory role focuses on the enforcement of rules. This officer makes sure that the offender abides by the conditions of probation or parole. Coercion and threats are used to ensure conformity to the rules.[15]

---

13. E. Czajkoski (1973, September). "Exposing the Quasi-Judicial Role of the Probation Officer," *Federal Probation 37*: 9–13.

14. Howard Abadinsky (2011). *Probation and Parole: Theory and Practice.* 11th Edition. Upper Saddle River, NJ: Pearson, 323.

15. Ibid., 342.

A new tool of supervision is **structured enforcement**. This practice allows the officer to have a structured, predictable way to enforce the rules. Sometimes an offender may violate conditions, but the violation may be less serious than a new arrest. The violation may be a positive drug test or repeated failure to report. The supervising officer should have a way to deal with this violation without the time and expense of a revocation hearing. Structured enforcement allows the agency administrator to impose immediate restrictions: "dirty" urine may result in weekend jail time; repeated failure to report or keep appointments may result in changing curfew to an earlier time, weekend jail time, or hours of community service. If the offender repeatedly disobeys the conditions, then the department will seek full revocation. With structured enforcement, the restrictions are imposed by the agency administrator.[16]

Issues Affecting Probation and Parole Officer Supervision

Officer Stress and Burnout

Burnout is the feeling of emotional, physical, and mental exhaustion related to high stress work environments that affects the ability to function and cope in situations. It can also cause a lack of commitment to the job. Burnout hinders the ability of the probation and parole officer to effectively manage offenders or deliver quality services to those offenders being supervised. Officers experience a number of stressors that may contribute to burnout, including:

1) job dissatisfaction,
2) communication problems with supervisors,
3) low salaries,
4) large caseloads and clients that are difficult to manage,
5) infrequent rewards,
6) job interference with family and social life,
7) a feeling of having little control over their work,
8) the public image of probation and parole officers,
9) job risks,

---

16. Clear and Dammer, *The Offender in the Community*, 337.

10) officer/client interactions, and
11) client failures.[17]

Many point to the organizational bureaucracy as the major reason for probation and parole officer stress and burnout. Probation and parole agencies are called upon to "do more with less." There are more probationers and parolees under supervision but fewer resources being allocated to these agencies. In addition to managing large caseloads, officers have other responsibilities, such as making court appearances, conducting investigations, writing reports, making client visits, and completing excessive paperwork. Although some degree of stress is expected because of the nature of the work with offenders, agencies and organizational heads can do more to reduce stress by identifying its causes and implementing strategies to reduce officer stress.

Prolonged exposure to a stressful work environment without strategies to relieve stress may lead to more serious problems, including:

- health and emotional problems
- risk-taking behavior
- disengagement from or over involvement in professional and personal relationships
- more cynical attitudes

At the organizational level, stress and burnout may lead to office conflict, job dissatisfaction, and high job turnover rates.[18]

Officer Victimization

Recently, there has been an increase in incidents of officer victimization. Officers are often required to visit high-risk clients or have clients arrested in high-risk neighborhoods. Recent data indicate increased attacks on officers who are being assaulted, threatened, and harassed. The most common forms of victimization are reported to be harassment, physical threats, and property loss. Studies reveal a disturbing pattern of officer victimization in many states. In a study of probation and parole officers in Pennsylvania, Parsonage and

---

17. Champion, *Probation, Parole and Community Corrections*, 408.
18. Calvin Simmons, John Cochran, and William Blount (1997). "The Effects of Job-Related Stress and Job Satisfaction on Probation Officers' Inclinations to Quit," *American Journal of Criminal Justice 21*(2): 213–229.

Bushey (1989) reported that 50% of the probation officers had been victimized at least once by assaults, threats, or other victimizations.[19] Over 50% of Texas probation officers have been victimized. These officers reported being attacked by dogs, threatened, or assaulted by a person.[20]

Some patterns of victimizations include that:

- Victimization incidents often take place in the community during field visits.
- Rural areas have higher rates of confrontations than urban densely populated areas.
- Probation and parole officers who carry weapons are more likely to be assaulted even though no weapon is used in about half of the attacks on officers.
- Some incidents take place outside the context of a normal visit, such as during a chance meeting in the community.[21]

Because of the increased number of victimizations, officers are more fearful and less effective on the job, they lack confidence, experience problems with personal and family relationships, and are more likely to carry a gun (both on and off duty). One of the most serious threats to the officer–client relationship is a lack of trust.[22]

Firearms Use by Officers

Because of the increase in assaults on probation and parole officers, many officers carry guns for their own protection even if agency policy does not support it. Many probation departments are adopting a law enforcement supervision style that requires officers to carry firearms and receive firearms training. Opinions are divided concerning whether probation officers should carry guns. Those who support firearms for probation officers point out that (1) probation and parole officers must be able to protect themselves when visiting seri-

19. W. Parsonage and W. Conway Bushey (1989). "The Victimization of Probation and Parole Workers in the Line of Duty: An Exploratory Study," *Criminal Justice Policy Review* 2(4): 372–391.

20. Dennis R. Longmire and Charles B. Wilson (1987). "Summary Report: Parole Division Survey," Huntsville, TX: Texas Correctional Association.

21. Paul Brown (1994). "Probation Officer Safety and Mental Conditioning," *Federal Probation 57*: 17–21.

22. Ibid., 19.

ous offenders in high crime areas during evening hours, (2) because warrant officers are often afraid to go into high crime areas, probation and parole officers are forced to serve their own warrants, and (3) offender populations have become more violent and more dangerous. Those who oppose firearms for probation and parole officers argue that (1) it creates role conflict for the officers who view their supervisory role as treatment agents, (2) when officers and offenders are armed, it could lead to violent confrontations with tragic consequences, and (3) innocent bystanders could become victims of these violent confrontations.[23]

Policies Regarding the Use of Firearms

Currently, three policies address the carrying of firearms by probation officers, depending upon where they serve.

1. Officers are not allowed under any circumstance to carry guns based on state law or agency policy. This policy is in effect in the states of Arizona, Maryland, South Dakota, and New Jersey.
2. Probation/parole officers are law enforcement officers but carrying firearms is restricted.
   a. Guns may be carried only in certain instances: when transporting a violator, making an arrest, entering a potentially dangerous situation, or responding to a threat on the officer's life.
3. Officers are law enforcement officers and the agency permits or requires officers to carry firearms and receive firearms training.[24]

The American Probation and Parole Association acknowledged that concern for officer safety should not be obscured by the rehabilitation versus law enforcement debate. Since probation and parole officers are charged with the dual responsibilities of providing community protection and promoting offender integration in the community, there must be well-defined policies to address officer safety. If the agency makes the decision for officers to carry firearms, the decision must be made by agency leadership and procedures must be identified and implemented. Nothing should be left to the discretion of individual officers except the decision to accept an assignment that requires carrying a weapon.[25]

---

23. Abadinsky, *Probation and Parole, 8th Edition*, p. 342

24. Champion, *Probation, Parole and Community Corrections*, p. 367.

25. American Parole and Parole Association (1994, January). "Position Statement: Weapons." Accessed at https://www.appa-net.org/eweb/Dynamicpage.aspx?site=APPA_2& webcode=IB_PositionStatement&wps_key=e2e80331-3bed-4d64-a044-ea98ee53bd17.

Critical Thinking Box 7.1

There has been growing concern for officer safety in the community. This has led to a debate regarding officers carrying firearms both on and off duty. Review the arguments for and against firearms. Which position do you take? Explain why.

Role Conflict

Probation and parole officers may experience **role conflict** in the performance of their duties. When probation and parole officers experience conflicting obligations in their roles, they might experience role conflict. Officers who are required to collect supervision fees experience some degree of conflict in their roles as rehabilitation agents and enforcers.[26] There are a number of reasons for this conflict. First, officers may perceive inconsistencies between their responsibility to enforce the rules and monitor the offender's behavior versus their role as a helping agent. Second, officers are also caught in the middle of the changing philosophies of the criminal justice system. On the one hand, the officer is viewed as an agent of rehabilitation; at other times, the officer's role is that of a law enforcement agent whose function is to "trail 'em, nail 'em, and jail 'em." [27]

> **Role conflict** is conflict that occurs when officers are expected to perform roles that are incompatible. Expectations to be law enforcers and treatment agents may cause conflict for the supervising officer.

Critical Thinking Box 7.2

Probation and parole officers are responsible for enforcing rules and regulations while promoting rehabilitation and integration of the offender back into society. Are these conflicting roles? How can balance be achieved between these conflicting roles?

Officers may also experience **role overload**. Role overload is the conflict between the demands of the organization, such as deadlines for client visits, reports, and court appearances,

> **Role overload** refers to the excessive work demands on the probation or parole officer.

---

26. Champion, *Probation, Parole and Community Corrections*, p. 411.

27. William White, David L. Gasperin, and Judi L. Nystrom (2005). "The Other Side of Burnout: An Ethnographic Study of Exemplary Performance and Health among Probation Officers Supervising High-Risk Offenders," *The Journal of the American Probation and Parole Association 29*(2): 26–31.

as well as unexpected emergencies, versus the critical needs of clients under supervision.[28]

Use of Volunteers

John Augustus, the first probation officer, was a volunteer. Augustus continued his volunteer work with offenders for 18 years. In the 1960s, Judge Keith Leenhouts, who had used volunteers in his municipal court, founded VIP, a national organization of volunteers in prevention, probation, and prisons.[29] Since that time, volunteers have assumed a vital part of the corrections system. A corrections volunteer is an unpaid person who performs services that supplement and assist correctional personnel. Volunteers may be college interns, retired educators, religious groups, or other individuals who choose to work with various correctional groups. Volunteerism on corrections is not without critics and criticisms. Champion (2008) identifies the criticisms associated with the use of correctional volunteers:

- Volunteers may be naïve about offenders, causing harm to those that they are trying to help.
- Volunteers do not make long-term commitments and may get tired and leave without giving adequate time to clients.
- Use of volunteers may reduce the need for paid employees.
- Most volunteers lack experience, expertise, and knowledge about probation and parole policies and rules.
- Since volunteers operate in an unofficial capacity, confidentiality might be an issue.
- Volunteers may create problems for corrections officials by aiding and abetting correctional clients.[30]

Although valuable, many volunteer programs have not been successful because of poor management, staff resistance, lack of volunteer training, inadequate communication between officers and volunteers, and the need for more support and supervision of volunteers. Volunteer programs must be planned with goals; staff must be involved at every level of program planning and operation; volunteers must be carefully selected, trained, supervised, and recog-

---

28. Champion, *Probation, Parole and Community Corrections.* p. 411.
29. Kevin Ogburn (1993). "Volunteer Program Guide," *Corrections Today 55*: 66–70.
30. Champion, *Probation, Parole and Community Corrections,* p. 411.

nized for their contributions; and the volunteer program must be continually evaluated for effectiveness.[31]

Caseload Sizes

A recurring concern that affects probation and parole officer supervision is caseload size. A caseload is the number of offenders supervised by probation and parole officers. As probation and parole populations have increased so have caseload sizes supervised by individual officers. It has been suggested that the caseload size affects the quality of supervision provided by the officer; the larger the number of offenders under supervision, the poorer the quality of supervision and the services provided by the officer to the client.[32] Large caseloads combined with additional duties can lead to inadequate offender supervision, increased risk of recidivism, officer stress and burnout, and more resignations by probation and parole officers.

Do smaller caseload sizes maximize the quality of officer supervision and minimize client failure? Intensive supervision programs feature smaller caseloads to maximize officer–client contact, supervision, and services to clients while minimizing the risk of offender recidivism. However, research findings are inconclusive about the effect of smaller caseloads and increased supervision on recidivism rates.

The National Institute of Corrections developed a five-principle model for caseload management. This model assists in identifying offender needs and risks and the appropriate supervision level based on those needs and risks. The five principles are to:

1. Accurately predict risk through the use of statistical risk assessment instruments. The use of statistical risk assessment instruments reduces the likelihood of over prediction of risk.
2. Systematically assess the offender's needs. By systematically assessing the needs of the offender, officers meet offenders' needs in a more consistent and comprehensive manner while avoiding subjective evaluations.
3. Using the risk and needs assessments, classify offenders into appropriate supervision levels. In this way, highest risk offenders with the greatest needs will receive the appropriate supervision.
4. Supervising officers must develop a supervision plan.

---

31. Ibid.
32. Champion, *Probation, Parole and Community Corrections,* p. 369.

5. Identify the workload of the agency and estimate the number of staff needed to carry out the workload.[33]

Recap and Review

- Probation and parole officers have three major functions: intake and screening, investigation, and supervision.
- Juvenile probation officers conduct intake and screening for juvenile cases that have been referred to juvenile court.
- An important aspect of the supervision process is identifying and managing offender risk and needs.
- Risk refers to the likelihood of a person committing a new crime.
- Supervision strategies should address offender needs and reduce and control offender risk.
- Risk control attempts to restrict the offender's opportunity to engage in criminal behavior, and risk reduction tries to reduce the motivation to commit crime.
- Stress and burnout, officer victimization, the use of firearms, role conflict, and role overload impact officers' ability to be effective in the supervision process.
- There has been an increase in probation and parole officer victimization by clients who may physically assault, verbally abuse, and threaten officers and damage the property of officers.
- Due to the increased incidence of victimization, officers experience more fear, lack of trust, and lack of confidence; they may carry guns on and off duty or leave their jobs.
- Burnout is the emotional, mental, and physical exhaustion that affects the officer's ability to effectively supervise clients.
- Stressors that lead to burnout may be individual and organizational.
- Stress and burnout may result in emotional and health problems and disengagement for the officer, and job dissatisfaction and high turnover rates for the organization.
- As concerns about officer safety have increased, some officers have taken to carrying firearms for personal protection.
- Those favoring arming officers state that officers must make field visits often in the evenings or serve warrants in high crime areas. Those

---

33. Ibid.

who oppose the practice indicate that arming officers creates role conflict for the officer and increases the likelihood of a confrontation with
clients in the community.
- Volunteers can make important contributions to corrections agencies
  by assisting and supplementing paid staff.
- Correctional volunteer programs may prove to be less successful because of poor management by the agency, staff resistance, and lack of
  training and supervision.
- Caseload size is another issue that affects the quality of probation and
  parole officer supervision and delivery of services to clients.

Questions for Review

1. Explain how officers may exercise a quasi-judicial role in the supervision
   process.
2. Discuss the three supervision models used by probation and parole officers.
3. Define risk control and risk reduction.
4. Explain the importance of officers' investigative roles for sentencing and
   parole release decisions.
5. Define role conflict and role overload. How can these affect the quality
   and quantity of services provided by probation and parole officers?
6. Discuss officer stress and burnout. Identify the stressors that can lead to
   officer burnout.
7. Discuss the problem of officer victimization by correctional clients. What
   are some of the effects of this victimization?
8. Discuss the arguments supporting and opposing the arming of officers
   with weapons.
9. Discuss the role of volunteers in corrections. What are some of the criticisms of these volunteer programs and volunteers?

Questions for Discussion

Please use these questions for discussion. Choose the response that you think
is most appropriate and explain your reasoning. Why are the other responses
not appropriate?

1. You have been on the job for a year and a half as the only female officer
   in the felony adult unit. You supervise a caseload of 150 clients and work

in the Presentence Investigation Unit. The Chief of Probation Services has asked you to revise the curriculum used in the DUI classes, restructure the classes and schedule Instructors to teach. Recently, one of the supervisors wrote you up after making a random check of your case files and finding that you had gotten behind on the paperwork for your cases. For the past 6 months, you have had sleeping problems, headaches, extreme fatigue, stomach pains and loss of appetite. You are absent at least one day each week. After the third visit and a conversation with your doctor, you discover that you are experiencing job related stress and burnout. Because your health is being affected, your doctor warns you that you must make changes. You decide to:

A. Resign from your job; your health is more important.
B. Continue without doing anything and hope that it will get better. You need the job.
C. File a lawsuit because you are a victim of discrimination.
D. Talk with your supervisors regarding your workload and the doctor's recommendations for changes.

2. As a field parole officer, you have been asked to verify the employment plan of an inmate who is being considered for parole. He has indicated that he would be working in maintenance at a wellness center. When you arrive, you discover that it is really a hospital that specializes in pain management, using narcotics as well as other techniques to manage chronic pain. You look at his file and discover that he has been convicted of possession of controlled substances. Further checking reveals that he has a past conviction for the sale of controlled prescription drugs. You decide to:

A. Say nothing because as a maintenance worker, he will not have access to drugs.
B. Provide the information as a part of your report to the institutional services.
C. Contact the inmate's family to ask for money to keep quiet about this information.
D. Contact the parole board directly to make sure that they get the information.

3. You have just discovered that one of your probationers, with a history of drug use, is HIV positive. As you discuss this issue with him, you discover that has not disclosed this information to anyone but you. You are also aware that he is married and has engaged in at least one extramarital relationship since being under your supervision. You are in a dilemma be-

cause you feel that you have a duty to warn these additional parties who might be at risk of being infected. Yet there are rules of confidentiality that must be followed. What do you do?

A.   Notify the wife and the girlfriend so that they can be tested.

B.   Request that probation be revoked so that he can go to prison where he can no longer be a risk to the population.

C.   Seek the advice of your supervisor and the department's legal counsel to find out the policy on disclosure of this information.

D.   Do nothing. He has probably already infected these significant others in his life.

4.   A recent college graduate who has been hired as a probation officer in your office believes that if he can gain the probationer's trust, they will cooperate and obey the rules. He confided in you that at least twice a week, he goes to happy hour with several of his male and female probationers. As an officer for the past 12 years, you respond by:

A.   Telling him to do whatever it takes to get the job done.

B.   Reporting his behavior to the department supervisor.

C.   Discussing with him the dangers of developing that kind of unprofessional relationship with probationers.

D.   Saying nothing. What he does after work is his business.

5.   As a broker working with probationers and parolees, your main goal is to:

A.   Understand and change the probationer or parolee's behavior.

B.   Find appropriate community services that can help meet the needs of the probationer or parolee.

C.   Campaign for the rights of probationers or parolees who have been unfairly treated by society.

D.   Enforce the court-ordered conditions of probation with no concern for changing behavior.

6.   Stress and burnout among probation and parole officers have been major concerns in the past years. Which of the following is *not* likely to be a cause of officer stress and burnout?

A.   pressures within the organizational bureaucracy

B.   low salaries/few rewards

C.   temptation to engage in criminal behavior

D.   interference with family and social life

7.   You discover that a volunteer working with you has been harassing probationers about attending church and Bible study. She has even used the

volunteer time with the probationers to teach Bible lessons. When probationers become frustrated with her constant harassment and warnings that they are "going to hell," they report the behavior to you. You decide to:

A. Have a meeting with the volunteer to discuss her behavior and warn her that future incidents will result in dismissal.

B. Do nothing.

C. Encourage the volunteer to continue but in a more discreet manner.

D. Encourage the probationer to sue the volunteer for violation of First Amendment rights.

8. An employer who recently hired one of your parolees for a construction job calls to report that the parolee "stole his tools." He was one the last to leave the construction site and didn't come to work the next day. The employer demands immediate action and you respond by:

A. Calling the police to have the parolee arrested.

B. Notifying the judge that you will be filing a motion to request revocation of parole.

C. Making contact with the parolee to see why he didn't report to work and what he knows about the missing tools.

D. Telling the employer that it is his responsibility to find his own tools because the parole department is not in the lost and found business.

9. A student intern for the Criminal Justice Department at the local university is working with you as a probation case aide. You discover that she has been reading and discussing the cases of several of her acquaintances that are on probation. When you discover this information, you:

A. Report her actions to your supervisor and the university internship coordinator and recommend termination.

B. Do nothing because she is a student and didn't know better.

C. Have her arrested for violating rules of privacy and confidentiality.

D. Start to look into her criminal history since she has several acquaintances who are probationers.

10. Most probation and parole officers feel uncomfortable in their roles as treatment agents largely because:

A. Society is opposed to the treatment approach in probation and parole.

B. They lack the skills and education necessary to "do therapy."

C. They have problems with the confidentiality of issues discussed in treatment sessions.

D. The majority of officers prefer a law enforcement approach.

11. In many jurisdictions, probation and parole officers are considered to be law enforcement officers and are required to carry firearms and receive firearms training. Which of the following arguments would support that position?

    A. Carrying firearms makes officers feel more powerful and authoritative.
    B. There has been an increase in officer victimizations in the community during field contacts.
    C. Showing a probationer or parolee a firearm helps to coerce them into compliance.
    D. Carrying firearms make officers feel equal to police officers.

12. If you were interviewing for a probation or parole officer position, which of the following characteristics do you think that supervisors will find most desirable?

    A. Being judgmental and hostile to clients
    B. Being intimidating and authoritative
    C. Being easily intimidated by opposition
    D. Being knowledgeable about the social and behavioral sciences

13. During the probationer's initial visit with the probation officer, which of the following is likely to be true of the meeting?

    A. The officer is likely to file a delinquency report to have probation revoked since the probationer is 30 minutes late.
    B. The probation officer explains the rules and conditions of probation.
    C. The officer modifies the conditions that he sees as unnecessary for this particular probationer.
    D. The probationer informs the officer that there are conditions that he will not follow because they interfere with his lifestyle.

14. A probationer, serving a five-year probation term for receiving stolen property, requests permission to move to another state where he has family and the promise of a job. He believes that moving would be in his best interest. You:

    A. Tell him that because he is on probation, he cannot move until he has served at least one-third of his probation term.
    B. Decide to terminate his probation in the convicting state and allow him to move.
    C. Allow him to move if the receiving state agrees to supervise.
    D. Ignore his request.

15. You have been appointed as a new probation officer with a caseload of 250 probationers, where 50%–60% are required to report either weekly, bi-weekly, or monthly. In addition, you are required to make field visits, write reports for the court, and conduct presentence investigations. Which of the following will be most valuable in surviving in your new job?

   A.   The ability to recognize and classify dangerous offenders.
   B.   Successfully convincing your supervisor to reduce your workload.
   C.   The ability to manage time and organize your work effectively.
   D.   The ability to represent yourself and the agency well in the community.

Case Studies

Case Study 1

Questions 1–3 are based on the following case.

Robert T. has been given a five-year probation term for burglary and for-gery. His PSI indicates that he is a known homosexual who made his living by dancing at gay bars. He is 19 years of age and dropped out of school in the tenth grade. The investigating probation officer indicated that when she in-terviewed him for the PSI, he came dressed in female attire: slacks and blouse and shoes. He has never been employed in a "real" job but claims that no one will hire him even though they will interview him. The probation officer also indicated that there is a man in the community who takes care of Robert and has made himself responsible for paying any fees that are owed. This man is well-respected and wants to remain anonymous. The PSI also indicates that Robert has displayed some violent tendencies. There have been several arrests for assaultive behavior. There are reports suggesting that Roberts carries a switchblade and will not hesitate to attack someone who might "provoke" him. His criminal history shows several arrests for assaultive behavior and alcohol related offenses.

1.   During the initial meeting in your office, Robert indicates that he has been fired from his previous dancing job and has had trouble finding other em-ployment. He further indicates that he really does want a job but has no skills. When he asks you for advice, you:

   A.   Dismiss him because he is not serious about wanting a job.
   B.   Look at his attire and think that he'll never get a job.

    C. Refer him to "Workforce" for career counseling and then require him follow through.

    D. Start preparing the paperwork to request revocation of probation.

2. One of Robert's conditions of probation is that he stay out of bars and taverns and stop dancing at gay bars. One night, you receive a call that he has been dancing frequently at the local bar. You respond by:

    A. Filing a delinquency report because this is a violation of probation conditions.

    B. Reminding Robert about his conditions of probation and the consequences of violating those conditions.

    C. Using other probationers to spy on him and report back to you.

    D. Requesting that police go into the bar undercover and arrest him if he is dancing.

3. Robert's presentence investigation report indicates previous problems with alcohol and some violent tendencies. How should the probation officer address these issues during the initial visit?

    A. The officer should wait until there is a problem with violence or alcohol before addressing these issues.

    B. The officer should inform Robert that he or she is aware of possible alcohol and violence problems and suggest counseling.

    C. The officer should refer the case back to the court for further processing.

    D. The officer should completely ignore these issues as possible problems.

Case Study 2

Questions 4–7 are based on the following case.

Larry is a 35-year-old male who has both a juvenile and an adult criminal record. As a juvenile, he was on probation twice and spent time in a juvenile institution. As an adult, he was incarcerated twice for burglary, receiving stolen property, and possession of cocaine. He admits that his crimes as a juvenile and an adult were related to his drug habit. He was addicted to cocaine, heroin, and Lortabs and would do whatever it took to get the drugs he wanted. He confesses that once he stole his mother's monthly money for bills to buy drugs.

During his last incarceration, he decided to apply for participation in a therapeutic community, a move that he admits saved his life. The program had intense individual and group drug therapy that helped him to confront his drug use and some of the reasons for that drug use. For the past six years, he has been clean. He is now married, employed, and serving as a counselor for a young men's organization in his community. He is also pursuing a degree in social work at the local university. He hopes to get a master's of social work degree to work as a juvenile social worker.

A year and a half ago, he applied to work as volunteer at the Probation and Parole Department. The volunteer coordinator has asked for your input and recommendation regarding allowing Larry's request. Reactions from officers in the department are mixed. Some of the office personnel see it as a positive because Larry can relate to offenders who come from the same environment and background. Others who oppose this practice argue that it is likely that Larry will identify too much with the probationers and it will ultimately cause problems.

4.   How can Larry be an asset to the probation and parole officers with whom he works?
     A.   He really can do nothing to assist in supervision since he has no training or qualifications.
     B.   He can help officers who may be from a different background.
     C.   He can understand clients and help offenders become more comfortable, open, and honest.
     D.   He can increase the costs of supervision, which sends a message to the administration that more money is needed.
     E.   He can help officers by finding out information about the illegal activities of clients.

5.   As the volunteer coordinator, you have discovered that there are some staff members who have refused to work with him or even allow him into their offices. How should you approach the situation?
     A.   Call a staff meeting to openly name and discuss the staff members in question and point out that Larry might one day have their jobs.
     B.   Meet with the staff members to discuss their concerns and reassure them that Larry can't and will not take their jobs.
     C.   Recommend the dismissal of these staff members.
     D.   Tell Larry that he cannot volunteer in order to maintain the morale of the department.

6.   Larry has been asked to work with one of your clients; the client was Larry's childhood friend. He had also served time with this young man in state prison when they both were 18 years old. He further admitted that he feels reluctant to volunteer with this former friend. How do you respond?
     A.   You suggest that Larry should work with the client and try to get information on any illegal behavior.
     B.   You dismiss Larry as a volunteer.

C. You understand Larry's dilemma and decide to give him another volunteer assignment.

D. You tell Larry that he has to work with the client or be fired.

7. One of your clients brags to Larry that he has been involved in some recent unsolved burglaries of local businesses. Businesses have lost quite a bit of money in these burglaries and the business community has been demanding that these crimes be solved. When Larry gives you this information, you decide to:

A. Keep your mouth closed because you have too much going on with your caseload without taking on additional stress.

B. Provide the information to local law enforcement authorities so they can investigate.

C. Tell Larry to demand "hush money."

D. Contact the businesses to determine if they have reward money and then make a decision about what to do with the information.

Chapter 8

Juvenile Justice

Key Terms

Automatic transfer
Breed Decision
Finding of fact
Intake
Judicial waiver
Parens patriae
Predisposition report

Preliminary hearing
Statutory exclusion
Status offense
Transfer hearing
Violent and Repeat Juvenile
   Offender Act

Learning Objectives
1. Explain a brief history of the early treatment of juveniles.
2. Explain the rise and function of juvenile court.
3. Examine the juvenile court process.
4. Identify correctional strategies used with juveniles.

Juvenile Justice in America

Juvenile Justice

The historical development of juvenile justice in America can be traced to early colonization, where colonists, influenced by the English model of juvenile justice, developed practices and ideas resembling the English system. Poor laws stipulated that poor, neglected, and abandoned children between the ages of 5 and 14 could be forced into governmental apprenticeship.[1] During the early years, fathers still maintained authority and control over children. Stubborn Child Laws, enacted in Massachusetts in 1646, stipulated that a child who continues to demonstrate stubborn and rebellious behavior could be brought

---

1. Robert Drowns and Karen Hess (2000). *Juvenile Justice*. 3rd Edition. Belmont, CA: Wadsworth Publishing.

Parens patriae is the legal right of the state to assume the parental role for the care and protection of children who cannot legally take care of themselves. It is a doctrine that maintains that the state must act in the best interest of the child and assume the role of parent if necessary.

to the Magistrates Court and put to death.[2] Americans adopted the English doctrine of *parens patriae* which was translated as "father of the country."

It is interpreted to mean that the state can act in the child's best interest by taking over the role of the parent if the parents are unable or unwilling to provide the proper treatment for the child at home. Because of this doctrine, a child could be removed from a home and placed in an alternative setting, not for punishment but for the betterment of the child.

In the early 1800s, houses of refuge were established to deal with children who were runaways or considered incorrigible. Although houses of refuge provided residents with education, training, and other assistance, they were prison-like organizations with strict discipline that was often oppressive and cruel. Two of the most well-known houses of refuge were the New York House of Refuge in New York City and the House of Reformation in Boston. These houses of refuge, initially established to separate juvenile offenders from adult offenders, housed dependent, delinquent, and neglected youth.[3]

Child-saving movements became prominent after the Civil War when many families migrated to cities to find work. Children were left unsupervised to roam the streets while parents worked long hours in the factories. Believing that these children would turn to crime, middle and upper class humanitarians would arrange for these youth to be moved across the country to work on farms. Amid growing criticisms of the treatment of children in houses of refuge and child-saving movements, reformers looked for alternative ways to handle delinquent, neglected, and dependent children. In response to the search for more humane ways to deal with children, a juvenile court was established in Cook County, Illinois, in 1899.[4]

The Development of Juvenile Court

The doctrine of *parens patriae* became the foundation for the establishment of this first juvenile court in 1899. States dealt with neglected and abused chil-

---

2. John Sutton (1981). "Stubborn Children: Law and the Socialization of Deviance in the Puritan Colonies," *Family Law Quarterly* 15(1): 31–64.

3. Barry Krisberg and James Austin (1993). *Reinventing Juvenile Justice.* Newbury Park, CA: Sage Publications.

4. Krisberg and Austin, *Reinventing Juvenile Justice,* 15.

dren, runaways, truants, and juveniles who had committed crimes. This idea caught on and by 1945, all states had a juvenile court (or family court) to manage abused and neglected children, status offenders, and delinquents.

> A **status offense** is conduct that is only illegal because a child is under a certain age. Examples of status offenses are running away, truancy, disobeying parents, and curfew violations. Until the 1960s, status offenders were treated in the same way as juvenile delinquents. Status offenders are no longer viewed as dangerous.

The underlying philosophy of juvenile court was that troubled and troublesome children should not be punished but treated. To use the punitive approach for juveniles would simply make juvenile court a criminal court for children. The founders of juvenile court wanted children going through juvenile court to avoid any kind of negative or stigmatizing experience. Therefore, the court process was informal, with a different terminology from adult court. Abadinsky notes the differences in terminology for the two courts: In adult criminal court, the term "defendant" is used to describe the individual who is charged with a crime and facing trial. In juvenile court, the individual is referred to as a "respondent." Instead of juveniles being "charged" or "indicted," there is a "petition"; the "trial" in adult court is replaced by an "adjudicatory hearing" in juvenile court, and the "verdict" becomes a "finding" in juvenile court.[5]

However, in the process of allowing children to avoid a criminal trial experience, juveniles were being denied the same procedural safeguards and due process protections granted to adults going through the criminal court process. The *Gault* decision,[6] decided in 1972 by the United States Supreme Court, gave juveniles rights in juvenile court and challenged the *parens patriae* doctrine. The Supreme Court ruled that juveniles are entitled to certain due process rights since those protections had already been extended to other groups such as probationers. In its decision, the Court recognized the noncriminal philosophy of juvenile court but acknowledged that being a child does not justify a "kangaroo court." Even a child cannot be denied reasonable standards of due process. As a result of this decision, juveniles were granted due process protections including:

a. a written notice of charges
b. the right to counsel
c. protection against self-incrimination

---

5. Howard Abadinsky (2003). *Probation and Parole: Theory and Practice.* 8th Edition. Upper Saddle River, NJ: Prentice Hall.

6. In Re Gault, 387 U.S. 1, 18 (1967).

    d. the right to confront and cross-examine witnesses
    e. the right to have written transcripts and appellate review

Juvenile Court Process

Intake

The juvenile court process begins with **intake**. Cases may be referred to juvenile court by police, parents, school officials, or other public or private agency personnel. It is estimated that each year, 1.6 million juvenile cases are referred to juvenile court.[7] In most jurisdictions, intake and screening are conducted by a juvenile probation officer. In some jurisdictions if there are criminal complaints, the case goes directly to the prosecutor's office. The intake officer conducts a number of interviews with the juvenile, the referring person or agent, and the child's parents or guardians and reviews court files and previous records. If it is a serious crime, the district attorney is also consulted. The intake officer takes two things into account before making a decision: (a) the alleged crime — its seriousness, the manner under which it occurred, and the child's attitude towards the offense and (b) the child's situation in the home and school and psychological and physical health.

If the case does not involve serious criminal behavior and the child admits to the behavior, the case is treated informally or unofficially. The probation officer places the child under probation supervision for 90 days to receive treatment, counseling, therapy, or whatever the officer feels is needed. There is no further processing in the juvenile court. If the juvenile has committed more serious criminal behavior, the case is treated as an official case. The probation officer files a petition through the court clerk or the prosecutor to set a date for the first of three types of juvenile court hearings. A decision to pursue the case is usually based on three things:

    a. the offense is serious and unofficial handling of the case is inappropriate
    b. the child or parents deny allegations
    c. informal probation has failed

There are three hearings for the juvenile who has committed a criminal offense and whose case will be adjudicated in a juvenile court. The **preliminary hearing**

---

7. Charles Puzzanchera, Benjamin Adams, and Melissa Sickmund (2010, March). *Juvenile Court Statistics, 2006–2007*. Pittsburg: National Center for Juvenile Justice.

is the first of three hearings where the judge informs the respondent and other parties of the charges and the rights of the respondent. The judge makes a decision about the detention of the child. If the respondent is believed to be a threat to his or herself and society or will not return to court voluntarily, detention will be ordered and the respondent remains in custody. The U.S. Supreme Court ruled in *Schall v. Martin*[8] that juveniles that are deemed dangerous can be detained prior to trial.

> The **preliminary hearing** may also be referred to as a detention hearing. The detention hearing is the juvenile court hearing to determine if the juvenile will be released or detained prior to the adjudicatory process.

The adjudicatory hearing is to decide if the juvenile should be made a ward of the court because he/she is delinquent, a status offender, abused, or neglected. With violations of law, the child makes a statement to admit or deny the charges in the petition. If there is a denial of the charges, evidence is presented to prove "beyond a reasonable doubt" that the delinquent act occurred. In a 1970 ruling, the Supreme Court established that the same standard of proof must be applied to the adjudicatory phase of a juvenile court case where a juvenile is charged with an act that would be criminal if committed by an adult (*In Re Winship*).[9] If the charges are found to be true, the judge makes a **finding of fact**, orders a predisposition report, and sets a dispositional hearing. Prior to making a decision regarding the disposition of the case, the judge orders a **predisposition report**. Similar to the presentence investigation report used in adult criminal court, the predisposition report includes information about the child's family, social and educational history, previous involvement with public or private agencies, and the physical and mental health of the child as determined by the court psychiatrist or psychologist.[10] The dispositional hearing, the final stage of the juvenile court process, is the sentencing stage for the case; the decision is made regarding what to do with the juvenile.

Juvenile court has always adopted the approach that disposition should be based on rehabilitation but not justice. However, as many jurisdictions take a hard line toward criminal behavior, many judges are looking at dispositions from a justice model—what the juvenile deserves—rather than the social service model—what the juvenile needs. There are a number of alternatives the judge may use with the juvenile: probation, community-based facilities that are noncustodial, group homes, training schools, and youth authority. According to Drowns and Hess (2000), there are several options available to the judge who can:

---

8. Schall v. Martin, 467 U.S. 253 (1984).

9. In Re Winship, 397 U.S. 385 (1970).

10. Robert Drowns and Karen Hess (2000). *Juvenile Justice*. 3rd Edition. Belmont, CA: Wadsworth Publishing, 311.

- dismiss the case,
- place the juvenile on probation,
- require community service,
- sentence the juvenile to a correctional facility, or
- refer the juvenile to a social service agency.[11]

Juvenile Probation

Probation is the most common disposition of juvenile court. Juvenile probation is similar to adult probation in that the juvenile offender is placed under the supervision of an officer of the court. The adjudicated delinquent is supervised by the probation department for community treatment. Juvenile probation is used in about 60% of the cases that have been judged delinquent. Recent data show that only 28% of adjudicated juvenile offenders are confined for violent offenses and 33% are confined for property offenses. In contrast, 78% of adults convicted of violent offenses and 68% convicted for property offenses are incarcerated.[12] More serious delinquents are placed on probation, not because it is the appropriate response, but because it is the only response available. Unless it is a serious offense, most states require that a child fail on probation before being sent to an institution. By the time a juvenile is placed on probation, he or she has already been in the juvenile justice system.

The goals of juvenile probation are to:

1. Promote rehabilitation of the juvenile.
2. Protect the community from the juvenile acts of the delinquent.
3. Make the juvenile accountable for the offenses committed.
4. To prepare juveniles to live responsible and productive lives by preparing them with education and job skills.

Conditions of probation include:

1. Staying away from other delinquents.
2. Obeying the law.
3. Attending school regularly or participating in vocational training.
4. Making restitution, which often takes the form of community service. If restitution is monetary, they must pay the victims back for some injury or damage. Juveniles may be placed in a restitution program.
5. Obtaining treatment at a child guidance clinic.

---

11. Robert Drowns and Karen Hess, *Juvenile Justice*, 314.
12. Abadinsky, *Probation and Parole*, 8th Edition, 290.

Institutional Placement

Outside of the death penalty, the most severe sanction involves sending a child to an institution. Approximately 22% of juveniles adjudicated as delinquent are sent to public or private institutional placements. Juvenile custodial facilities may include detention centers, group homes, camps, training schools, or residential treatment centers. Institutional placement may be in a private residential treatment facility or a state institution. According to statistics, 69% of juveniles are held in public facilities.[13] Most facilities that house adjudicated offenders are minimum security facilities with a small population and emphasis on treatment and education. At one time, jurisdictions would confine a child until age 21, but this resulted in the child being incarcerated for a long period of time, longer than an adult for the same offense. Laws in some states specify that a child can only be committed from one to three years.[14]

Another issue for policy makers has been the overrepresentation of minorities who are incarcerated in juvenile facilities. The Juvenile Justice Delinquency Prevention Act of 1988 requires states to examine the disproportionate representation of minority juveniles in institutions. If there is disproportionate representation, states must develop strategies to address and minimize the disproportionality.[15]

Juvenile Parole: Aftercare

A juvenile may be placed in an aftercare program after being released from custodial care to supervised services in the community. In some states, such as New York, the same parole officers supervise both convicted adult felons and violent juvenile felons who have been released from correctional facilities. In most states, the released juvenile offender is supervised by a youth parole officer under the administration of a youth parole review board. There are rules and regulations to govern the behavior of the juvenile; violation of the rules may result in being returned to the secure setting of a correctional facility.[16] Juvenile aftercare is important because it helps to control behavior while the juvenile is confined, reduces the sentence, and prevents overcrowding. The possibility

---

13. Clear, Cole, and Reisig, *American Corrections*, p. 444.
14. Ibid.
15. Ibid., 451.
16. Howard Abadinsky (2000). *Probation and Parole.* 7th Edition. Upper Saddle, NJ: Pearson Publishing, 79.

of being released early and entering aftercare (juvenile parole) encourages good behavior and conformity to the rules while the juvenile is confined.[17]

Other Juvenile Related Sanctions

Within the past two decades, new juvenile programs have been implemented. Restorative justice, also referred to as the balanced approach, attempts to balance offender accountability, community protection, and development of competencies. Intensive supervision for juveniles and boot camp are two intermediate sanctions have become popular alternatives for juvenile sentencing.

Restorative Justice and the Balanced Approach

Restorative justice and the balanced approach in juvenile justice emerged as a response to the swinging pendulum between rehabilitation/treatment for juveniles and retribution/punishment. This balanced approach attempts to integrate a number of goals: (a) community protection, (b) accountability of the juvenile (making the juvenile responsible for his or her actions), (c) competency (teaching the juvenile basic skills and vocational skills), and (d) balance.[18] Pranis (1988) points out that being accountable requires the offender to understand how the behavior affected others, acknowledge the harmful nature of the behavior, seek to make restitution and repair for the harm, and modify behavior to avoid repeating the behavior in the future.[19] This approach also suggests that community protection and attention to the victim should be priorities. The community should be protected from the potential criminal behavior of the juvenile offender. Further attention must be balanced between the victim, the community, and the offender, with the victim being given the opportunity to participate in the court processing. Finally, this approach advocates the development of basic competencies so that juvenile offenders can be productive and responsible citizens in the community.[20]

---

17. Abadinsky, *Probation and Parole*, 78.
18. Gordon Bazemore and Mark Umbreit (1994). *Balanced and Restorative Justice* (Summary). Washington, DC: U.S. Department of Justice, Office of Juvenile Justice and Delinquency Prevention, 2.
19. Kay Pranis (1998). *Guide for Implementing the Balanced and Restorative Justice Model.* Washington, DC: U.S. Department of Justice, Office of Juvenile Justice and Delinquency Prevention, 10.
20. Bazemore and Umbreit, *Balanced and Restorative Justice*, 2.

Intensive Supervision Probation for Juveniles

Just as with adult intensive supervision, juvenile intensive probation is a structured program that serves as an alternative to incarceration; it emphasizes increased supervision and surveillance for the juvenile offender. Program features include small officer caseloads; increased face-to-face contacts per month; greater emphases on counseling, vocational, and employment training; participation in education programs; and finding more support groups for the juvenile.[21]

Boot Camp

Boot camps are short-term institutional correctional programs that impose harsh, military-style training and discipline on younger offenders. The goal of the military training is to break down the street identity of the juvenile and impose discipline into the lives of juveniles.

In 1991, the Office of Juvenile Justice and Delinquency Prevention (OJJDP) awarded three boot camp grants to the Boys and Girls Clubs of Greater Mobile, Alabama; New Pride, Inc.; and the Cuyahoga County Court of Common Pleas in Cleveland, Ohio, to implement juvenile boot camp programs.[22] These programs were intermediate sanctions that provided an alternative to long-term institutionalization for nonviolent juvenile offenders who were at risk for future criminal behavior. The program consisted of three phases: (1) intake and screening, (2) a three-month intensive training period, and (3) a six to nine month aftercare period in the community. The primary feature of the boot camp was the 90-day residential intensive training period that focused on military-style physical training; drug abuse counseling; and completion of high school education, vocational education, job preparation, and development of life skills.[23]

Juveniles and the Death Penalty

In colonial America, children had no rights and were subject to the absolute control of their father, who had the right to kill children who were considered

---

21. Dean Champion (2008). *Probation, Parole and Community Corrections.* Upper Saddle, NJ: Pearson Publishing, 626–627.

22. Daniel Felker and Blair Bourque (1996). "The Development of Boot Camps in the Juvenile System: Implementation of Three Demonstration Programs," in *Correctional Boot Camps: A Tough Intermediate Sanction*, edited by Doris L. McKenzie and Eugene Herbert, 143–158.

23. Ibid., 147.

to be incorrigible. Juveniles aged seven and older who committed serious crimes were tried and punished as adults in criminal courts. Laws specified that the death penalty was an appropriate punishment for disobedient children.[24] The first recorded execution of a juvenile occurred in 1642, when Thomas Graunger, age 16, was executed in Plymouth, Massachusetts. The youngest juveniles to be executed in the United States were James Arcane, a Native American male executed in 1885 who committed robbery and murder at age 10, and George Stinney, a black male executed in 1944 for the murders of two white girls when he was 14.[25] From the first legal execution in 1642 until 2004, there have been 366 executions of juveniles in 38 states and the federal government. In the modern era of capital punishment, approximately 227 death sentences were imposed for juvenile crimes; 22 executions of juveniles were carried out during this same period. Thirteen (59%) of the 22 juvenile executions occurred in the state of Texas.[26]

When juvenile court was first established, the vision for the court was that it would be a social welfare agency that would remove children under 16 from adult criminal court jurisdiction, reduce the incarceration of juveniles in adult jails and prisons, and implement a policy of reform and treatment for juveniles based on the medical or treatment model.[27] Although provisions were made for the transfer of juveniles committing serious crimes to adult court, efforts were made to keep juveniles out of adult criminal court, as the rehabilitation of juvenile delinquents replaced the goal of punishment.

In 1972, the U.S. Supreme Court addressed the issue of capital punishment, but did not specifically address the issue of juveniles and the death penalty. It was not until 1988 that the Supreme Court ruled on the constitutionality of the death penalty for juveniles in the case of *Thompson v. Oklahoma*.[28] At age 15, Thompson participated in the murder of his former brother-in-law, who was shot and stabbed. He was prosecuted in adult criminal court, convicted, and given the death penalty because of the heinous and cruel nature of the crime. The Supreme Court ruled that the execution of juveniles who committed crimes prior to and at age 15 was unconstitutional and violated the Eighth Amend-

---

24. Robert Drowns and Karen Hess (2000). *Juvenile Justice.* Belmont, CA: Wadsworth, 7.

25. Victor Streib (1998, Autumn). "Moratorium on the Death Penalty for Juveniles," *Law and Contemporary Problems 61:* 55.

26. Victor Streib (2004). "The Juvenile Death Penalty Today: Death Sentences and Executions for Juvenile Crimes from January 1, 1973–April 30, 2004." Accessed at http://www.law.onu.edu/faculty/streib.

27. Drowns and Hess, *Juvenile Justice,* 14–15.

28. Thompson v. Oklahoma, 487 U.S. 815 (1988).

ment. The Court concluded that the execution of juveniles who had committed crimes before their sixteenth birthday constituted cruel and unusual punishment. The earlier decision was affirmed in *Stanford v. Kentucky* where the Court ruled that executions of juveniles aged 16 or older is constitutional and does not constitute cruel and unusual punishment.[29]

Up until 2005, the United States was one of seven countries that still permitted the executions of juveniles. In 2004, the U.S. Supreme Court once again addressed the constitutionality of the death penalty for juveniles. In 2003, the Missouri Supreme Court ruled in the case of *Roper v. Simmons*[30] that the execution of juvenile defendants under the age of 18 constituted cruel and unusual punishment and was therefore unconstitutional under the Eighth Amendment. Furthermore, the Missouri court highlighted that most states, excluding Texas, Oklahoma, and Virginia, had not sentenced or executed a juvenile defendant since 1993. Additionally, the death penalty for juveniles had been rejected by international, social, and religious communities.[31] Following the decision by the Missouri Supreme Court, the U.S. Supreme Court addressed the issue of the constitutionality of the death penalty for juveniles under age 18 in *Roper v. Simmons*.[32] In a five-to-four vote, the Supreme Court overturned the *Stanford* decision and declared that the death penalty for juveniles who had committed crimes before the age of 18 was clearly in violation of the cruel and unusual provision of the Eighth Amendment.[33]

Juveniles in Adult Criminal Court

As public fear of juvenile crime escalated, the public demanded tougher treatment for these "superpredators." In response to increases in juvenile violent crimes, legislation was enacted to allow juvenile court judges to waive jurisdiction over the case and transfer it to adult court for prosecution. These actions that undermined the goals of juvenile court were based on the belief that violent juveniles were beyond hope of rehabilitation and necessitate prosecution in adult criminal court. As a result of this legislation, states lowered the age at which ju-

---

29. Stanford v. Kentucky, 492 U.S. 361 (1989).
30. Roper v. Simmons, 112 S.W.3d 397 (2003).
31. Scott Vollum, Rolando del Carmen, et al. (2015). *The Death Penalty: Constitutional Issues, Commentaries, and Case Briefs.* 3rd Edition. Waltham, MA: Anderson Publishing, 112–113.
32. Roper v. Simmons, 543 U.S. 551 (2005).
33. Vollum, del Carmen, et al. (2015), p. 114.

veniles could be transferred to adult criminal court and expanded the offenses eligible for transfer. In Wisconsin, Kansas, Indiana, and Vermont, children as young as age 10 are eligible for transfer. Despite increased public awareness of juveniles being prosecuted in adult criminal court the number of transferred juveniles has been decreasing since the early 1990s. In 1992, an estimated 1.6% of all juveniles were transferred; in 2005, that number had dropped to .5%.[34]

Types of Transfers of Juveniles to Adult Criminal Court

There are three mechanisms available to transfer juveniles to adult court: statutory exclusion, judicial waiver, and prosecutorial discretion.

Statutory Exclusion. Most states have statues that exclude some crimes from juvenile court jurisdiction; juveniles committing these crimes are transferred to adult criminal courts. Juveniles accused of violent crimes, especially capital crimes, cannot be held or have their cases heard in juvenile court.[35]

Judicial Waiver. All states permit juvenile court judges to waive their jurisdiction over certain juvenile offenders. In a decision to waive jurisdiction over a case, juvenile court judges consider factors such as age, type of offense, prior criminal record, previous responses to treatment, and dangerousness.[36] In order for juvenile court judges to waive jurisdiction over a case and transfer the case, there must be a **transfer hearing**. In *Kent v. United States*, the Supreme Court ruled that when juvenile court judges waive jurisdiction over juvenile cases, juveniles are entitled to a waiver hearing, a statement of reasons for the waiver, and the assistance of counsel.[37]

Judicial waiver —
The process whereby the juvenile court judge gives up authority over a case and transfers it to adult criminal court.

Prosecutorial Discretion. In some states, prosecutors can charge juveniles in either juvenile or adult courts. This discretion may be limited by statutory criteria such as age and type of offense. Unlike judicial waiver, there is no hearing to determine which court should be selected for filing and there is no formal procedure for the transfer.[38]

---

34. Gerard A. Rainville and Steven K. Smith (2003). *Juvenile Felony Defendants in Criminal Courts*. Washington, DC: U.S. Department of Justice, Office of Justice Programs, Bureau of Justice Statistics.

35. Patrick Griffin, Sean Addie, Benjamin Adams, and Kathy Firestine (2011, September). *Trying Juveniles as Adults: An Analysis of State Transfer Laws and Reporting. National Report Series*. Washington, DC: U.S. Department of Justice, Office of Juvenile Justice and Delinquency Prevention, 2.

36. Ibid., 2.

37. Kent v. United States, 383 U.S. 541 (1966).

38. Griffin, Addie, Adams, and Firestine, *Trying Juveniles as Adults*, 2.

In response to increased violent crimes committed by juveniles in the 1980s and 1990s, at least 34 states passed **automatic transfer** legislation that made it easier to transfer juveniles to adult criminal court. This legislation stipulated that once a juvenile had been prosecuted in adult criminal court, they will forever be an adult; they could not return to juvenile court jurisdiction. According to these statues, "once an adult, always an adult."[39]

Critical Thinking Question 8.1

It has been argued that juveniles are more violent and more of a threat to society than ever before. In 1997, Orin Hatch introduced the **Violent and Repeat Juvenile Offender Act**, which advocated a "get tough" approach to juveniles. One part of this act recommends trying juveniles as adults and sending violent and repeat juveniles to adult institutions for punishment. At the same time, research shows that trying juveniles as adults and sending them to adult prisons increases recidivism and threats to public safety. What is your position on getting tough on juveniles? When should juveniles be sent to adult criminal court, tried as adults, and sent to adult facilities?

Issues Related to Transfer

Protection of Juvenile Rights. Transfer procedures must be careful to avoid violating the rights of juveniles. To make sure that juveniles are protected and not subject to double jeopardy, all waivers must be done in accordance with the ruling in *Breed v. Jones*.[40] Trying a juvenile in adult court must be within the guidelines of the *Breed* decision. Breed was a 17-year-old who was the subject of a juvenile court petition alleging armed robbery. After the preliminary and adjudication hearings had been completed, the judge declared at the disposition hearing that Breed was not a suitable candidate for the programs available through juvenile court. His case was transferred to criminal court where he was tried as an adult and found guilty of armed robbery. The case was appealed to the Supreme Court that ruled that the action in this case violated the Double Jeopardy Clause of the Fifth Amendment because he was tried twice for the same offense.[41]

---

39. Ibid., 7.

40. Breed v. Jones, 421 U.S. 519 (1975).

41. Richard Redding (2010, June). "Juvenile Transfer Laws: An Effective Deterrent to Delinquency?" *Juvenile Justice Bulletin.*

Racial Disparity. Questions of racial disparity have arisen because of the disproportionate number of minority juveniles who are tried as adults. The Bureau of Justice Statistics (1998) reported that 67% of the juvenile defendants who are transferred to adult criminal court for prosecution are black. Seventy seven percent (77%) of the juveniles convicted in criminal court and sent to prison are black (60%) and Hispanic (15%). Most minority juvenile defendants in adult court are charged and sentenced for drug offenses despite the fact they use drugs at a lower rate than white juveniles.[42]

Critical Thinking Question 8.2

The criminal justice system has been charged with being a system of injustice where the poor and minorities are treated more punitively. As it stands, the system is instrumental in maintaining the subordination of minorities. Those supporting this position would argue that the racial disparity in the transfer of juveniles to adult court for prosecution is further evidence of the racial disparity that permeates the entire criminal justice system. What is your position?

Juveniles in Adult Prisons. Evidence shows that approximately 63% of juveniles transferred to adult courts are convicted, but only 23% are sentenced to prison. Incarcerating juveniles in adult prisons has consequences. Juveniles are more likely to be physically and sexually abused, more likely to be attacked with a weapon, and more likely to commit suicide. In many instances, they do not receive the education and other services appropriate for their age group.[43]

Negative Consequences. The transfer of juveniles to adult courts for prosecution has disadvantages and long-term consequences. Juveniles may receive longer and more severe sentences since there are fewer sentencing options available in adult court. They are also less likely to desist from criminal behavior.[44] Rearrests numbers are higher and these juveniles are more likely to be rearrested at a faster rate than juveniles who have not been prosecuted in adult

---

42. Malcolm Young and Jenni Gainsborough (2000). *Prosecuting Juveniles in Adult Court: An Assessment of Trends and Consequences*. Washington, DC: The Sentencing Project.

43. Howard Snyder (2003, December). "Juvenile Arrests, 2001," *Juvenile Justice Bulletin*. U.S. Department of Justice, Office of Juvenile Justice and Juvenile Delinquency.

44. Edward Mulvey and Carol Schubert (2012, December). "Transfer of Juveniles to Adult Court: Effects of a Broad Policy in One Court," *Juvenile Justice Bulletin*. U.S. Department of Justice, Office of Juvenile Justice and Juvenile Delinquency, 3.

courts.[45] Additionally, transfers increase racial disparity; there is more stigma attached to a conviction in criminal court and records are harder to seal, and there may be social, emotional, and developmental consequences. Once juveniles have been transferred, they may lose voting rights, have limited educational and employment opportunities, and become a greater threat to public safety.[46]

Finally, there is little evidence to demonstrate that transferring juveniles to adult courts for prosecution reduces criminal activity. Instead, evidence indicates the opposite to be true. When children who have been transferred are compared to those who remained under juvenile court jurisdiction, criminal activity increased. Rearrest rates for violent and other types of crime increase for juveniles tried in adult courts.[47] These findings suggest that tougher treatment for juveniles may do more harm than good.

Life without the Possibility of Parole

In 2010, the U.S. Supreme Court addressed the issue of juvenile incarceration, specifically the sentencing of juveniles to life in prison without the possibility of parole. In Florida, 17-year-old Terence Graham was sentenced to life without parole for violating probation conditions. The Court ruled in the case of *Graham v. Florida* that it is unconstitutional to sentence a juvenile to prison for life without parole if that juvenile had not committed murder or been convicted of the intent to murder. The sentence was unconstitutional and violated the terms of *Roper v. Simmons*. Furthermore, the Court acknowledged that to impose a sentence of life in prison without the possibility of parole fails to take into account the fact that juveniles change with maturity and does not offer "reasonable opportunity" for rehabilitation.[48] In 2012, in the case of *Miller v. Alabama,* the U.S. Supreme Court ruled that mandatory sentences of life without parole are unconstitutional for juveniles. The ruling in this decision went further than the *Graham* case, which had ruled that juvenile life without parole sentences were unconstitutional for crimes excluding murder.[49]

---

45. Ibid., 10–11.

46. Patricia Allard and Malcolm Young (2002). *Prosecuting Juveniles in Adult Court: Perspectives for Practitioners and Policymakers.* The Sentencing Project, http://sentencingproject .org/doc/publications/sl_prosecutingjuveniles.pdf.

47. Ibid.

48. Graham v. Florida, 130 S. Ct. 2011 (2010).

49. Miller v. Alabama, 567 U.S. (2012).

Recap and Review

- Early Houses of Refuge were established to provide education and training to children who were runaways or incorrigible. They often became prison-like, with oppressive and cruel discipline.
- The doctrine of *parens patriae* became the foundation for the development of juvenile court. Under this doctrine, the state can take the place of the parent when parents are unable or unwilling to act in the best interest of the child.
- The first juvenile court was established in Cook County, Illinois, under the leadership of Judge Julian Mack.
- Juvenile court was based on the philosophy that troubled juveniles should be treated and not punished and that the juvenile court process should be informal.
- The *Gault* decision resulted in juveniles receiving rights and protections when being processed though juvenile court.
- The juvenile court process includes three hearings: preliminary, adjudicatory, and dispositional hearings.
- If the juvenile is adjudicated as delinquent, the judge has several sentencing options, including probation, institutional placement, or intermediate sanctions. Probation is the most common sanction used in juvenile court; approximately 59% of all juveniles adjudicated in juvenile court are given probation.
- There are three types of transfers: statutory exclusion, judicial waiver, and prosecutorial discretion.
- All transfers must be done in accordance with the *Kent* and *Breed* decisions. The *Kent* decision stipulates that before judges can transfer cases, there must be a waiver hearing. The *Breed* decision protects transferred juveniles from double jeopardy or having their cases tried twice.
- Automatic transfer statues require juveniles of certain ages who commit certain types of crimes to be transferred automatically to criminal court. They do not appear before a juvenile court judge. These statutes avoid the judicial requirements of *Kent* by taking the transfer decision out of the juvenile court judge's hands altogether.

Questions for Review

1. What is the doctrine of *parens patriae*? How was the concept related to the development of juvenile court?

2. Who was Judge Julian Mack?
3. Describe the intake process for juveniles who have been referred to juvenile court? What factors might influence the probation officer to treat the case as a formal case?
4. Describe the three hearings in juvenile court. What is the finding of fact?
5. What is the pre-disposition report? How is it similar to the presentence investigation report?
6. Describe the use of probation in juvenile court. What are the goals of probation? Identify some conditions of probation.
7. What was the purpose of the Juvenile Justice Delinquency Prevention Act of 1988?
8. What is aftercare and why is it important?
9. What is balanced probation? How does it differ from regular juvenile probation?
10. What is juvenile boot camp? How would you describe its purpose?
11. What are the three ways that juveniles may be transferred to adult criminal court?
12. How do "automatic transfer" and "once an adult, always an adult" statues affect transfer practices?
13. Discuss the issue of racial disparity in the transfer of juveniles to adult courts for prosecution.
14. What are some of the consequences associated with the transfer of juveniles to adult courts for prosecution?

Questions for Discussion

Please use these questions for discussion. Choose the response that you think is most appropriate and explain your reasoning. Why are the other responses not appropriate?

1. John, an 18-year-old male on your caseload, lives with his sister in a neighborhood known for extensive criminal activity. He has been arrested several times, always in this neighborhood and with his best friend, Walt, who is also known as a major player in the drug business. He could live in a stable neighborhood with his mother who has tried repeatedly to get him to move. He refuses. His mother, fearful that her son will die in this neighborhood, comes to you for help. You respond by:
   A. Telling her that there is nothing you can do because he is an adult.
   B. Requesting that the judge amend the probation order to require him to move out of this neighborhood.

    C. Writing a delinquency report requesting that probation be revoked for violation of probation conditions.

    D. Waiting until he gets arrested and the recommending revocation and prison time.

2. A juvenile that you supervised on juvenile probation committed a new offense—a robbery. The case was treated formally in juvenile court and went through the juvenile court process. After the case had been adjudicated and was in the dispositional phase, the judge decided that juvenile court had exhausted its efforts to rehabilitate this young man. He decided to waive jurisdiction and transfer the case to adult criminal court. As you read the comments of the judge, you become alarmed because:

    A. You know that this young man will never survive in an adult prison.

    B. You are afraid that he will only become a better criminal in adult prison.

    C. You know that his family cannot afford to hire a criminal defense lawyer.

    D. You know that this is a case of double jeopardy—he can't be tried twice for the same crime.

3. John, aged 15, has been placed on your juvenile probation caseload for two burglary cases. Previously, he was under informal supervision for theft and disorderly conduct. When informal methods didn't work, the family court judge placed him on formal juvenile probation. Although you have doubts that he will do well under supervision, you prepare for his initial visit. What would you do in this case?

    A. You share your doubts with him and tell him that you plan to refer him to the Department of Youth Services at the first violation of the rules.

    B. You feel that the judge made a mistake and you send the case to the prosecutor for transfer to adult criminal court.

    C. You develop a plan for supervision and treatment and inform him that you will be strictly enforcing this plan.

    D. Prepare to go over the rules and regulations and hope that he will violate soon so that you can get rid of the case.

4. Walter, aged 14, has been under court-ordered supervision since he was referred for simple assault and theft. You have supervised him for the last three months. Over the last month, you have noticed several things about Walter's behavior. He seems to be suffering a mild case of depression. Further, the school counselor has informed you that he is exhibiting signs of attention deficit hyperactive disorder. As his supervisor, you decide to:

   A. Do nothing because he only has a short time remaining under supervision.

   B. Refer him to the court psychologist for evaluation and guidance for a treatment plan.

   C. Make a recommendation to the judge for Walter's transfer to the Department of Youth Services.

   D. Make a recommendation to the court for Walter's release from supervision.

5. You have just received Mary's case from family court. Although she is only 15, she has been arrested 10 times for prostitution. Mary has lived in foster care since her mother was first incarcerated for drug possession. Her records indicate that Mary was molested for several years by her father who has been incarcerated for the past 10 years. Although she was sentenced to a one-year probation term, you don't believe that this is sufficient. You decide to:

   A. Recommend placement in a group home with psychological counseling.

   B. Recommend placement in another foster home.

   C. Just enforce the probation rules as ordered.

   D. Do nothing and wait for the term to end.

6. Bryan comes from a good home where both parents are supportive of Bryan and his brother and sister. Bryan has been arrested twice for selling drugs at school. For the first charge, the case was treated informally, and he was placed on unsupervised probation with recommended counseling for him and his family. Bryan's father is the judge's pastor; therefore, the judge wants you to treat the case informally again and place Bryan on unsupervised probation to avoid further embarrassment to the family. As the intake officer, you are faced with a dilemma and you decide to:

   A. Seek advice from another judge in juvenile court.

   B. Make your decision based on the information and allow the case to proceed formally through juvenile court.

   C. Relent to the judge's wishes and drop the case before it proceeds through the juvenile court process.

   D. Report the judge's request and behavior to the American Bar Association.

Case Studies

Case Study 1

Questions 1–3 are based on the following case study.

Randy, a 15-year-old male, has been in juvenile court several times since he was 10 years old, always appearing before the same juvenile court judge. At age 10, he was referred to the court for habitual truancy from school. Then he began associating with a "bad crowd," and his delinquent behavior began. He was next before the juvenile court for shoplifting. He was placed on six-months of probation. During his probation period, he was suspected of several burglary offenses. He was eventually charged with one burglary. At age 14, he was placed in the Mt. Vernon Juvenile Institution. After seven months, he was released on parole. During the next year, he was arrested four times for underage drinking, public intoxication, DUI, and disorderly conduct. He violated his conditions of parole and spent another four months in Greensville State School for Boys.

After being released, he stayed out of trouble for about three months before being arrested again for burglary. Loss of property was estimated at $15,000. The state wants the juvenile tried as an adult so that he may receive adult punishment and incarceration in a state facility. The district attorney feels that to do this is in the best interest of the community because Randy has not responded to the care, treatment, and supervision of the facilities of juvenile court.

Once the juvenile court has waived its jurisdiction, the case will be sent to the grand jury for indictment. Because of Randy's record and the fact that the case is a felony, the result is sure to be incarceration in prison. The juvenile court judge has several concerns: (a) Can Randy recover from the experience in an adult prison? (b) What is his responsibility as judge to protect the community? and (c) Should the severity of the case warrant Randy being tried as an adult or should he be protected under juvenile court in an effort to rehabilitate him?

As the juvenile probation officer who has done intake on Randy as well as been his probation officer, the judge has requested a conference with your seeking advice about the case.

1. As you read the information that has been given to you again you pay close attention to the case and conclude that:
   A. Randy does not seem to be deterred by punishment.
   B. His delinquent behavior is due to the lack of care and concern for him by others.

C. Randy has a pattern of aggressive behavior that should be controlled.

D. Juvenile prison has made him what he is; his felonies began after placement in a juvenile institution.

2. Based on case history, you present all of the reasons to the judge why Randy should be given another chance in juvenile court. Which of the following would be your strongest argument for keeping him under juvenile court jurisdiction?

A. There is no program or punishment left in juvenile court to deter him.

B. Statistics indicate that juveniles placed in adult prisons are often beaten, sexually assaulted, or learn to be better criminals.

C. It costs twice as much to house a juvenile in an adult facility than an adult.

D. Randy's incarceration will protect society from his uncontrolled criminal behavior.

3. If you believed that this case should be transferred to adult court, what would be your argument for more severe punishment?

A. Randy is only 15 and believes that these are childish pranks.

B. The offenses are only property offenses and should not receive severe punishment.

C. Randy has not been deterred by the punishment or rehabilitation efforts juvenile court; life in prison with the possibility of parole is the appropriate sentence.

D. Randy is too young and immature to understand the seriousness of his behavior.

Case Study 2

James Allen Morton, Jr. is a 14-year-old male who is facing transfer to adult criminal court for an armed robbery case. On August 8, Buddy's Food Mart located at 101 37th Street in Tuscaloosa was robbed by a lone black male who entered the store. He was armed with a handgun and demanded the store's money. The clerk placed the money in the bag and the male took the money and ran from the store.

Once the male left the store, the bag tore open, leaving money and food stamps at the scene. Police investigating the offense recovered most of the food stamps and money. A tip called in to Crime Stoppers led to the defendant, who was later arrested at his grandmother's house. The defendant states that one day he was at home and decided to go to the laundromat. While there, he states that he met a guy that he did not know. He got into the car with this guy and rode around smoking marijuana and drinking alcohol. They went across town to Buddy's Food Mart. He says that this guy told him that this looked like an easy store to rob. "I went in with the intention of getting beer, but I got scared and I showed the clerk the gun. She asked if I wanted the money. Then, she gave me all the money." The defendant states that he ran out of the store and into some bushes, threw the gun away, and got in the car. Regarding the offense, the defendant further states that, "I couldn't believe that I did it. I didn't have a reason for doing it. I was drunk; I was stupid. I am so sorry that I did it."

In 1996, he was taken to juvenile court for public intoxication and was given 24 hours of community service. In 1997, he was referred to juvenile court for trespassing. He attempted to go to an ex-girlfriend's house while under the influence of alcohol. He was sent to the High Intensity Training (HIT) Program for 28 days. He completed the program successfully. The defendant has no felony arrests or convictions. The present offense is the only felony arrest on his criminal record.

His father is James Allen Morton, Sr. He grew up in Houston, Texas, and is presently employed as a mental health worker. He and James' mother are presently separated after being married for 18 years. He has no criminal record. The defendant has never had a good relationship with his father; his father never spent much quality time with him while he was growing up. James, Jr. grew up being almost completely ignored by his father. He grew up feeling rejected by his father who, even now, has shown little concern for his son's present legal difficulties. His mother is Mrs. Alma Morton. She grew up in Anniston, where she attended school. She is presently a teacher in the Tuscaloosa City School System with the Program Future Alternative School. She is an active member of the Borderline Baptist Church where she has been a member all of her life. She is a youth advisor for Youth Fellowship and a member of the hospitality committee. She has no criminal history. Mrs. Morton, however, is very supportive of her son. She says that she has always had a good relationship with him and tried to compensate for the lack of the relationship with his father. Mrs. Morton asserts that she has taught her children Godly principles and Christian values. She emphasized the importance of having good attitudes and being productive. Keeping them involved in church activities including Sunday School and youth activities has always been a priority. James had been active in church activities until about one year ago. Approximately one year ago, he started to show signs of rebelliousness. At that time she started to have some difficulty with him. He started to hang around with boys in the streets and stay out later than permitted. Even in the present difficulty, Mrs. Morton still supports her son. She still believes in him and believes that he can get back to those values and principles that she has taught. James has one sister, Alice, who is a third grader at Kelly Elementary School. He has a stepsister, Freda Adler, aged 20, who is a student at Jacksonville State University. James has no contact with his stepsister. He also has a large extended family including his grandparents, aunts, and several cousins. All of his family members are supportive of this young man and desire to see him get his life back on track.

James Allen Morton, Jr., the oldest child of James Allen Morton, Sr. and Alma Morton, was born in Tuscaloosa, Alabama, on July 1, 1981. He is 19 years old. He is not married, nor does he have children. He attends Borderline Baptist Church where he has participated in the youth ministry of the church. Although his attendance and participation had become sporadic within the past year and a half, he has begun to get active again with the youth ministry. James attended Tuscaloosa County High School but dropped out as an eleventh grade student. Since his arrest, he has been attending classes to secure his GED. He describes himself as a below average student who had no major discipline problems or attendance problems while attending school. Except for playing basketball in eighth grade and playing football in the tenth grade, he had no extracurricular activities. James has been employed at Wendy's since September where he works approximately 30 hours per week. He states that his employers are not aware of his present legal difficulties. He also reports that he has had good comments and reports about his work. Prior to his job at Wendy's, he was unemployed.

Physical Health. James has been diagnosed as having scoliosis; however, he is not presently receiving treatment for this condition. He has used drugs and alcohol and describes himself as a recovering alcoholic. He spent one month at the Bradford Center and seven weeks at the Start Alcohol and Drug Rehabilitation Center. He reports that he has been clean and sober since November of this year.

Mental/Psychological Health. At age nine, James was diagnosed with Attention Deficit Hyperactive Disorder (ADHD) and placed on Ritalin for approximately six months. Since that time, he has been under the periodic care of psychiatrists. Much of this treatment has focused on his suicidal thoughts. He reports that he thinks about suicide quite a bit. His mother states that when he was younger, his drawings depicted death and dying themes.

Case Study 3

Victor Allen Washington is a 16-year-old male who is being considered for transfer to adult criminal court for Robbery I.

On March 21, 2002, university police were called to a sorority house on the University of Alabama campus. Witnesses reported that a female victim had been robbed by a lone black male who approached her and hit her in the head with a handgun and took her purse. He then ran down Campus Drive with university police in pursuit. While he ran, he threw the gun and the purse under a nearby car. When apprehended by police, he confessed and was taken back to the scene of the crime. Although the victim was unconscious, witnesses identified the attacker. The victim was transported to Regional Medical Center where she was treated for a concussion and released after three days. The offender was transported to Tuscaloosa City Jail and later transferred to Tuscaloosa County Jail where he was charged with aggravated robbery.

The defendant stated that he had been at home on the day of the incident because he did not attend school and had taken off work. He had not slept at all the night before and had been restless all day. He smoked marijuana that day and drank almost an entire bottle of Jack Daniels whiskey. He left home to visit a friend in hopes of getting more marijuana. He stayed at his friend's house for approximately two hours. His friend later dropped him off near the university campus where he had planned to visit another friend. He remembered walking in the direction of sorority row, but he does not remember robbing and hitting the victim or running away from the scene. When he came to himself, he was in the back of a police cruiser being transported to Tuscaloosa City Jail. He states that even though he cannot remember the incident, he is remorseful for the injury and fright to the victim. He also regrets the shame that he has brought to his family.

The defendant has no felony arrests or convictions. The present offense is the only felony arrest on his criminal record. However, he has been investigated for credit card theft and a robbery that occurred at McFarland Mall. When he was a senior in high school, he was accused of firebombing a classmate's car after the classmate called him a "fag" one day at school. When his parents agreed to pay $7,000 for damage to the car, the victim decided not to file charges. The entire incident was dropped and the defendant was never charged.

His father is Dr. James Washington. He grew up in Mobile, Alabama, and is presently in private practice as a psychiatrist. He and Victor's mother have been married for 25 years. He has no criminal record and is a well-respected citizen of the community. He is a member of the Borderline Baptist Church where he serves as head of the scholarship committee. The defendant states that he has never had a good relationship with his father; his father never spent much quality time with him while he was growing up. Victor states that being the oldest son, his father expected much of him but failed to provide the guidance that he needed.

When he could not meet his father's expectations, his father seemed to reject him. He stated that he grew up being almost completely ignored by his father.

His mother is Mrs. Helen Washington. She grew up in Anniston, where she attended school. She is presently the office manager for her husband's practice. She is active in the community and is often called upon to be a motivational speaker. She is an active member of the Victory in Praise Church where she has been a member for the past five years. She is a praise team leader and a member of the education committee. She has no criminal history.

Victor's family is very prominent in the city. Not only is his father a doctor, but he has two uncles and an aunt who are also physicians. Although Victor and his father have never had a close relationship as father and son, his father is hurt by his son's present legal difficulties. He feels that Victor has failed to take advantage of many of the opportunities available to him. Dr. Washington also states that he now sees how his treatment of his son could have contributed to feelings of rejection and perhaps his present legal troubles. He remarked that "sometimes you are so busy diagnosing everyone else's problems that you miss the glaring ones in your own life. I wish that I could go back and start all over with my son." Mrs. Washington, however, is very supportive of her son. She says that she has always had a good relationship with him and tried to compensate for the lack of the relationship with his father. Mrs. Washington asserts that she has taught her children Godly principles and Christian values. She emphasized the importance of having good attitudes and being productive. Keeping them involved in church activities including Sunday School and youth activities has always been a priority. Victor is a trained vocalist and had been active in church activities until about one year ago. Approximately one year ago, when he got his car, he started to show signs of rebelliousness. He started to hang around with boys in the streets and stay out later than permitted. He moved out of the house and into an apartment. They took his car and sold it, but his behavior still did not improve. Even in the present difficulty, his parents still provide moral support for their son. They still believe in him and believe that he can get back to those values and principles that they taught him.

Victor has one sister, Ventrice, who has just completed medical school and is in her first year of residency at John Hopkins Medical Center. He has one brother, Billy, aged 19, who just completed his second year as a theater major at New York University where he received a full four-year scholarship. He also has a large extended family, including his grandparents, aunts, uncles, and several cousins. All of his family members are supportive of this young man and desire to see him get his life back on track.

Victor Allen Washington is the oldest son of Dr. and Mrs. James Washington. He was born in Tuscaloosa, Alabama, on July 1, 1981. He is 21 years old.

He is not married, although he has a three-year-old daughter. He has no plans to marry his baby's mother and has seen the relationship worsen over the last six months. He attends Borderline Baptist Church where he has participated in the music ministry of the church. His attendance and participation had become sporadic within the past year and a half. Since his arrest for the present offense, he has begun to get active again.

Victor is a sophomore at Thomas High School although he seldom attends. He states that he does not like school, and the teachers don't like him. After he was accused by one of his teachers of stealing her credit card, he stopped attending on a regular basis. Although no charges were ever filed, he states that the embarrassment was too much for him. His choral teacher states that Victor is a gifted vocalist who could "make it" if he would stop feeling sorry for himself and focus on his goals.

Since ninth grade in high school, Victor has been employed part time in his father's practice as a janitor and file clerk. His mother states that up until about February, he was good worker. After then, Victor would often miss work, show up late, or leave early.

She had planned to terminate him the same week that the offense occurred. Since the arrest, he has gone back to work at the office and attends an alternative school. His work habits have improved; he works overtime and on weekends if needed.

Physical Health. His physical health is good, and there are no medical problems. Although he has used marijuana and cocaine, he does not see himself as an addict. Since his arrest, he states that he has not smoked or snorted. He has also used alcohol but states that he does not have a problem.

Mental/Psychological Health. At age five, Victor was diagnosed with Attention Deficit Hyperactive Disorder (ADHD) and placed on Ritalin for approximately one year. At age 16, he was treated for depression and suicidal thoughts. He reports that sometimes he still thinks about suicide. He did not tell his family or get any other kind of help. He states that he started "drinking and drugging more to ease his emotional pain."

Please review the two cases being considered for transfer to adult criminal court and answer the following questions.

1. Summarize the details of each case.
2. Compare and contrast the two cases. How are they similar? How do they differ?
3. Would you recommend transfer for the cases or retaining them in juvenile court?
4. Write a brief report to the judge with a recommendation for each case. Please justify your recommendation.

Chapter 9

Supervising Special Needs Populations

Key Terms

Criminalization of mental illness	Miscellaneous offender
Cybersex offender	Preferential cybersex offender
Dabbler	Synthetic Officer
Drug-defined crimes	Therapeutic Officer
Drug-related crimes	Time Server
Law Enforcer	Traveler

Learning Objectives
1. Identify three groups of offenders that require special treatment in the criminal justice system.
2. Identify challenges associated with supervising these special populations.
3. Outline supervision strategies that have been developed to supervise special populations.

Supervising Special Needs Populations

Over the years, agencies supervising probation and parole populations have become more aware of offender populations with special needs. Innovative supervision strategies and programs have been devised to address the needs of these offenders. Mentally ill offenders, drug users, HIV/AIDS-infected offenders, sex offenders, and the elderly all require special attention and programs. This chapter focuses on mentally ill offenders, alcohol- and drug-addicted offenders, and sex offenders.

Mentally Ill Offenders

In the 1960s, when sociologists discovered the long-term consequences of labeling someone as criminal or mentally ill, progressives encouraged "de-institutionalization," or an "away from the institution" movement. These diversion programs would allow people to avoid the stigma associated with being in prisons and mental hospitals. The landmark Supreme Court decisions *Shelton v. Tucker*, 364 U.S. 479 (1960), and *O'Connor v. Donaldson*, 422 U.S. 563 (1975),[1] supported this movement when the majority opinion in *Shelton v. Tucker*[2] stated that patients diagnosed as mentally ill cannot be detained in a restrictive environment if it is not needed for treatment.

While the deinstitutionalization of the mentally ill was well-intentioned, there were several concerns:

1. The poor mentally ill living in the community were not able to get the medications that they needed to address their mental health conditions.
2. Mental health facilities were unwilling to provide long-term care for the mentally ill.
3. When the mentally ill sought treatment in these facilities, they were only kept for the minimum amount of time necessary to stabilize their medications before being released back into the community.
4. Finally, the number of mentally ill exceeded the available mental health services.[3]

Criminalizing mental illness occurs when persons with severe mental illnesses commit criminal offenses and are placed in jails and prisons where their illnesses are left untreated.

In the 1970s, the emphasis was on incapacitation, deterrence, and punishment and that led to the **criminalization of mental illness**. In the community, the mentally ill were often arrested for misdemeanors such as public drunkenness, disorderly conduct, and malicious mischief. The initial arrest for a misdemeanor began a cycle of repeated contacts with criminal justice agencies.[4] Three factors were important in mental illness becoming criminalized:

a. A shortage of mental health facilities.

---

1. O'Connor v. Donaldson, 422 U.S. 56 (1975).
2. Shelton v. Tucker, 364 U.S. 479 (1960).
3. H. R. Lamb and L. E. Weinberger (1998). "Persons with Severe Mental Illness in Jails and Prisons: A Review," *Psychiatric Services 49*: 483–492.
4. L. A. Teplin (1983). "The Criminalization of the Mentally Ill: Speculation in Search of Data," *Psychological Bulletin 94*: 54–67.

b. Public fear of the mentally ill.

c. A police culture that emphasized arresting mentally ill misdemeanants rather than referring them to the mental health system.[5]

As a result, more mentally ill offenders were incarcerated in jails and prison instead of hospitals. These factors worsened the criminalization, incarceration, and the overcrowding in America's jails and prisons by the mentally ill who were more in need of treatment than punishment. By early 2000, approximately 200,000 mentally ill offenders were incarcerated in jails and prisons. An additional 600,000 received mental health treatment while under probation supervision. With the inclusion of the mentally ill in correctional populations, two major concerns emerged: exploding prison health care costs and the lack of expertise by criminal justice personnel in dealing with the mentally ill and their special needs.[6]

Criminalizing Mental Illness

The National Alliance on Mental Illness published the following facts about the criminalizing of mental illness in a 2010 publication:

1. About two million people with serious mental illnesses are booked into local jails each year. About 30 percent of female and 15 percent of male inmates in local jails suffer serious mental illnesses with schizophrenia or bipolar disorder being the most predominant. The majority of arrests are for non-violent offenses such as disturbing public order or property offenses. Many have been homeless.[7]

2. Seventy percent of youth in the juvenile justice system also experience mental health disorders, with 20 percent experiencing disorders so severe that their ability to function is significantly impaired.[8]

3. In prisons, almost 25 percent of inmates live with serious mental illness, but their conditions are often under-treated—or not treated at all. Harsh conditions, isolation, and noise, can "push them over the edge" into acute psychosis. An estimated 70,000 prisoners suffer from psychosis on any given day.[9]

---

5. H. R. Lamb and L. E. Weinberger (1998). "Persons with Severe Mental Illness in Jails and Prisons: A Review," *Psychiatric Services 49*: 483–492.

6. Teplin, "The Criminalization of the Mentally Ill," 54–67.

7. National Alliance on Mental Illness. "Fact Sheet 2010." Accessed at http://www.nami.org/Template.cfm?Section=press_room&template=/ContentManagement/ContentDisplay.cfm&ContentID=109504.

8. Ibid.

9. Ibid.

4. Fifty percent of people with mental illness who have previously been in prison are rearrested and returned to prison not because they have committed new offenses, but because they have not been able to comply with conditions of probation or parole — often because of mental illness.[10]

5. In prison, people with mental illness lose access to Medicare, Medicaid, and Social Security benefits. Even when benefits can be restored upon release, reapplying can be time-consuming and complex. Without case management and community assistance, individuals with mental illness are at risk of requiring costly emergency medical services or going back to jail or prison.[11]

Supervising Mentally Ill Probationers and Parolees

Eleven million people are arrested each year in the United States. Six hundred thousand of those arrested have an acute mental illness and approximately seven million have a substance abuse problem and/or a mental illness.[12] About 600,000 mentally ill offenders are supervised on probation and parole. The number of mentally ill probationers and parolees might be two times higher than those not on probation.[13] When supervising mentally ill offenders under probation and parole, officers are faced with four distinct challenges:

1. Mentally ill have special treatment needs and needs for other services. Officers may be called upon to find housing and other social services.

2. The mentally ill offender may not be capable of following the rules of supervision because of limited mental ability. They find it difficult to respond to the conditions of probation or understand their legal status or obligations.[14]

3. Mentally ill offenders may also have substance abuse problems that make supervision even more difficult.

4. The probation officer is required to supervise the mentally ill offender to ensure compliance to both standard and special conditions of probation. Making sure that the mentally ill offender obeys the condi-

10. Ibid.

11. Ibid

12. John Petrila (2002). *The Effectiveness of the Broward Mental Health Court: An Evaluation*. Louis de la Parte Florida Mental Health Institute, University of South Florida.

13. Lauren Babchuk, Arthur Lurigio, Kelli Canada, and Matthew Epperson (2012, September). "Responding to Probationers with Mental Illness," *Federal Probation 76*: 2, 41–48.

14. Ibid.

tions of probation is overwhelming and time consuming to the probation officer who may have a caseload of 100–200 offenders.[15]

When mentally ill probationers are placed on regular probation caseloads, they have higher rearrest, violation, and revocation rates. Thirty-five percent (35%) of mentally ill probationers do not complete probation. Rearrests for mentally ill probationers may be as high as 54%, compared to 30% for probationers without mental illness. Recidivism rates and outcomes are much worse for mentally ill probationers than for probationers without mental illnesses.[16]

Probation officers are not skilled to understand and deal with complicated psychiatric and mental disorders. However, the officer's supervision style may possibly affect outcomes for the mentally ill probationers. In his typology of probation officer supervision styles, Klockars suggests that the supervision approach that works best for mentally ill probationers is a style that combines the law enforcer with the therapeutic agent.[17]

Carl Klockars' Probation Officer Supervision Styles: Law Enforcers are concerned with strictly enforcing the wishes of the court combined with concerns related to public safety and performing police-like tasks. The Therapeutic Agent supervises by seeking resources to aid in the rehabilitation and treatment of the probationer. Understanding problems and seeking solutions to those problems are important to this supervision style. Time Servers avoid the law enforcer and treatment supervision styles. Instead, they do the minimum to meet job demands and view their job as just a job. Synthetic Officers may employ law enforcement or treatment supervision style as the situation requires.[18]

Specialized Probation Caseloads

Many jurisdictions have implemented specialized probation programs to manage the mentally ill probationer. Specialized probation officers may supervise a reduced specialized probation caseload and work with community agencies to provide mental health care, substance abuse counseling, and other social services.

Specialized probation caseloads often have the following components:

• Caseloads are mental health caseloads. Probation officers exclusively handle mentally ill probationers in need of mental health services.

15. Arthur Lurigio (2009). "Comorbidity," In *Encyclopedia of Psychology and Mental Health*. Edited by Nancy A. Piotrowski. Pasadena, CA: Salem Press, 439–442.

16. Lauren Glaze and Thomas Bonczar (2010). *Probation and Parole in the United States, 2010*. Washington, DC: Department of Justice, Office of Justice Programs, Bureau of Justice Statistics.

17. Carl Klockars (1972). "A Theory of Probation of Probation Supervision," *Journal of Criminal Law, Criminology and Police Science* 63(4): 550–557.

18. Ibid.

- Caseload sizes are reduced. They may range in size from 30–50 probationers.
- Probation officers are provided with intensive and specialized training in mental health issues. Training consists of two major components: (a) developing and maintaining relationships with the probationer and community-based services and (b) identifying problem-solving and correctional strategies for supervising the mentally ill probationer.
- Probation officers use internal and external services to meet probationer needs. Probation officers serve as brokers, coordinating social services to meet the needs of probationers.
- Probation officers develop strategies for identifying obstacles associated with non-compliance to conditions and problem-solving techniques for addressing probationers' failure to comply with probation conditions.[19]

Effectiveness of Specialized Probation Caseloads

Although research data on specialized caseloads are limited, findings suggest that specialty caseloads can reduce the number of probation violations, create a better relationship between the probation officer and the probationer, and provide better probation outcomes.[20] These programs are more effective when the relationship between the client and officer is based on trust, caring, fairness, and toughness. These specialty programs are most effective when the probation officer can combine correctional practices of fairness and firmness with caring and problem-solving strategies. Threats and coercion are not effective in the specialized approach to supervising mental health offenders.[21]

Substance Abusers

Probationers and parolees often have similar histories of alcohol or drug abuse. Two-thirds of all probationers have drug or alcohol problems and over 50% of inmates in the United States who will be released will be returning to the community with drug and alcohol problems.[22]

---

19. Babchuk, Lurigio, Canada, and Epperson, "Responding to Probationers with Mental Illness," 43–44.
20. Ibid.
21. Ibid.
22. Laura Maruschak (1999). *DWI Offenders under Correctional Supervision*. Washington, DC: U.S. Department of Justice, Office of Justice Programs, Bureau of Justice Statistics.

Alcohol-Dependent Probationers

Of the 1.5 million people arrested each year for DWI, a majority will be granted probation. In 1999, the Bureau of Justice Statistics reported that 454,000 convicted DWI (Driving While Intoxicated) offenders were being supervised on probation.[23]

When DWI offenders are granted probation, they are required to follow standard conditions including:

- Weekly reporting to the probation officer
- Maintaining employment
- Committing no new offenses
- Submitting to home visits from the probation officer

They may also be required to follow special conditions. Probationers may be ordered to:

- Complete community service
- Attend DWI classes
- Install ignition interlock devices on their vehicles
- Be subjected to random alcohol testing
- Attend AA meetings
- Receive alcohol treatment

Failure to abide by these conditions of probation may result in revocation of the probationer's sentence and the probationer being sent to prison.

Although most of the DWI probationers are low-risk offenders, there is a small group of chronic offenders who are at a high risk for having subsequent DWIs. This small group of chronic offenders account for the majority of the drunken driving incidents, arrests, and fatalities. The chronic DWI offender is usually a white male between the ages of 30 and 44 years old, employed, and with low educational attainment. He is often unwilling to acknowledge the problem, make an effort to change, and modify his poor attitude about punishment. Being a chronic drunk driver is less about an overall alcohol or drug use disorder and more associated with an unwillingness to change, acknowledge a problem, and seek help.[24]

---

23. Ibid.

24. Michael DeMichele and Brian Payne (2010). *Predicting Repeat DWI: Chronic Offending, Risk Assessment, and Community Supervision.* Retrieved from http://www.appa-net.org/eweb/docs/APPA/PRDWI-DRAFT.pdf.

Drug Abusers

Drug-defined crimes are crimes that violate laws that prohibit the possession, distribution, and manufacture of illegal drugs.

Drugs may be related to crime in three ways: drug-defined crimes, drug-related crimes, and a drug-related lifestyle associated with drug use. The drug-related lifestyle emphasizes a deviant lifestyle where drug users are encouraged to participate in illegal economic activities rather than a legitimate economy.[25]

Drug-related crimes are crimes committed by users who need money to buy more drugs or the distribution of drugs.

Characteristics of Drug Offenders on Probation and Parole

In comparing drug offenders on probation with probationers who are not drug offenders, there are some differences:

- Drug offenders on probation supervision tend to be non-white.
- Drug offenders have higher school drop-out rates and lower incomes.
- Criminal histories differ between both groups with most drug offenders having at least one prior conviction for drug abuse and a higher frequency of drug abuse prior to conviction.
- Drug offenders receive a longer probation sentences and are required to do community service, receive drug treatment, and submit to random urinalysis testing but are less likely to pay supervision fees or court costs.[26]
- Regarding case outcomes, drug offenders on probation have a higher revocation rate than non-drug probationers and are more likely to be revoked for technical violations. Non-drug offenders have more revocations resulting from new arrest violations. Drug offenders have lower rearrests for new offenses or serious offenses.[27]

Supervision of Drug Offenders

Intensive supervision probation with frequent monitoring and intense surveillance has been used for drug offenders on probation. Drug offenders are forbidden to use drugs, subjected to more supervision and surveillance, and are

---

25. Amy Craddock, James Collins, and Anita Timrots (1994, September). *Fact Sheet: Drug Related Crime.* Washington, DC: U.S. Department of Justice, Office of Justice Programs, Bureau of Justice Statistics.

26. Ibid.

27. Ibid.

required to get drug treatment and frequent drug testing. Research reveals that drug probationers on ISP have a higher number of drug-related technical violations, which may be attributed to closer surveillance and no guaranteed access to drug treatment.[28]

More recently, the National Institute of Corrections has recommended a more strategic approach to supervising drug probationers and parolees who violate the rules. If probationers and parolees violate conditions, problem-solving interventions can be identified to prevent future criminal behavior while saving the costs of revocation and incarceration.[29]

Supervision Strategies for Chronic Offenders

Regular supervision strategies are less effective in reducing recidivism for chronic or repeat offenders. Some strategies that have worked include:

a. **Intensive supervision probation (ISP).** Probationers are subjected to increased supervision and surveillance by probation officers who manage a reduced caseload. Intensive probationers are required to receive intensive therapy and participate in treatment programs. Although few studies have been conducted of ISP programs for chronic DWI offenders, preliminary results indicate that ISP offenders have lower recidivism rates than DWI offenders not supervised in ISP programs.[30]

b. **Electronic monitoring (EM).** Offenders are ordered to remain at home and only allowed to leave for work or treatment. They are monitored by a transmitter on a band that is strapped to their ankles. The monitor verifies that the offender is at home. Study results have shown that electronic monitoring can reduce recidivism rates for DWI offenders on probation for two to three months; recidivism rates increased when electronic monitoring ended. Other benefits of using electronic monitoring with house detention for DWI offenders are: it allows the offender to be home; the curfew keeps the offender off the road during DWI hours; and it can be adjusted for employment

---

28. Joan Petersilia and Susan Turner (1993). "Intensive Probation and Parole," *Crime and Justice 17*: 281–335.

29. Peggy Burke, Linda Adams, and Becki Ney (1990). *Policy for Parole Release and Revocation: The National Institute of Corrections, 1988–1989.* Technical Assistance Project. Washington, DC: National Institute of Corrections.

30. Ralph Jones, Connie Wiliszowski, and John Lacey (1996). *Evaluation of Alternative Programs for Repeat DWI Offenders.* Washington, DC: National Highway Traffic Safety Administration, Office of Program Development and Evaluation. 1–35.

hours, AA meetings, and counseling sessions. It is also less expensive than jail.[31]

c. **Day Reporting Centers (DRCs).** DRCs are highly structured, non-residential facilities that provide counseling, supervision, employment, education, and community resource referrals to DWI probationers. Research results show that the DRC is not effective in reducing recidivism but facilitates offenders' reintegration into society and is less expensive than jail.[32]

Treatment Issues for Probationers and Parolees

When developing drug treatment plans for probationers and parolees, there must be consideration of a number of issues:

1. A previous history of failure in drug treatment.
2. Stress caused by overwhelming financial responsibilities.
3. Keeping the probationer or parolee motivated to continue treatment.
4. The possibility of drug relapse.
5. Recidivism. This is concern for parolees, who account for 35% of all prison admissions. Two thirds of all parolees are arrested within three years of release.
6. Violation of probation and parole conditions.[33]

Critical Thinking Box 9.1

In many jurisdictions, probation departments are responsible for the supervision of offenders processed through mental health courts and drug courts. Supervision often requires specialized treatments and specially trained officers. Many probation departments are being required to "do more with less" because of limited resource allocation. Is it really fair to the probation department to be called upon to supervise mentally ill and drug addicted offenders who have needs beyond the expertise of most line officers?

---

31. J. Robert Lilly, Richard Ball, G. David Curry, and John McMullen (1993, October). "Electronic Monitoring of the Drunk Driver: A Seven-Year Study of the Home Confinement Alternative," *Crime and Delinquency* 39(4): 462–484.

32. Ibid. Jones, Wiliszowski and Lacey (1996). *Evaluation of Alternative Programs for Repeat DWI Offenders*, p. 26.

33. Ibid.

Sex Offenders

Sex offenders are generally referred to as anyone convicted of a sex crime. In most states, sex offenses may be broadly classified as forcible sex offenses and non-forcible sex offenses. Forcible sex offenses are those where the victim may be sexually assaulted as a result of force or the threat of the use of force. Non-forcible sex offenses are committed against victims who are incapable of giving consent. These criminal offenses may be committed against underage victims or victims with physical or mental impairments. Supervision of sex offenders poses unique challenges. Convicted offenders must register as sex offenders. Their names, identifying information, addresses, and descriptions of their crimes are kept in an online searchable database maintained by the Department of Public Safety in most states. Housing may be a challenge due to the residency restrictions. Most states prohibit sex offenders from living close to schools, playgrounds, daycare centers, or any other place where children may spend time. Probation and parole officers are required to investigate living arrangements and police are required to notify community residents of the presence of a sex offender.

Sex offenders on probation and parole often have unstable living arrangements which may increase the likelihood of recidivism. These probationers are at a higher risk for unemployment, drug and alcohol abuse, absconding, and recidivism.[34]

There are also unintended consequences of housing restrictions, sex offender registration, and community notification on reentry.

a. Sex offenders often experience unemployment, loss of relationships, threats, harassment, assaults, and property damage. They have reported experiencing shame, embarrassment, depression, and hopelessness.
b. They may be forced to move from a home that they have owned or rented and prevented from returning to that home after release from prison. Housing instability and frequent moves cause the sex offender to become disengaged from family and community and increases the likelihood of general and sexual recidivism.[35]
c. When sex offenders have strong social bonds, they are more likely to desist from criminal behavior. Employment, marriage, constructive re-

---

34. Jill Levenson, Kristin Zgoba, and Richard Tewksbury (2007). "Sex Offender Residence Restrictions: Sensible Crime Policy or Flawed Logic?" *Federal Probation* 71(3): 2–9.

35. Richard Tewksbury (2004). "Experiences and Attitudes of Registered Female Sex Offenders," *Federal Probation* 68(3): 30–34.

lationships, and a stable lifestyle increase the likelihood of desistance from criminal behavior.[36]

The Cybersex Offender on Probation

In the age of technology, probation agencies are being required to supervise a new offender—the **cybersex offender**. There are three types of cybersex offenders. The dabbler may be an adult who has gained new access to child pornography or the adolescent who stumbles onto and downloads child pornography while searching for pornography. The preferential cybersex offender is a sexual deviant who has a variety of sexual interests or a pedophile who prefers children. The miscellaneous offender may be the prankster or an individual who possesses child pornography as a misguided attempt to investigate or expose others engaged in child pornography.[37]

> The **cybersex offender** uses a computer to store or distribute pornography and communicate with potential victims.

Supervision of the cybersex offender and appropriate probation and parole conditions should consider the following:

1. the jurisdiction's probation/parole law
2. conviction offense
3. the offender's computer knowledge/skills
4. prior criminal behavior involving computers
5. the offender's need to have a computer and internet access
6. necessity of the offender having computer/internet access
7. the offender's access to a computer and the internet[38]

More restrictive conditions of probation and parole are given to pedophiles who have victimized children or those who show a likelihood of doing so. This may include sex offenders who travel across state lines to have sex with a minor. The most restrictive conditions include a complete ban on computer use and internet access; the offender may be completely restricted from computer or internet access. The offender must also submit to warrantless searches of his or her home, office, or car by the probation officer if there is reason-

> A **traveler** is a sex offender who travels across state lines to have sex with a minor.

---

36. Richard Tewksbury (2005). "Collateral Consequences of Sex Offender Registration," *Journal of Contemporary Criminal Justice* 21(1): 67–82.

37. Jill Levenson and Leo Cotter (2005). "The Effect of Megan's Law on Sex Offender Reintegration," *Journal of Contemporary Criminal Justice* 21(1): 49–66.

38. D. A. Andrews and James Bonta (2003). *The Psychology of Criminal Conduct.* 3rd Edition. Cincinnati, OH: Anderson Publishing.

able suspicion that there is a violation of this condition. Failure to allow a search constitutes a violation of probation conditions and may be grounds for revocation. The offender may be given access to the computer and online sites only with the written permission of the probation officer. The least restrictive conditions grant the offender access to a computer but the offender must submit to unannounced random examinations of the computer and must provide accurate information about the computer system and hardware, passwords, and internet provider. Standard conditions may include limited contact with minors, mental health and/or substance abuse treatment, and polygraph testing.[39]

Recap and Review

- In the 1960s, there were concerns about the long-term consequences of labeling someone criminal or mentally ill. This perspective encouraged a deinstitutionalization, or an away from the institution, movement.
- The criminalization of mental illness was first recognized when the mentally ill committed petty offenses and were housed in jails because mental health services were not available.
- It is estimated that about one million mentally ill offenders are processed through the criminal justice system each year and 600,000 are supervised on probation and parole.
- The mentally ill probationer or parolee may pose special supervision challenges, including having special treatment needs and having difficulty following the rules of supervision and managing substance abuse problems and mental illness.
- There are various probation and parole officer supervision styles that may ultimately affect the outcome for mentally ill probationers and parolees.
- Some jurisdictions use specialized caseloads with specially trained probation officers to supervise mentally ill clients.
- Approximately 454,000 DWI offenders are supervised on probation each year.
- Most DWI offenders are low-risk offenders but there is a small percentage of chronic alcohol offenders who account for a majority of the alcohol related arrests and fatalities.

---

39. Art Bowker and Michael Gray (2004). "An Introduction to the Supervision of the Cybersex Offender," *Federal Probation* 68(3): 3–6.

- Drug offenders have higher probation revocation rates and are more likely to be revoked for technical violations than non-drug probationers.
- Strategies to supervise drug offenders who violate probation or parole include intensive supervision, electronic monitoring, and day reporting centers.
- Sex offenders are required to register as sex offenders, providing their names, addresses, identifying information, and descriptions of their crimes. Registrations are kept in an online searchable database.
- Supervising sex offenders poses challenges for probation and parole officers because of housing concerns. Sex offenders are restricted from living in areas where children may live or spend time. Police are also required to notify the residents of a community about the presence of a sex offender.
- In an age of technology, cybersex has become a major problem. Cybersex offenders are categorized as one of three types: the dabbler, the preferential cybersex offender, and the miscellaneous offender.
- Conditions for cybersex offenders may completely restrict all access to the computer or may grant limited access to the computer with random examinations of the computer.

Questions for Review

1. Identify the three ways that drugs are related to crime.
2. What does "criminalization of mental illness" mean?
3. What are three factors that contributed to mental illness being criminalized?
4. What are four challenges associated with the supervision of mentally ill probationers and parolees?
5. Describe Klockar's four officer supervision styles for the mentally ill: Law Enforcer, Therapeutic Agent, Timer Server, and Synthetic Officer.
6. Identify the three strategies used to supervise chronic alcohol and drug offenders.
7. Why does housing pose a challenge in the supervision of sex offenders?
8. Who is the cybersex offender?
9. What supervision strategies and conditions are used for cybersex offenders?

Questions for Discussion

Please use these questions for discussion. Choose the response that you think is most appropriate and explain your reasoning. Why are the other responses not appropriate?

1. A probationer who has had alcohol problems in the past informs you that she has started drinking again and needs some help before the problem gets worse. You respond by saying that:

    A. She should violate probation conditions so you can recommend revocation.
    B. She should try to solve her own problem.
    C. You will refer her to a community resource that can help her with her problem.
    D. You will prepare a violation report for the courts to have probation revoked.

2. You receive notice that a probationer who has been ordered to receive drug treatment has been denied participation in a non-profit mental health program that could address his drug addiction. The regulations of these programs prohibit services being offered to those convicted of felony offenses. Since you view yourself as an advocate for the probationer, you decide to:

    A. Leave it up to the probationer to find a program that will accept him.
    B. Investigate to see how agency regulations can be changed so that these programs can address the needs of probationers.
    C. Inform the judge that the probationer cannot receive the services in the community and should be revoked and sent to prison to receive services.
    D. Encourage the probationer to sue the agencies that denied him services.

3. After a night of drinking, two young men steal a tractor and drive it down the middle of one of the main streets in the city. After they attempt to steal a telephone booth, they are arrested and charged with felony theft of property and trespassing. Information in the presentence investigation report indicates that there have been some "alcohol issues" in the backgrounds of both of these young men. When given probation, which of the following special conditions is the judge likely to impose?

    A. They must attend school or get a GED.
    B. They must not get within 100 feet of any place where there are children.
    C. They must attend Alcoholics Anonymous meetings.
    D. They must do 500 hours of community service.

4. You have just received a new probationer on your caseload. In reading the file, you discover that there are some mental health concerns. He had spent the six months prior to probation in jail awaiting trial. During that time, he underwent extensive psychiatric evaluations in which the findings were inconclusive. The first three months of supervision consisted of him coming to your office each week and talking to himself for approximately 15

minutes. He can't complete the probation report form or communicate with you. At first, you think that it is just a game, but as you re-read his case file, you recognize that there is a problem. You decide to:

A.   Request revocation of probation because there is nothing you can do to help him.

B.   Refer the case back to the court psychiatrist for further evaluation, reporting his behavior over the past three months.

C.   Let him continue to do what he was doing, it makes your job easier because you don't have to do much.

D.   File a complaint against the judge who placed the young man on probation knowing that he was mentally incompetent.

5.   Annie, a 55-year-old probationer on your caseload, is an alcoholic. In the three years that you have supervised her, she has been to drug rehabilitation four times. She reports to you that for the past 10 years her husband, who is also an alcoholic, has abused her. She also says that he has become more violent, and she has become more and more afraid. You have suspected it and her presentence investigation information indicated an abusive relationship. You decide to:

A.   Do nothing; she is used to the abuse.

B.   Ignore her; it is probably the alcohol making her imagine things.

C.   Refer her to the court for provoking the assaults from her husband.

D.   Refer her to the domestic violence shelter for battered women.

Case Study

Otis is a 40-year-old male who was convicted of the sexual assault of his 14-year-old male student. He was sentenced to 10 years in prison but was released on parole after serving five years. He is on your parole caseload. He has two master's degrees, one in music and one in educational leadership. He is a former schoolteacher and church minister of music. As you interview him during his initial visit, he informs you that he has been out of prison for a month and has not registered as a sex offender because he feels that he was wrongfully convicted and should not have to endure further punishment and public humiliation for a crime that he did not commit.

Although this was his first felony offense, he previously served 30 days in county jail on worthless checks charges. His mother and father have been divorced for about 20 years; she has had little contact with Otis and never visited him while he was in prison. He lives with his father, who is 85 and in poor health.

He has a brother and sister. His brother is a successful businessman who owns an auto supply store and repair center. His sister is married and lives in another city. Neither wants to be associated with him since their parents always favored Otis when they were growing up. In addition, he states that he cannot keep the parole condition that requires him to be employed. Teaching and music are all he knows and did not receive training to do anything else while in prison. He organized the prison choir and worked in the library. He was married briefly; his wife left when she discovered that he was gay, which he denies. You impress upon him the seriousness of his parole conditions, especially the requirement to register as a sex offender. After being on parole for six months, you get information that he is hanging with some of his old friends and has been using cocaine. He is still unemployed but claims that he is looking for work.

1. What do you see as the greatest challenges to supervising this case?
2. What are his chances for being successful under parole supervision?
3. Write a plan of supervision that will include recommendations for employment and counseling.

Chapter 10

Current Controversies

Current Controversies

Specialty Courts

The rise of specialty courts can be traced to therapeutic jurisprudence that began in the late 1980s. The main objective of therapeutic jurisprudence is to reduce recidivism through rehabilitative, therapeutic means. The therapeutic jurisprudence philosophy suggests that courts might assist rehabilitative efforts by making adjustments to the criminal procedure, including:

a. making sure that judges, attorneys, and other legal personnel are aware of therapeutic options;
b. making sure that offenders have a central role in the process and require them to assist in the creation of their treatment plans; and

Therapeutic jurisprudence ideology suggests that courts can promote rehabilitation for criminal offenders by making adjustments to the criminal process and using therapeutic rather than non-therapeutic responses to criminal behavior.

   c.   giving courts the authority to order offenders to participate in programs that will help their rehabilitation.[1]

Creation of Specialty Courts

In recent years, courts have experienced an increase in the number of cases
with complex social and psychological problems. These cases require the courts
to resolve disputed issues of fact and attempt to solve a variety of human problems that are responsible for the offender being in court. These courts are typically referred to as specialty courts or problem-solving courts.[2] Juvenile court,
the first of which was established in 1899, developed the problem-solving court
model with the focus on the rehabilitation of juvenile offenders. Other specialty courts, including drug courts and mental health courts, followed that
model. The first modern-day specialty court was the drug court, first developed
in 1989, which emphasized drug treatment over punishment. Other specialty
courts that have developed in recent years include:

- domestic violence courts
- re-entry courts
- dependency courts
- youth courts
- mental health courts.[3]

The criminal justice system uses problem-solving courts to better understand "human problems" of domestic violence, drug addiction, and mental
illness. Understanding these problems leads to better treatment models and
reduced recidivism. Specialty courts also play an advocacy role for needed resources within a community such as shelters and inpatient and outpatient
treatment facilities. Once resources are available, specialty courts can work
with community agencies to improve the effectiveness of the treatment that is
provided.[4] The discussion in this chapter will focus on two of those courts:
mental health courts and drug courts.

---

   1. A. McGaha, R. A. Boothroyd, N. G. Poythress, J. Petrila., and R. G. Ort (2002).
"Lessons from the Broward County Mental Health Court Evaluation," *Evaluation and Program Planning 25*: 125–135.

   2. Kathryn Morgan and Crystal Null (2010). "Outcomes of Mental Health Court: Results from a Southeastern State." Unpublished Manuscript.

   3. Bruce Winick (2003). "Therapeutic Jurisprudence and Problem Solving Courts," *Ford-
ham Urban Law Journal 30*: 1055–1090.

   4. A. Christy, N. G. Poythress, R. A. Boothroyd, J. Petrila, and S. Mehra (2005). "Evaluating the Efficiency and Community Safety Goals of the Broward County Mental Health
Court," *Behavioral Sciences and the Law 23*: 227–243.

Mental Health Courts

Mental health courts were established to provide an alternative to punishment for those mentally ill offenders who commit minor crimes when not on medication. These courts were developed to focus on treatment rather than punishment for the mentally ill offender when it became apparent that confining the mentally ill to jails and prisons for the accepted goal of punishment did not work. For rehabilitation and deterrence to work, there must be treatment programs and services available, and the offender must be able to participate in the process.

> The traditional purposes of punishment are retribution, deterrence, incapacitation, and rehabilitation.

The first mental health court was established in Broward County, Florida, in 1996. Recent data indicate that there are now over 500 mental health courts in the United States. The number of courts continues to increase as the awareness of the problem and the number of mentally ill offenders increases. These courts have helped to improve judicial efficiency and provide more focused treatment for defendants.[5]

To be eligible for processing in a mental health court, the individual must have committed a crime and been diagnosed with a severe mental illness such as schizophrenia. Offenders must volunteer to have their cases processed in mental health court before a judge instead of in criminal court. Once the offender becomes a "client" in a mental health court, supervision is performed by case managers who may function as probation officers. Case managers administer drug tests when necessary, refer clients to community treatment programs, advocate for the clients in the community and before the judge, and ensure client compliance to the guidelines of their individual treatment programs. Judges attempt to maintain an active role in the treatment process of mental health clients.[6]

Clients of a mental health court progress through three phases that begin with constant supervision and surveillance in Phase I and culminate with graduation from the program in Phase III. A precondition of moving from one phase to the next is the successful achievement of tasks in the previous stage. Graduation from the program is contingent on the completion of treatment goals, payment of all restitution, and approval of a treatment aftercare plan by the mental health court judge.[7]

---

5. Ibid.
6. Morgan and Null, "Outcomes of Mental Health Court," 6.
7. Ibid.

If participating clients fail to comply with the requirements of the program, sanctions may include retention in the current phase of completion for a longer period of time, demotion to a previous phase, judicial review of the case, or expulsion from the program. If the client commits a new offense while under supervision, the judge decides if the client should remain under the supervision of the mental health court.[8]

Studies of mental health courts and outcomes for participants of mental health courts reveal that:

1. Program participants are usually males aged 18 to 72. Whites, Hispanics, and blacks are equally represented among offenders supervised by mental health court.[9]

2. Misdemeanants in mental health court are usually homeless and may have greater access to community resources than mentally ill misdemeanants who are processed in regular court.[10]

3. Participants in mental health courts often have been diagnosed with severe mental illnesses including bipolar disorder, schizophrenia, and depression prior to entering mental health court. The most common diagnoses are schizophrenia and severe depression. Many participants also have drug and alcohol addictions.[11]

4. Graduates from the mental health court program are usually white males who had been under supervision for approximately 734 days and had fewer incarcerations and hospitalizations prior to entering the mental health court and during the supervision period. Nongraduates were black males who had been supervised for considerably less time (437 days) and experienced an increase in incarcerations and hospitalizations during the supervision period.[12]

5. When graduates of mental health court are compared with similar offenders being processed through regular court, mental health court graduates have lower re-arrest and incarceration rates, less psycho-

---

8. Ibid., 7.

9. Susan Ridgley, John Engberg, Michael Greenberg, Susan Turner, Christine De-Martini, and Jacob Dembrosky (2005). *Justice, Treatment, and Cost: An Evaluation of the Fiscal Impact of Allegheny County Mental Health Court*. Rand Corporation: Technical Report.

10. John Petrila (2002). *The Effectiveness of the Broward Mental Health Court: An Evaluation*. Louis de la Parte Florida Mental Health Institute, University of South Florida.

11. Susan Ridgley et al. (2005). *Justice, Treatment, and Cost*, p. 35.

12. Jennifer Teller, Christine Ritter, Mark Munetz, Kristen Marcussen, and Karen Gil (2004). "Akron Mental Health Court: Comparison of Incarcerations and Hospitalizations for Successful and Unsuccessful Participants in the First Cohort," *Ohio Forensic Newsletter 22*: 4–6.

logical distress, lower levels of substance abuse, and fewer probation violations than those in regular court or non-graduates.[13]

6. Mental health courts are cost-effective. They provide short term savings by processing seriously mentally ill offenders through the mental health court system rather than through traditional courts. In the long term, substantial savings may result from reduced recidivism by offenders.[14]

Critics point out that while there are some advantages in using mental health courts, there are several disadvantages associated with the use of these specialty courts. As voluntary participants of mental health courts, offenders are required to plead guilty to be eligible for participation. Because of the increased demand for treatment services, there might be a lack of mental health treatment opportunities to accommodate this demand.

The Impact of the Fiscal Crisis on Mental Health Courts

As states struggle with restricted budgets, mental health courts are being affected. The growing fiscal crisis in many states has forced a reduction in the allocation of resources for many programs and the closure of some programs. In other cases, funding is being denied to jurisdictions to implement new mental health courts. Some states are closing mental health facilities in favor of mainstreaming the mentally ill into the community. Preliminary indications are that this move will be devastating for mentally ill criminal offenders who will again be housed in jails and prisons where they are unlikely to get needed treatment. Mentally ill misdemeanants are overcrowding jails and increasing medical care costs. County sheriffs in several jurisdictions have indicated that their jails are the largest mental health care providers in the area because often over 50% of the jail's residents have been diagnosed with a mental illness or have sought treatment for mental illness. Even the smallest reduction in the number of inmates would save local jails over $300,000 each year.[15]

---

13. Patricia Tobias (2007). "Idaho Drug Courts Reduce Recidivism, Save Dollars, and Protect Idaho Communities," Special Report. Idaho Supreme Court.

14. Ibid., 6.

15. Kathryn Morgan (2012). "Outcomes of a Mental Health Court: Results from a Southeastern State." Unpublished manuscript.

Drug Courts

Drug courts represent another type of problem-solving court. Drug courts have existed since 1989, when the first court was established in Dade County, Florida. The drug court concept caught on quickly, and by 1999, 492 drug courts had been established in the United States. A more recent count of drug courts revealed that by mid-year 2012, approximately 3,000 drug courts existed throughout the United States.[16]

The drug court model encompasses different components including:

- offender assessment
- case management
- drug testing
- judicial status hearings
- judicial interaction
- multidisciplinary decision making
- treatment practices[17]

Participation in drug court is available for offenders who have a non-violent or drug possession offense and test positive for drugs at arrest. Most states prohibit violent offenders from eligibility in drug court.

Drug courts may be administered following one of two models: deferred prosecution and post-adjudication programs. Deferred prosecution programs do not require the defendant to plead guilty and stop further prosecution if the defendant completes drug court successfully. In post-adjudication programs, offenders are required to plead guilty, and their sentences are suspended while they participate in drug court. Once drug court has been completed successfully, the sentence may be waived. Under both models, failure to complete drug court results in prosecution and sentencing for the defendant.[18]

Drug Court Success

Evidence from a number of studies indicates that drug courts have success in lower recidivism rates, cost savings, and reduced drug use.

---

16. Janine Zweig (2010). *Drug Court Policies and Practices and How They Relate to Offender Outcomes.* Washington, DC: Urban Institute, Justice Policy Center, 6.

17. Ibid.

18. National Institute of Justice (2006). "Drug Courts: The Second Decade." Accessed at www.ojp.usdoj.gov/nij.

Recidivism. Findings from several studies indicate that drug court graduates have lower arrest and reconviction rates than those not participating or graduating from drug court.

Studies of recidivism rates for drug court graduates after two years, three years, four years and longer reveal a significant decline in rearrests and reconvictions. These studies show that reductions in rearrest rates may be as high as 70%.[19]

Cost savings. Evaluations of drug courts reveal that these courts are more cost effective than regular probation and incarceration. The annual average cost to supervise one person in drug court is approximately $4,300 as compared to $23,000 in annual incarceration costs. Cost savings are largely due to reduced recidivism rates, reduced incarceration, and lower victim costs. Evaluations of drug courts reported that cost savings may range from $400,000 to over 1 million dollars per year.[20]

Reduced drug use. Evaluations indicate that drug court reduces drug use and drug relapse. When drug court participants are compared to drug users who did not participate in drug court, drug court participants were les likely to report using drugs in the six- and eighteen-month follow-up periods. Drug court participants were less likely to test positive for drugs during those periods. Even in cases where there was self-reported drug use, drug court participants used drugs less frequently than those who did not participate in drug court. [21]

Other benefits of participation in drug court include:

- reduced frequency of drug use
- improvement in the individual's mental health
- increased employment
- improved economic situations
- improved family relationships
- increased use of aftercare treatment programs[22]

19. Ibid., 6.

20. Ibid., 8–9.

21. Shelli B. Rossman, John Roman, Janine Zweig, Michael Rempel, and Christine Lindquist (2011, November). *The Multi-Site Adult Drug Court Evaluation: Executive Summary.* Washington, DC: The Urban Institute, Justice Policy Center.

22. Shelli B. Rossman, John Roman, Janine Zweig, Michael Rempel, and Christine Lindquist (2011, November). *The Multi-Site Adult Drug Court Evaluation: Executive Summary,* p. 8.

Critical Thinking Box 10.1

Critics maintain that these specialty courts such as drug and mental health courts become another way to excuse deviant and criminal behavior and allow criminals to avoid punishment. How do we explain the importance of these courts to the criminal justice system and the supervision of offenders?

Challenges of Prisoner Reentry

Recent data on correctional populations indicate that approximately 1.5 million inmates are incarcerated in state and federal prisons.[23] At least 95% of those prisoners will return to their communities. It is estimated that 600,000 prisoners are released back into their communities each year.[24] It is also a well-known fact that many of those released reoffend and are returned to prison. Langan and Levin (2002) found that two-thirds of the prisoners released from prison are rearrested and returned to prison within three years of release as a result of technical violations or committing a new offense.[25] Recidivism rates are especially high for males between ages 20–40 who have at least one prior conviction and some with three or more prior convictions.[26] For many of these released prisoners, prison becomes a revolving door. Many prisoners being released back into society are churners who have been recycled through probation and parole.[27] Prisoners returning to society after a prison stay are likely to face many challenges and disadvantages associated with their incarceration.

Recidivism is re-offending or a return to criminal behavior.

Churners are parolees who have failed at reentry for previous releases from prison.[28]

---

23. Anne Carson and William Sabol (2012). *Prisoners in 2011*. Washington, DC: U.S. Department of Justice, Office of Justice Programs, Bureau of Justice Statistics, http://bjs.gov/content/pub/pdf/p11.pdf.

24. J. Petersilia (2004). "What Works in Prisoner Reentry? Reviewing and Questioning the Evidence," *Federal Probation* 68(2): 4–8.

25. Patrick A. Langan and David J. Levin (2002, June). *Recidivism of Prisoners Released in 1994*. Washington, DC: U.S. Department of Justice, Office of Justice Programs, Bureau of Justice Statistics.

26. Ibid.

27. James P. Lynch and William Sabol (2001, September). "Prisoner Reentry in Perspective," *Crime Policy Report 3*. Washington, DC: The Urban Institute.

28. Ibid., 15.

Physical and Mental Health Problems. Many inmates have chronic illnesses and communicable diseases while incarcerated. When inmates experience physical and mental illnesses while incarcerated, they have access to state-provided health care even though that health care may not be the best health care.[29] Upon release, they no longer have access to that care. As a result, released prisoners entering the general population might spread HIV, tuberculosis, and other infectious diseases.[30] Visher (2007) found that among Returning Home project respondents, males have the most serious mental and physical health problems, such as hepatitis, asthma, depression, and high blood pressure.[31] Once released, they do not seek help because they distrust the mental health system; they are often afraid of being returned back to prison.[32]

Substance Abuse Problems. Approximately 75% of returning inmates report a history of drug abuse, with addictions to heroin, cocaine, and other drugs prior to entering prison; they identify drug abuse as the major problem contributing to their incarceration. Many of these inmates also have a dual diagnosis of substance abuse and mental illness. Few report getting treatment while in prison with the result being that they return to society still addicted to drugs.[33]

Family Instability. When parents, especially mothers, go to prison, it affects children who are left behind. Often, mothers are sent to facilities in different geographic locations, making it difficult to maintain contact with their children. Research indicates that if parents can maintain family relationships while incarcerated, it can improve outcomes for the prisoners when they are released. Mothers who are released from prison may be homeless, unemployed, and have difficulty finding child care for their children.[34] Beck (1993) makes this

29. Kathryn D. Morgan (2013). "Issues in Female Inmate Health: Results from a Southeastern State," *Women & Criminal Justice, 23*: 2, 121–142.

30. Joan Petersilia (2000). "When Prisoners Return to the Community: Political, Economic, and Social Consequences," *Sentencing and Corrections: Issues for the 21st Century.* Papers from the Executive Sessions on Sentencing and Corrections. Washington, DC: National Institute of Justice.

31. Christy Visher (2007). "Returning Home: Emerging Findings and Policy Lessons about Prisoner Reentry," *Federal Sentencing Reporter 20*(2): 93–102.

32. Bureau of Justice Statistics (1999). *Mental Health and Treatment of Prisoners and Probationers.* Washington, DC: U.S. Department of Justice, Office of Justice Programs, Bureau of Justice Statistics.

33. Theodore Hammett, Cheryl Roberts, & Sofia Kennedy (2001). "Health-Related Issues in Prisoner Reentry." *Crime & Delinquency 47*(3): 390–409. Petersilia. (2000). When Prisoners Return to the Community: Political, Economic, and Social Consequences, p. 4.

34. Petersilia. (2000). When Prisoners Return to the Community: Political, Economic, and Social Consequences, p. 4.

observation regarding the children of parents who have been incarcerated and released:

Children of incarcerated and released parents often suffer confusion, sadness, and social stigma, and these feelings often result in school related difficulties, low self-esteem, aggressive behavior, and general emotional dysfunction. If the parents are negative role models, children fail to develop positive attitudes about work and responsibility. Children of incarcerated parents are five times more likely to serve time in prison than are children whose parents are not incarcerated.[35]

Employment and Economics. Employment is perhaps the toughest challenge facing released inmates. Many inmates are released from prison with limited educational and vocational skills and few prospects for employment. Employers are reluctant to hire "ex-cons," making the employment picture for released offenders even more dismal. Losing a job or being unable to gain meaningful employment has implications for other areas.[36] Substance abuse, child abuse, and family violence may be related to the released inmate's economic and employment status and frustration with the inability to find employment.

Return to Socially Disorganized Communities. Parolees return to neighborhoods that are characterized by high rates of social disorganization. These neighborhoods experience high crime rates and increased opportunities for crime. Prison admissions from these communities have increased over the years. Gang affiliations that began in prison often continue once parolees return to their neighborhoods.[37]

Other challenges facing returning prisoners include homelessness, loss of political rights, exclusion from housing areas and professions, and a return to criminal behavior. According to Petersilia (2001), many prisoners lack the motivation while in prison to participate in programs that will address employment, educational, and vocational needs once they leave prison.[38] As a result of these challenges facing the released prisoner, many return to crime and ultimately return to prison. Recidivism rates for released inmates are high.

---

35. Alan Beck (1993). *Survey of State Prison Inmates 1991.* Washington, DC: U.S. Department of Justice, Office of Justice Programs, Bureau of Justice Statistics; Bureau of Justice Statistics (1999). *Mental Health and Treatment of Prisoners and Probationers.* Washington, DC: U.S. Department of Justice, Office of Justice Programs, Bureau of Justice Statistics.

36. Joan Petersilia (2001, September). "Prisoner Reentry: Public Safety and Reintegration Challenges," *The Prison Journal* 81(3): 360–375.

37. Joan Petersilia (1999). "Parole and Prisoner Reentry in the United States," *Crime and Justice 26*: 479–529.

38. Petersilia, "Prisoner Reentry," 360–375.

Additionally, inmates being released from prison are older (over 35), have served longer sentences, have prior criminal convictions and previous probation and parole terms, are less likely to have participated in educational and vocational programs while in prison, and are drug violators who are addicted to drugs (it is estimated that up to 75% of offenders released have drug and alcohol problems). Post-prison supervision or a lack of supervision may affect reentry success. Parole caseload sizes are increasing (70:1 or 1 officer for 70 parolees; the ideal is 35:1) and at least 80% of parolees are placed on regular caseloads. This means one or two 15-minute face-to-face visits per month. The public does not support rehabilitation and there is confusion about the mission of the parole department. The public is more fearful of parolees and the likelihood of being victimized. More parolees are violating parole conditions and absconding from supervision. Finally, many inmates are being released under mandatory release guidelines, which means that many are released without being screened and assessed for risk by a parole board. There is no post-custody supervision; one of five released inmates does not have post-custody supervision.

To address the reentry problem, many states and the federal government have implemented offender reentry initiatives on the national and state levels to address the challenges that face returning prisoners.

Offender reentry is the return of prisoners or ex-inmates from jail or prison back into the community.

Federal and State Reentry Programs

Starting in 2001, the federal budget included money (approximately $100 million) for prisoner reentry initiatives. Federal reentry programs include the National Institute of Corrections implementing the *Transition from Jail to Community Project* and the *Returning Home Project* being implemented by the Urban Institute in 12 states. The National Institute of Justice has encouraged more partnerships between corrections and academic communities to develop ideas and provide evaluation of programs once implemented.

On the state level, initiatives include:

* the Parallel Project (Missouri);
* the Preventing Parole Failure Project (California);
* the Coerced Abstinence Program (Maryland); and
* the Prison Reform and Inmate Work Act (passed to create a reentry program in Oregon).

Critical Thinking Box 10.2

It costs approximately $10,000–$25,000 to maintain one prisoner in prison for one year. Despite incarceration costs, inmates return to the community addicted to drugs, unemployable, homeless, and with mental and physical health problems. Many states and communities find it necessary to spend more money to develop reentry strategies to assist these former inmates with reintegration back into society. If prisons did a better job of not just punishing offenders but preparing them for reentry, would these programs be necessary?

Measuring Recidivism in Community Corrections

How do you measure whether a person was unsuccessful in a program? Recidivism is the return to criminal behavior. The definition is not the problem. The problem is trying to measure recidivism. Measuring recidivism is not a problem when an offender in a community-based program commits another serious crime and is reconvicted for that crime. It becomes more difficult when different situations occur. What about probationers who are arrested for technical violations or the probationer who is arrested because police suspect criminal activity? Often, rearrests of probationers or parolees may occur if the police suspect involvement in a crime or if the probationer or parolee lives within close proximity to where a crime has been committed. In many of these cases, these offenders are never officially charged with any crime. Yet, they are certainly in violation of program conditions, which stress that the offender should not be rearrested.[39]

Race and Probation and Parole

One of the most important controversies in criminal justice and criminology today focuses on whether or not there is disparate treatment of racial and ethnic minorities by decision-making authorities in the criminal justice system. This controversy in the criminal justice system raises questions about the impact of race on decision-making by decision-makers. It has been suggested

---

39. Kathryn Morgan (1995). "Factors Influencing Probation Outcome," *Journal of Criminal Justice* 22(4): 341–354.

that there is racial disparity at every level of processing where criminal justice authorities have the power to make discretionary decisions. Police are more likely to arrest, verbally and physically abuse, harass, and profile racial and ethnic minorities; prosecutors are more likely to charge and prosecute minorities for felonies; courts are more likely to convict and sentence minorities to a term of incarceration.[40]

The controversy has recently focused on two key issues: (a) the impact of race on probation and parole decisions, and (b) the question of racial disparity in granting probation and parole. Previous research suggests that race is an important variable at every level of processing where criminal justice authorities have the power to make discretionary decisions. Does race influence who is sentenced to probation or selected for parole? Blacks and Hispanics are disproportionally represented at every phase of the criminal justice system. Of the 1.6 million prisoners incarcerated in state and federal prisons in 2009, blacks and Hispanics represented over 1 million of that total prison population.[41]

Race and Probation

At the end of 2012, there were about 4.7 million adults under probation supervision in the United States. Whites comprised 55% of the probation population while 30% of the population was comprised of black defendants and 17% were Hispanic.[42] In some states, such as Texas and Oklahoma, the percentage of whites on probation increases to as high as 69% and the percentage of blacks on probation falls to 20%. Evidence shows that presentence reports may be more favorable to whites, resulting in many judges granting probation

40. Joan Petersilia (1983). *Guideline-Based Justice: Implications for Racial Minorities*. A report prepared for the National Institute of Corrections. Santa Monica, CA: Rand Corporation; Jeffrey Reiman, (1998). *The Rich Get Richer, The Poor Get Prison*. Boston: MA: Allyn and Bacon; Michael Tonry (1994). "Racial Politics, Racial Disparities and the War on Crime," *Crime and Delinquency 40*; Samuel Walker, Cassia Spohn, and Miriam DeLeon (2004). *The Color of Justice*. 2nd Edition. Belmont, CA: Wadsworth.

41. Lauren Glaze and Thomas Bonczar (2010, December). *Probation and Parole in the United States, 2009*. Washington, DC: U.S. Department of Justice, Office of Justice Programs, Bureau of Justice Statistics.

42. Laura M. Maruschak and Thomas P. Bonczar (2013, December). *Probation and Parole in the United States, 2012*. Washington, DC: U.S. Department of Justice, Office of Justice Programs, Bureau of Justice Statistics.

to white defendants more than minority defendants.[43] In California, 71% of the whites convicted of a felony are placed on probation compared to 67% of blacks and 65% of the Hispanics convicted of a felony.[44] In studies of sentencing patterns in Michigan courts, "borderline" cases, in which judges could impose long probation sentences or short prison terms, results show that most of the time, whites are given probation terms and blacks are being sentenced to prison.[45]

Drug policies associated with the War on Drugs dramatically increased the number of incarcerated blacks and Hispanics. Approximately two-thirds of the drug users are white, but blacks comprise 62% of those incarcerated for drug offenses and whites make up only 36% of those in prison for drug charges. Blacks are often sent to prison for drug offenses and serve as much time in prison for a drug offense as whites serve for a violent offense.[46] Clear and Dammer (2000) suggest that there is a bias that operates in the selection process for discretionary community programs such as probation that results in the exclusion of black defendants. Black offenders are likely to be young, poor, uneducated, unskilled, and have a more serious criminal history than their white counterparts. Therefore, they are viewed as less suitable for these programs.[47]

The pattern persists with juvenile defendants; white juveniles may be granted probation while black juveniles are sentenced more severely. A study of juvenile probation presentence reports reveals that the delinquency of black juveniles is viewed as the result of negative attitudes and personality disorders, and the behavior of white juveniles is explained as the product of the school and family problems. As a result, white delinquents are sentenced to probation because their behavior problems can be addressed through community treatment and intervention programs. Since personality disorders are less responsive to such interventions, black juveniles are incarcerated in order to protect the community.[48]

---

43. L. Carroll and M. Mondrick (1976). "Racial Bias in the Decision to Grant Parole," *Law and Society Review 11*: 3–107.

44. Joan Petersilia (1985). Racial Disparities in the Criminal Justice System: A Summary. *Crime and Delinquency 31*: 15–34.

45. Cassia Spohn and Susan Welch (1987). The Effect of Prior Record in Sentencing Research: An Examination of the Assumption that Any Measure Is Adequate. *Justice Quarterly 4*: 287–302.

46. Samuel Walker, Cassia Spohn, and Miriam DeLeon (2004). *The Color of Justice*. 2nd Edition. Belmont, CA: Wadsworth.

47. Clear and Dammer, *The Offender in the Community*, p. 156.

48. Marc Mauer (2006). *Race to Incarcerate*. New York: The New Press.

The fact that fewer blacks and Hispanics are sentenced to probation is not only a race issue, but a class issue. More blacks and Hispanics remain in jail pending trial unable to afford monetary bail. Many of these same defendants use court-appointed attorneys and are tried by juries of whites because blacks from lower-class neighborhoods are less likely to report for jury duty.[49]

Race and Parole

At the end of 2012, there were 851,000 adults under parole supervision in the United States. Forty-one percent of the parole population was white. Blacks comprised 39% of the parole population, and 17% of those on parole were Hispanics. Although black inmates make up approximately 62% of the prison population, only 39% of those released on parole are black.[50] Studies reveal that race has an impact on parole release decisions. In a study of racial discrimination in three states, Petersilia (1985) found that black and Hispanic defendants received more severe sentences than white defendants who had similar criminal records and were convicted of similar crimes. They also consistently served longer sentences than whites sentenced to prison. Black inmates serve longer sentences, are less likely to receive parole, and often have additional criteria to satisfy.[51]

When parole decisions are compared for black and white inmates, several findings become apparent:

a) Black inmates not only served longer sentences before being paroled but had to show proof of participation in and completion of some institutional treatment program. This criterion was not required for white inmates being considered for parole.[52]

---

49. M. Lynch and B. Groves (1989). *Primer in Radical Criminology*. Albany, NY: Harrow & Heston Publishers; C. Mann (1993). *Unequal Justice: A Question of Color*. Bloomington, IN: Indiana University Press; S. Walker, C. Spohn, and M. DeLeon (2004). *The Color of Justice*. 2nd Edition. Belmont, CA: Wadsworth.

50. Laura M. Maruschak and Thomas P. Bonczar (2013, December). *Probation and Parole in the United States, 2012*. Washington, DC: U.S. Department of Justice, Office of Justice Programs, Bureau of Justice Statistics.

51. Petersilia. *Racial Disparities in the Criminal Justice System: A Summary*, p. 28.

52. Leo Carroll and Margaret Mondrick (1976). "Racial Bias in the Decision to Grant Parole," *Law and Society Review 11*: 3–107.

b) When first-time offenders are being considered for discretionary re-
    lease, black first-time inmates usually serve four months longer than
    whites (62 months versus 58 months).[53]

c) In a study of the parole release process in Alabama, race was not a sig-
    nificant predictor of parole release decisions. However, black inmates
    served more time before being considered for parole release. While two
    times more black inmates than white inmates were eligible for parole
    release and selected for a parole release hearing, fewer black inmates
    were actually chosen for parole release by the parole board.[54]

d) Race does not influence parole release decisions. Instead, legal, so-
    cial, and institutional variables are the most significant predictors of
    parole release decisions. Elion and Megargee (1978) studied 958 youth-
    ful offenders and found no differences in the actual amount of time
    served, but a significantly higher percentage of whites than blacks were
    granted parole. Blacks who were granted parole served a smaller por-
    tion of their sentences than did whites who were granted parole. Blacks
    who were denied parole served a greater portion of their sentences
    than whites who were denied parole. They suggest that these differences
    are attributed to social, legal, and institutional variables and not race.[55]

e) Black and white inmates are likely to be paroled at the same rate when
    they commit similar offenses. Parole boards make no distinctions be-
    tween races when considering inmates for parole.[56]

Because blacks and Hispanics are less likely to be granted probation and parole, there are implications for individuals, families, and communities. When
defendants are granted probation, they maintain community ties and continue
jobs or secure employment with the assistance of the supervising probation
officer. When individuals are incarcerated, they are removed from the labor
force. Released with few job prospects, these ex-offenders are viewed in a negative manner by employers who are often unwilling to hire individuals who
have been incarcerated. Failure to secure and maintain suitable employment

53. Timothy Hughes, Doris Wilson, and Alan Beck (2001). *Trends in State Parole: 1990–2000.* Washington, DC: U.S. Department of Justice, Office of Justice Programs, Bu-reau of Justice Statistics.

54. Kathryn Morgan and Brent Smith (2005, May–June). "Parole Decisions Revisited," *Journal of Criminal Justice 33*(3): 277–287.

55. Victor Elion and Edward Megargee (1978). "Racial Identity, Length of Incarcera-tion, and Parole Decision Making," *Journal of Research in Crime and Delinquency 16*: 233–245.

56. Joseph Scott (1974). "The Use of Discretion in Determining the Severity of Pun-ishment for Incarcerated Offenders," *Journal of Criminal Law and Criminology 65*: 214–224.

may result in individuals violating conditions of parole and returning to prison. The economic impact affects the offender and dependents. Incarceration affects family stability and the socialization and psychological well-being of children. Children feel humiliation, guilt, and shame when a parent is incarcerated, often believing that they contributed to the parent's incarceration. Children may be labeled and stigmatized.[57]

Some recommendations to address this disparity include reserving prison for serious or violent offenders and expanding the use of intermediate sanctions, especially for non-violent minority offenders. There should also be a racial impact statement for every change in justice policy. These statements would prospectively assess the implications that the policy shift would have on minority involvement in the justice system so the policy can be evaluated on the basis of its consequences. Finally, it is evident that more empirical investigation needs to focus on decisions made at crucial decision points in the criminal justice system.

Critical Thinking Box 10.3

In his book, *The Myth of a Racist Criminal Justice System,* William Wilbanks points out that the notion that the criminal justice system is racist is incorrect, although some individual police officers, attorneys, judges, and correctional workers may act in a racist manner. Instead, he argues that blacks and Hispanics are more likely to receive long prison sentences and whites are more likely to get probation or some other community placement because black and Hispanic offenders have more severe criminal histories and commit more serious crimes. This, not racial bias, explains the differences in sentences.[58]

Do you agree with this assessment? Why or why not?

---

57. Jeremy Travis, Elizabeth McBride & Amy Solomon (2006). *Families Left Behind: The Hidden Cost of Incarceration and Reentry.* Washington, DC: The Urban Institute, Justice Policy Center. February. Petersilia. (2000). When Prisoners Return to the Community: Political, Economic, and Social Consequences, p. 4.

58. William Wilbanks (1987). *The Myth of a Racist Criminal Justice System.* Monterrey, CA: Brooks/Cole.

Recap and Review

- The rise of specialty courts can be traced to therapeutic jurisprudence ideology that suggests making changes in the criminal justice process in order to promote rehabilitation.
- Specialty courts are problem-solving courts used to address a variety of human problems that may be contribute to a person's involvement in the criminal justice system.
- Juvenile court was the first specialty court and was established in 1899 to promote rehabilitation for juvenile offenders. The first modern-day specialty court was drug court, established in 1989.
- Mental health court is a specialty court that provides an alternative to punishment for mentally ill offenders who commit minor offenses when not on their medications.
- The first mental health court was established in Broward County, Florida, in 1996. There are over 500 mental health courts throughout the United States.
- Studies of mental health courts reveal that overall these courts have high graduation rates, reduce rearrest rates for participants, and are cost effective.
- Disadvantages associated with mental health courts include defendants being required to plead guilty in order to participate, an insufficient number of mental health services to meet the demand, and that defendants may serve longer sentences than they otherwise would.
- The first drug court was established in Dade County, Florida, in 1989. By the middle of 2012, there were 3,000 drug courts in the United States.
- Inmates returning from prison face many challenges. Many leave prison with mental and physical health problems, addicted to drugs, uneducated, and unskilled. In addition, inmates return to unstable family life and communities that experience high rates of social disorganization and gang activity.
- Because of determinate sentencing, a substantial percentage of inmates are being released without supervision. Parole caseloads have increased and time spent monitoring and providing services to parolees has decreased.
- Reentry initiatives have been developed by several states and the federal government to deal with the challenges of ex-convicts returning to the community.

- One of the major controversies in criminal justice is the racial disparity in sentencing defendants to probation or incarceration. Of the approximately four million under probation supervision, blacks and Hispanics comprise 30% and 13% of the probation population, respectively.
- Drug policies have contributed to the increased incarceration rate for blacks and Hispanics. Blacks and Hispanics are more likely to be convicted and sentenced to prison for drugs even though two-thirds of drug users are white.
- Parole numbers show a similar pattern. Although 62% of the inmates in prison are black, blacks make up only 39% of the parole population.
- Some argue that there is no race or class bias in the criminal justice system. Blacks receive severe sentences and prison more often because they have more severe criminal histories and commit more serious crimes.

Questions for Review

1. What are the deferred prosecution and post-adjudication models for administering drug court?
2. Identify some of the major challenges that face offenders returning to the community after a prison term.
3. Identify some of the characteristics of inmates returning home after serving time in prison.
4. What is the philosophy underlying the creation of specialty courts?
5. Describe the process for becoming a "client" in mental health court.
6. Discuss the three areas of success for drug courts: lower recidivism rates, reduced drug use, and cost savings.
7. Identify some of the major challenges facing prisoners returning home after incarceration.
8. Discuss the difficulties associated with measuring recidivism in community corrections.
9. Discuss research findings related to race and parole decisions.

Case Study

Questions 1 and 2 are based on this case.

Daniel is a 25-year-old male who was convicted of theft. He volunteered for drug court and was given a probation term. He and a friend stole the night deposit from the manager of Golden Fried Chicken as she was making a deposit at the bank. He confessed and apologized to the victim. He later stated that he regretted even leaving his home that night. He and his friend had been "getting high" most of the day. His friend admitted that it was not Daniel's idea to steal from the manager. He has no juvenile or adult criminal history. This was his first offense.

Daniel, who has three sisters and one brother, grew up in a lower-middle class neighborhood and a stable family. The family is close and surprised by Daniel's criminal behavior. He is not married but has a girlfriend that he hopes to marry one day. Daniel dropped out of school in the ninth grade; he was a poor student who was absent from school much of the time. Since he has been on probation, he has worked at a gas station. His employer describes him as a dependable employee who is good at organizing and taking care of equipment and tools; recently his employer has offered him the position of tool supervisor. He has a heart problem and, therefore, cannot do work that involves heavy labor.

His family has planned to move to Indiana because his father's job has transferred him to another office. Daniel is totally dependent upon his family for financial and emotional support. He does not want to leave his job or his girlfriend but he doesn't know if he can make it without his family.

1. Daniel received a five-year probation term for theft. There may be a number of reasons for this decision by the court. Explain why each of the following factors make him a good candidate for drug court and probation.
    A. He is a first-time offender.
    B. He accepted responsibility, expressed remorse, and apologized to the victim.
    C. He has a stable family and strong family support.
    D. He was under the influence of drugs at the time of the offense.

2. What would be the advantage of Daniel moving with his family?
    A. It allows him to keep his job, have more stability, and become emotionally and financially independent.
    B. It allows the probation department to keep an eye on him since there is a high risk of recidivism.
    C. It makes it easier to revoke him if he violates conditions of probation.
    D. There are no advantages; Daniel needs to be on his own.

Chapter 11

Legal and Liability Issues in Probation and Parole

Key Terms

Absolute immunity	Immunity doctrine
Civil liability	Negligence
Good faith defense	Qualified immunity

Learning Objectives
1. Identify issues related to probation officers' civil and criminal liability.
2. Examine the immunity doctrine as it relates to probation and parole officers.
3. Examine how legal decisions have impacted the probation and parole process.

Legal and Liability Issues in Probation and Parole

Probation and Parole Officer Liability

Probation and parole officers may be held criminally or civilly liable for actions that occur in the context of their relationships with clients or a third party. Criminal liability occurs when an officer commits a criminal act under federal or state law, such as assaulting, harassing, or threatening a client or a member of the client's family; injuring a client by using excessive force with malice; or participating in criminal behavior with a client, such as allowing a client who is a drug dealer to continue in their criminal behavior in exchange for a percentage of the profits.[1] A probation or parole officer may be held civilly liable or sued in state court for negligence or malpractice. Im-

> **Civil liability** occurs when there is a civil wrong and the injured party receives damages or compensation for wrongs.

---

1. Marilyn McShane and Wesley Krause (1993). *Community Corrections.* New York: MacMillan Publishing Company.

portant to civil lawsuits are issues of negligence. A charge of **negligence** by the victim is based on the victim's belief that loss or injury occurred as a result of the defendant's failure to adhere to a particular standard of care.[2] Negligence may be used to establish civil liability in officers' relationships with clients or officers relationships with the public, which is called third party liability.[3]

Civil Liability in Officers' Relationships with Clients

Officers may be sued in civil court for injury to the client. These cases are called torts. On February 19, 1990, at California's Camp O'Neal, a privately owned juvenile institution, three youth fell through a thin layer of ice on Convict Lake and drowned. Two counselors and two others who attempted to rescue them also drowned. The boys, who were on an outing with 16 other boys and two counselors, wandered away from the group. The report indicated that one counselor had used marijuana five hours before the incident, and it was the other counselor's first day on the job. There were no criminal charges filed because there was not enough evidence to prove guilt beyond a reasonable doubt. However, the incident was blamed on a lack of appropriate supervision and care by the staff. Although the staff could not be held criminally liable, the parents of the three victims filed a civil suit alleging wrongful death against the camp. The state revoked the license and closed the Camp.[4]

The officer may take some action that is a violation of a client's civil rights such as inventing or misusing conditions in a way designed to harass the client. The client will usually file a civil suit rather than criminal charges if the officer excessively enforces regulations because of the client's, race, sex, or religion. When this occurs, the officer may be sued under the Federal Civil Rights Act, which prohibits an individual from acting on behalf of the government in violating a citizen's constitutional rights. The most commonly used defense against civil rights lawsuits is the **good faith defense**. To establish good faith, it must be shown that (1) the officer was acting sincerely and believed that he/she was doing what was lawful, and (2) the judge or jury must accept that this belief was reasonable.[5]

> The **good faith defense** is a defense to a lawsuit stating that the plaintiff acted in a manner sincerely believed to be lawful and reasonable.

---

2. Robert J. Watkins (1989). "Probation and Parole Malpractice in a Noninstitutional Setting: A Contemporary Analysis," *Federal Probation* 73:(3) September 29–34.

3. Ibid., p. 29.

4. Richard Mallard. (2011). *Convict Lake: A True Account of the Convict Lake Rescue.* CreateSpace Independent Publishing Platform.

5. Ibid. Robert J. Watkins (1989). "Probation and Parole Malpractice in a Noninstitutional Setting: A Contemporary Analysis," p. 2.

Civil Liability in Officers' Relationships with the Public

In the performance of supervisory duties, probation and parole officers may incur civil liability for injuries caused by their clients to a third party. These lawsuits have focused on the officer's failure to warn a third party or victim about the potential dangers posed by a probationer or parolee and that failure to warn resulted in harm or injury to the victim.

There are two liability issues that are important in the officer's relationship with the general public or a third party. The first liability issue focuses on the (a) legal duty of the officer to supervise and control the behavior of the offender; and (b) failure to warn a victim of the potential danger from the offender.[6] The third party claims that the officer's negligence or failure to control an offender or failure to warn about the potential dangers posed by the offender resulted in injury to the victim. The injured party may sue the individual officer, the probation/parole department, or the state parole board for damages if the victim believes that the board or officer's negligence is the cause of injury.[7] Liability for negligence requires finding three things:

a. The professional had a legal duty to the injured party or the general public.
b. The professional failed to perform a duty according to a required standard of care.
c. The failure was the cause of the injury or harm to the victim.[8]

Lawsuits Based on Officer's Failure to Control the Offender

The courts have awarded punitive damages to victims when the probation or parole officer had a legal duty to supervise and control the offender but failed in that duty. In the case of *A.L. v. Commonwealth* (521 N.E.2d 1017, 1988),[9] the Supreme Court of Massachusetts found a probation officer to be negligent when a child molester with two previous convictions for child molestation was placed on probation for the third conviction with the condition that he was not allowed to associate with young boys. When the probationer obtained employment as a middle school teacher and subsequently molested several boys at the school, parents of the victims sued the probation officer. Parents

---

6. Ibid.
7. Kathryn Morgan, Barbara Belbot, and John Clark (1997). "Liability Issues Affecting Probation and Parole Supervision," *Journal of Criminal Justice* 25(3): 211–222.
8. Watkins, "Probation and Parole Malpractice," p. 29.
9. *A.L. v. Commonwealth*, 521 N.E.2d 1017 (1988).

were awarded damages after the court ruled that although the probationer falsely informed the officer that he was employed as a salesman, the officer had a responsibility to verify the employment and failed to make a reasonable effort to fulfill that responsibility. Because the conditions of probation ordered the probationer to refrain from association with young boys, there was a special relationship between the probation officer and the victims and the officer had a legal duty to protect the victims. She failed in her responsibility. In a similar case, *Taggart v. State* (822 P.2d 243, 1992),[10] the Washington State Supreme Court found a supervising parole officer negligent in her duty to supervise and control parolee Lou Brock, who assaulted Victoria Taggart, causing serious injuries. The parolee, who had convictions for sexual and alcohol related offenses, was released from prison with the conditions that he seek drug counseling and submit to random drug testing. The supervising officer failed to make sure that the parolee submitted to random drug testing or continue substance abuse counseling. The parole officer only saw the parolee in the office once weekly, did not make collateral contacts, and did not follow up on information provided by his girlfriend that he was drinking on a regular basis and had assaulted his ex-wife's new husband. The court ruled that there existed a special relationship between the parole officer and the parolee where the supervising officer had a duty to exercise reasonable and responsible control over the parolee's behavior. She failed in that responsibility.

Lawsuits Based on Officer's Failure to Warn

Some lawsuits have been based on an officer's failure to warn a victim of potential harm. The officer has a duty to warn a third party of the possible dangers posed by an offender under supervision.

The oldest case that focuses on a failure to warn is *Goergen v. State* (718 N.Y.2d 193, 1959).[11] The New York State court determined that a parole officer was liable for failure to disclose information about a violent parolee that he recommended for employment. The female employer, who had no knowledge of the parolee's violent tendencies, was assaulted by the parolee. In its decision for the plaintiff, the court ruled that the parole officer was negligent because he recommended the parolee for employment but failed to disclose information about the inmate's violent tendencies.[12] In the case of *Johnson v. State* (447 P.2d 352,

---

10. *Taggart v. State*, 822 P.2d 243 (1992).

11. *Goergen v. State*, 718 N.Y.2d 193 (1959).

12. Morgan, Belbot, and Clark, "Liability Issues Affecting Probation and Parole Supervision," 216.

1968),[13] a foster parent, attacked by her juvenile foster child, sued a parole officer who failed to disclose that the juvenile had a background of violent and homicidal tendencies. The parole department had a "duty to warn" the foster parent of the risk of accepting the juvenile parolee. The parole department was held liable for the injury because the failure to warn resulted in the assault. The most well-known case of third party liability in parole supervision is *Reiser v. District of Columbia* (563 F.2d 462, 1977).[14] Rebecca Reiser, a female apartment manager, was killed by a parolee whom she employed as a maintenance man at the apartment complex. The parole officer assisted the parolee in securing employment but failed to disclose information about the parolee's violent history or the fact that he was a suspect in two rapes and a third rape and murder of a little girl. One night, the parolee entered the female manager's apartment and raped and murdered her. The victim's family sued the parole department alleging that the parole officer had a duty to inform management of the parolee's prior violent sex offenses in order to prevent harm to the tenants of the apartment complex. According to the court's ruling, since the parole officer assisted the parolee in securing employment at the apartment complex, there was a "duty" to disclose the offender's prior criminal record.[15]

Immunity for Probation and Parole Officers

Historically, the **immunity doctrine** grants immunity to state officials for personal injuries caused in the performance of their duties; they cannot be held personally liable for these injuries. According to the immunity doctrine, state officials are immune from personal liability for injuries resulting from acts performed in their official duties. The belief is that public officials should be able to perform their duties unhindered by the threat of lawsuits and the drain on resources to defend public officials who have been sued.[16]

Judges, legislators, and prosecutors enjoy absolute immunity in the performance of their judicial capacities; they cannot be sued. In the last few years, there has been an attempt to

Absolute immunity is the freedom from civil liability claims for acts committed as a part of their official duties.

---

13. *Johnson v. State*, 447 P.2d 352 (California, 1968).

14. *Reiser v. District of Columbia*, 563 F.2d 462 (1977).

15. Morgan, Belbot & Clark, "Liability Issues Affecting Probation and Parole Supervision," 216.

16. Morgan, Belbot, and Clark, "Liability Issues Affecting Probation and Parole Supervision," 218.

balance immunity for those in public service with a need to allow injured parties to seek remedy for injuries. As a result, there may be exceptions to the immunity doctrine.[17]

Qualified immunity protects a public servant from personal civil liability as long as they do not violate the law. Sometimes, officials protected under qualified immunity doctrine may be sued or they may not be.

In some circumstances, probation and parole officers may have protection from liability for negligent acts. Because they perform tasks that are an important part of the judicial process, they enjoy qualified immunity. Some states have granted absolute immunity to parole boards for the decisions made to release an inmate on parole.[18] In *Martinez v. California* (444 U.S. 277, 1984),[19] the Supreme Court ruled that a state can grant absolute immunity to the parole board who makes a decision that results in harm or injury to a third party. Martinez, a mentally disturbed sex offender, was released by the parole board even though there was no recommendation for parole. He raped and kicked a 15-year-old girl within five months of his release. Her family's claims of negligence were dismissed because California grants immunity to parole board members. The cases of *Tarter v. State* (New York) and *Taggart v. State* (Washington) demonstrate how states have granted absolute immunity to parole boards for decisions that resulted in harm to a third party.

Most states continue to protect parole boards and their members from liability for release decisions based on the quasi-judicial doctrine. There are exceptions, however, as evidenced in the cases of *Grimm v. Arizona Board of Pardons and Paroles* (564 P.2d 1227, 1977), *Donahoo v. Alabama* (479 So. 2d 1188, 1985), and *Grantham v. Mississippi Department of Corrections* (522 So. 2d 219, 1988). In *Grimm v. Arizona Board of Pardons and Paroles* (564 P.2d 1227, 1977), the Arizona Supreme Court considered a wrongful death and a personal injury claim against the board by the parents of a man killed by a parolee during a robbery and by another man injured during the same incident. They alleged the board had information indicating the parolee was mentally ill and extremely dangerous, but decided to release him despite the knowledge of his mental state. Ruling for the victims, the Arizona Supreme Court held the board owed a duty to the public when making a parole release decision. Since the prisoner's record showed violent propensities and no reasonable basis for a belief that he had changed, a decision to release him was grounds for liability.[20]

---

17. Champion, *Probation and Parole*, p. 471.
18. Ibid., 471.
19. *Martinez v. California*, 444 U.S. 277 (1984).
20. *Grimm v. Arizona Board of Pardons and Paroles*, 564 P.2d 1227 (1977).

Similar cases were decided by both the Alabama and Mississippi Supreme Courts. In *Donahoo v. Alabama* (479 So. 2d 1188, 1985), the wife of a man murdered by two parolees sued the parole board alleging that the members acted negligently and incorrectly interpreted the state's good time laws in releasing the murderers. The court acknowledged the discretionary nature of decisions to release prisoners on parole and a state statute that granted immunity to public officials for discretionary acts. The court concluded, however, that the allegations of misinterpreting the law removed the shield of absolute immunity for discretionary acts.[21]

In Mississippi, the victim of an assault by a parolee sued the parole board and its members, alleging negligence and reckless disregard for the safety of the public (*Grantham v. Mississippi Department of Corrections*, 522 So. 2d 219, 1988). The victim charged that the board failed to review all the important information concerning the parolee and his prior record. The Mississippi court also ruled that although the board's decision was discretionary, the allegations of gross neglect of duty removed absolute immunity.[22] In these three cases, the boards were charged with failing to review and consider information important to their decisions.

Critical Thinking Question 11.1

A parole board may decide to release an inmate against recommendations of prison personnel who have provided information that the inmate is dangerous and poses a foreseeable risk to a third party. When that inmate injures or kills someone, should the victims or victim's family be allowed to sue the parole board or should the parole board enjoy immunity from lawsuits resulting from the decision to release the inmate? Justify your response.

Legal Decisions Affecting the Probation and Parole Process

Legal decisions have influenced the probation process in the areas of probation conditions and probation revocation.

---

21. *Donahoo v. Alabama*, 479 So. 2d 1188 (1985).
22. *Grantham v. Mississippi Department of Corrections*, 522 So. 2d 219 (1988).

Probation Conditions

While sentencing judges have discretion in setting probation conditions, they cannot set conditions that violate the probationer's constitutional rights. Furthermore, the conditions must be legitimate, clearly understood, and related to the purposes of rehabilitation. Legal challenges to probation conditions have provided clarity regarding limits placed on judges' discretion in imposing probation conditions.

Owens v. Kelley

In this Georgia probation case, Owens protested probation conditions that required him to attend emotional maturity instruction classes and to take a lie detector test. According to the lawsuit, the first condition violated his First Amendment rights because of the religious content of the course. The U.S. Court of Appeals for the Fifth Circuit ruled that a probation condition that requires a probationer to participate in a class which advocated acceptance of religion violated First Amendment rights. The *Owens* lawsuit further alleged that the condition which required him to submit to a lie detector test when so ordered by the probation officer violated his Fifth Amendment rights of protection against self-incrimination. The same court rejected this claim because Owens was not required to answer incriminating questions. During the test if there was a question that required a self-incriminating answer, he was free to assert Fifth Amendment rights.[23]

In Re Judge Thomas P. Quirk *(1998)*

In a 1998 decision, *In Re Quirk*, the Louisiana Supreme Court upheld the ability of a Louisiana judge to impose church attendance as a probation condition. The court ruled that Judge Thomas Quirk did not violate 1,200 probationers' constitutional rights by requiring weekly attendance at religious worship services. The court argued that Judge Quirk gave probationers a choice to attend whatever religious service they desired. Further, they equated the choice to attend religious services to that of attending a self-help group.[24]

---

23. *Owens v. Kelley*, 681 F.2d 1362 (1982).
24. *In Re Judge Thomas P. Quirk*, 705 So. 2d 172 (1997).

Beardon v. Georgia

In *Beardon v. Georgia*, probation was revoked and the probationer sent to prison when he was unable to pay the balance of a $500 fine and $250 restitution. He had been laid off from work and unable to find employment even after repeated efforts. The Supreme Court ruled that probation cannot be revoked and the probationer sent to prison if there have been efforts to pay, and despite those efforts, the probationer still lacks the ability to pay. Probation cannot be revoked for not paying restitution or fines if the probationer is indigent and cannot pay. This ruling also extended to probation supervision fees. A probationer can be revoked for refusal to pay but not for inability to pay supervision fees.[25]

Anderson v. State

Probationer Anderson was revoked after failure to pay probation supervision fees. He was employed but chose not pay the probation fees that was imposed by the court. He appealed the decision to a higher court which upheld the judge's decision to revoke. Anderson was able to pay, but refused.[26]

Probation Revocation

When probationers face possible revocation of probation, they are in danger of losing the privilege of conditional freedom granted by the court. Therefore, the Supreme Court has ruled that these probationers are entitled to certain due process protections. In the case of *Mempa v. Rhay*, Mempa's probation was revoked after he confessed to his involvement in a burglary while under supervision. He appealed the decision citing that he did not have an attorney present at the revocation hearing nor was he asked if he wanted representation by counsel. The United States Supreme Court ruled that a person is entitled to an attorney at every stage of criminal proceedings where rights of the offender might be affected. Sentencing is considered a crucial stage of the criminal process. Since Mempa was sentenced at the revocation hearing, he was entitled to be represented by counsel.[27]

In a similar case, *Gagnon v. Scarpelli*, Gerald Scarpelli was sentenced to seven years in prison after his probation was revoked for robbery. He claimed that

---

25. *Bearden v. Georgia*, 461 U.S. 660 (1983).
26. *Anderson v. State*, 624 So. 2d. 362 (1993).
27. *Mempa v. Rhay*, 389 U.S. 128 (1967).

he was denied due process because he was revoked without a hearing and without the presence of counsel, with which the Supreme Court agreed. The Court ruled that although probation revocation is not a stage of criminal prosecution, it does result in the loss of liberty. Therefore, the probationer must be given certain due process rights. The probationer is entitled to three things: (1) a written notice of alleged violations, (2) a preliminary hearing to see if there is enough reason to believe that conditions have been violated, and (3) a revocation hearing where the probationer has the right to testify and confront and cross-examine witnesses.[28]

Critical Thinking Question 11.2

Both *Owens v. Kelley* and *In Re Quirk* involved potential violations of First Amendment rights. However, the ruling in each case was different. What was the ruling in the *Owens* case? How did it differ from the *Quirk* decision? Do you believe that the appellate court erred in either case? Should judges have the discretion to impose conditions such as attending church if they believe that it will contribute to the rehabilitation of the offender?

Legal Decisions Affecting the Parole Process

For many years, parole operated without any interference from the judiciary. In the 1970s, the New York Court of Appeals ruled on a case regarding parole release and parole revocation hearings. This represented the first judicial involvement in parole matters. In 1972, the Supreme Court ruled in the landmark case *Morrissey v. Brewer*.

Menechino v. Oswald, 1970. Menechino received 20 years to life for murder in New York. He was paroled but was returned to prison as a parole violator 16 months later. The basis of revocation was association with criminals and giving the parole officer misleading information. Two years later, he appeared before the parole board seeking release but was denied. He appealed, claiming that his rights had been violated because he was denied representation by counsel at the revocation and parole release hearings. The U.S. Court of Appeals in

---

28. *Gagnon v. Scarpelli*, 411 U.S. 778 (1973).

New York addressed the issue of legal counsel present in the parole release and parole revocation hearings.

Regarding the parole release hearing, the court ruled that because the inmate was already in prison, there was no "present private interest" that needed to be protected. There were no rights to be protected; he was already in prison seeking the privilege of early release. The parole release hearing is not a fact-finding hearing but an evaluation hearing where the board makes its decision based upon many different pieces of information. The release hearing, which lasts about 10–15 minutes, is only a small part of the process. Therefore, the parolee is not entitled to representation in the release hearing.

In addressing the presence of counsel in the parole revocation hearing, the decision stated that at this stage, an inmate does have a present private interest to be protected—conditional freedom. Therefore, some procedural safeguards must be provided. The court of appeals ultimately ruled against Menechino because he initiated actions regarding both the release hearing and the revocation hearings. If he had initiated actions regarding only the revocation hearing, he would have won. This represents the first time that the judiciary got involved in parole matters. The parole board had previously operated without interference from the courts.[29]

Menechino v. Warden, 1971. In 1971, Menechino filed a case alleging violation of due process rights because he did not have representation by counsel at the revocation hearing. This time, the New York Court of Appeals ruled that parolees should be granted some rights at parole revocation hearings: the right to counsel and the right to call their own witnesses. The court wrote in its opinion that probationers and juveniles had already received some due process protections at hearings that might result in the loss of freedom, but parolees had not been granted those protections. This protection should be extended to parolees. This ruling only applied to parolees in the state of New York.[30]

Morrissey v. Brewer, 1972. This case is important for two reasons; (1) in its ruling, the Supreme Court extended due process protections to parolees in all states, and (2) this case represents the first involvement by the Supreme Court in the parole process. Up until June 1972, the Supreme Court had not ruled in this area. Morrissey was sentenced to a seven-year prison term for forgery but was paroled after serving one year. Seven months after being paroled, he was arrested after violating several conditions of parole. He purchased and operated a car under an assumed name without notifying the parole officer, and

29. *Menechino v. Oswald New York Court of Appeals*, 430 F.2d 403 (1970).
30. *Menechino v. Warden*, 27 N.Y.2d 376, 318 N.Y.S.2d 449, 267 N.E.2d 238 (1971).

he gave false information to police and an insurance company following a traffic accident. He was returned to prison without a preliminary or revocation hearing. The supervising officer justified the return by saying that Morrissey failed to justify the violations adequately. The Supreme Court ruled that a number of parolees (30%–40%) are having their parole revoked and being returned to prison each year. With these numbers being as high as they are, there must be some protection of parolees' rights. Regarding the revocation process, the Court ruled that the revocation process should be a two-stage process:

   a.   arrest of parolee and preliminary hearing and
   b.   the revocation hearing.

In the preliminary hearing, the hearing officer should be someone who has no involvement in the case. It does not have to be a member of the parole board. The parolee should be given a written notice of charges. Witnesses who have given unfavorable testimony should be questioned in the parolee's presence. The hearing process should be informal.[31]

Critical Thinking Question 11.3

It is accepted that inmates seeking parole have limited due process protections in the parole release process because parole is a privilege and they have nothing to lose at that point. Do you agree with this position?

Recap and Review

- Probation and parole officers may be held criminally liable if the officer assaults or threatens the client or the client's family, injures the client by using excessive force, or participates with the client in criminal activity for financial gain.
- Officers may be sued for monetary damages if the officer has a legal duty to control the offender or warn a third party about potential danger and the failure to do so results in injury or harm to a third party.
- Officers may use the good faith defense in civil lawsuits. To establish a good faith defense, the officer must demonstrate that there was a sincere belief that the actions were lawful.

---

31. *Morrissey v. Brewer*, 408 U.S. 471, 485–86 (1972).

- Several lawsuits have resulted in officers being found negligent in their failure to control the offender under supervision or the failure to warn a third party about the potential danger posed by the offender.
- Historically, parole boards have enjoyed immunity from being sued for decisions that may result in injuries to a third party. In recent years, there have been exceptions to immunity protection allowing victims and victims' families to sue parole boards for discretionary decisions that resulted in injury or death.
- Probation conditions must be reasonable, clear, and must not violate the U.S. Constitution.
- When probationers are ordered to attend a religious service as a condition of probation, it is in violation of First Amendment rights. However, when probationers are ordered to attend a religious service of their choice, similar to attending a self-help group, it is not in violation of their constitutional rights.
- Although probationers can be revoked and sent to prison for failure to pay assessed fees, they cannot be revoked when there is inability to pay after there have been efforts to meet financial responsibilities.
- Because the revocation process is a critical stage of criminal justice proceedings, probationers are entitled to certain due process rights including right to counsel, right to a revocation hearing, and the right to confront and cross examine witnesses.
- Parole operated without involvement from the judiciary until 1971. The New York Court of Appeals first ruled on a parole case in 1970 in the case of *Menechino v. Oswald* followed by the first Supreme Court ruling in *Morrissey v. Brewer* (1972).
- The Supreme Court justified its involvement by pointing out the number of parolees revoked and returned to prison annually. Their due process right must be protected in the revocation process.
- According to the Supreme Court, the revocation process should be a two-stage process with a preliminary hearing and a revocation hearing. The hearing officer should be someone not associated with the case.
- Parolees are not entitled to due process protections in parole release hearings because they have no present private interests to be protected.

Questions for Review

1. Distinguish between criminal and civil liability for probation and parole officers.
2. Under what circumstances can an officer be held criminally liable in a relationship with a client?
3. Officers may be held criminally or civilly liable for violation of a client's civil rights. Explain.
4. Identify the three requirements for a finding of negligence.
5. Discuss civil liability that may result from the officer's relationship with a client.
6. What is the immunity doctrine and how does it apply to probation and parole officials?
7. What are at least three requirements for setting probation conditions?
8. What was the basis of Owens' appeal? How did the appellate court rule on his appeal?
9. What was the ruling in the *Beardon* decision regarding fees?
10. In the *Gagnon* decision, the Supreme Court ruled that the probationer facing revocation is entitled to three things. What are they?
11. According to the appeals court, why are probationers entitled to due process protections?
12. How is the concept of present private interest related to the parole release process?
13. What parole case included present private interest as a part of its ruling?
14. Why did the New York Court of Appeals rule against the plaintiff in the case of *Menechino v. Oswald*?
15. Why is the *Morrissey v. Brewer* case important to parole administration and process?
16. Why did the Supreme Court become involved in the parole revocation process?

Questions for Discussion

Please use these questions for discussion. Choose the response that you think is most appropriate and explain your reasoning. Why are the other responses not appropriate?

1. A probationer convicted of grand larceny finds employment as a clerk at a local convenience store without the assistance of the probation officer. He

fails to inform his new employer of his criminal record. After being employed for six months, he is promoted to shift manager. Shortly after the
promotion, he steals $2,500 from the store. The employer sues the probation
department for failure to warn about the offender's criminal record. Should
the probation department be responsible for the offender's actions?

A. Yes, because they had a duty to inform the employer.
B. No, because probation and parole officers are immune from being sued.
C. Yes, because there was a failure to provide adequate supervision.
D. No, because the probationer secured the job without the assistance or
   knowledge of the probation department.

2. The wife of a probationer calls you to ask if you could request that the
   court amend her husband's probation order to include "mandatory church
   attendance." She states that this is probably the reason for her husband's
   problems — he won't go to church. You respond by:

   A. Requesting an amended probation order including the condition of
      mandatory church attendance.
   B. Making him think that he must attend church as condition of probation or face probation revocation.
   C. Informing his wife that the judge cannot order mandatory church attendance since it would be in violation of his First Amendment rights.
   D. Doing nothing after telling her that you would take care of the matter.

3. A probationer on probation for possession and use of drugs confides to his
   probation officer that he has started using drugs again and he needs some
   help. He informs the officer that he has been driving while under the influence. He has gone to a local drug counselling program asking for help
   but is told that he cannot enter the program without a referral by the probation officer. While driving under the influence of drugs and alcohol, he
   has a head-on collision with a car. The collision kills the probationer, the
   husband and a five-year-old child. The family sues the probation department alleging that the officer failed to provide adequate supervision to the
   probationer who informed him of his drug relapse. Can the probation department be held liable for the probationer's acts?

   A. No, because the probation department did not make him use drugs
      and drive.
   B. Yes, the probation officer had a duty to provide supervision and control of the offenders behavior.
   C. No, because the probation department is always immune from lawsuits.
   D. Yes, because the officer encouraged him to use drugs to help relieve stress.

4. A parolee who was recently released from prison told another parolee that he was planning to harm his wife who cheated on him while he was incarcerated. The wife also informs you that he has been making accusations and threats on her life. As the officer, you believe that they are just having some adjustment issues because of his time in prison. His wife contacts you to tell you that he has bought a gun in violation of his parole conditions. You still delay hoping that they can work out their difficulties. You receive a call from the Sheriff's Department at 2:00 AM to inform you that the parolee has killed his wife and her mother. Six months later, you are notified that you and the parole department are being sued by the victims' family. Do they have a basis for a lawsuit?

   A. No, because the officer sincerely believed that the parolee was not serious in his threats to harm his wife.
   B. Yes, the officer knew that there was a potential danger to the victim by the parole but did nothing to control the offender.
   C. No, because the parole officer and department enjoy unqualified immunity.
   D. No, because the officer did nothing to violate the victims' civil rights.

Cases Cited

A.L. v. Commonwealth, 521 N.E.2d 1017 (1988).

Anderson v. State, 624 So. 2d. 362 (1993).

Beardon v. Georgia, 461 U.S. 660, 103 S. Ct 2064 (1983).

Donahoo v. Alabama, 479 So. 2d 1188 (1985).

Gagnon v. Scarpelli, 411 U.S. 778 (1973).

Goergen v. State, 718 N.Y.2d 193 (1959).

Grantham v. Mississippi Department of Corrections, 522 So. 2d 219 (1988).

Grimm v. Arizona Board of Pardons and Paroles, 564 P.2d 1227 (1977).

In Re Judge Thomas P. Quirk, 705. So. 2d 172 (1997).

Johnson v. State, 447 P.2d 352 (California, 1968).

Martinez v. California, 444 U.S. 277 (1984).

Mempa v. Rhay, 389 U.S. 128 (1967).

Menechino v. Oswald, 430 F.2d 403 (1970).

Menechino v. Warden, 27 N.Y.2d 376, 318 N.Y.S.2d 449, 267 N.E.2d 238 (1971).

Morrissey v. Brewer, 408 U.S. 471, 485–86 (1972).

Owens v. Kelley, 681 F.2d 1362 (1982).

Reiser v. District of Columbia, 563 F.2d 462 (1977)

Taggart v. State, 822 P.2d 243 (1992).

Tarter v. State, New York 503 N.E.2d 84 (1986).

Chapter 12

Looking Ahead: Challenges and Trends in Probation and Parole Practice

Key Terms
Broken windows probation
Evidence-based practice

Learning Objectives
1. Identify recent trends in probation and parole.
2. Understand challenges to probation and parole.
3. Identify future directions and priorities in probation and parole practices.

At the end of 2011, statistics indicated that the correctional population was declining. The Bureau of Justice Statistics showed that the total correctional population was 6.98 million, a decline of almost 100,000 offenders. The year 2011 marked the third year of a decline in the correctional population that started in 2008 and included correctional offenders in state and federal prisons, jails, and on probation and parole.[1] Much of the decline in the correctional population was due to the decline in probationers under supervision. In 2011, the probation population decreased by almost 82,000 offenders for the third consecutive year.[2]

Probation and Parole Trends

Recent trends have shown a declining probation population. After 2008, when the probation population reached 4.8 million under supervision, the

---

1. L. Glaze and Erika Parks (2012, November). *Correctional Populations in the United States, 2011*. Washington, DC: U.S. Department of Justice, Office of Justice Programs, 1.
2. Ibid.

probation population began a steady decline that has continued over the past three years. According to the Bureau of Justice Statistics, the population fell below four million for the first time since 2002.[3] In 2011, the most significant decline in probation populations occurred in five states: California, Florida, Texas, Michigan, and Georgia, which accounted for 56% of the decrease in the probation population. Maryland and Alabama had the largest increases in the probation population in 2011. These two states alone accounted for over 50% in the probation population increase.[4] While the probation population is declining, the number of those leaving probation through completion of supervision or early discharge remains stable. Since 2008, the exit rate for probationers has remained stable at 36 per 100 probationers and the average time spent on probation is 22 months. Decreasing crime rates has been suggested as one of the main reasons for the decrease in the probation population. According to recent data published in the Uniform Crime Report, violent and property index offenses have declined significantly. Since 2007, the violent crime rate decreased by 15.7%; property crimes decreased by 11%.[5] Fewer crimes being committed results in fewer offenders being processed by the criminal justice system and being punished. Since probation has been criticized for being too lenient, criminal justice officials may opt for more severe sentences. As a result, more offenders are being given incarceration sentences rather than being placed on probation.

While there has been a declining probation population, the parole population has shown slight increases over the past three years. The parole population declined in 2009 but increased in 2011 by 1.6%, or 13,300 offenders.[6] The most significant decreases in the parole population were in New York, Michigan, Pennsylvania, and Massachusetts. These four states accounted for a 55% decline in the parole population. The largest increases in the parole population occurred in California and Texas. Although federal parole was phased out by 1992, federal offenders may be granted supervised release by the federal courts and the number of federal offenders under supervised release also contributed to the increase in the parole population.[7]

---

3. Laura Maruschak and Erika Parks (2012, November). *Probation and Parole in the United States, 2011.* Washington, DC: U.S. Department of Justice, Office of Justice Programs.

4. Ibid., 4.

5. *Crime in the United States, 2011.* US Department of Justice, Federal Bureau of Investigation, Criminal Justice Information Services Division. Retrieved August 18, 2014.

6. Maruschak and Parks, *Probation and Parole in the United States, 2011,* 7.

7. Ibid., 7.

Challenges to Probation and Parole

Attack on Rehabilitation

As crime rates rose in the 1960s, the public became concerned about the rising crime rates and the failure of rehabilitation and treatment programs to deter or prevent crime. Critics attacked the indeterminate sentence, probation, and parole and demanded tougher and longer sentences for career and violent offenders.[8] By the 1970s, high recidivism rates signaled that crime prevention and rehabilitation programs were not effective in reducing crime. Robert Martinson published the results of a controversial study in which he reviewed 231 evaluations of rehabilitation programs that all had the same finding: "The program shows no appreciable effect on recidivism." "Nothing works," Martinson concluded. While the majority of these evaluations related to prison rehabilitation programs, it resulted in a general attack on all rehabilitation programs.[9]

That attack on rehabilitation and the emergence of the crime control model indicated a return to a philosophy of punishment, retribution, and deterrence. In the 1980s, criminologists and politicians promoted a "get tough" approach to crime. Legislatures enacted laws that would institute "sentencing guidelines" and set mandatory sentencing for certain offenses, allowing little opportunity for judicial discretion. Increased public fear of crime and concerns about crime and recidivism rates resulted in several states and the federal system abolishing parole and replacing indeterminate sentencing with determinate sentencing structures.[10] Despite the attacks, the probation and parole population continued to increase because it is cheaper to supervise offenders under probation and parole than to incarcerate them in prison.

Organizational Diversity

There is much organizational diversity among probation and parole agencies in this country. Probation and parole agencies do not represent a single unified system but more of a "fragmented, heterogeneous collection of organizations

---

8. Todd Clear, George Cole, and Michael Reisig (2012). *American Corrections*. 10th Edition. Belmont, CA: Wadsworth Publishing.

9. Robert Martinson (1974). "What Works? Questions and Answers about Prison Reform," *Public Interest 35*: 22–54.

10. Camille Camp and George Camp (1999). *The Corrections Yearbook 1999*. Middletown, CT: Criminal Justice Institute.

found at the federal, state, county and municipal levels, housed in the judicial and executive branches."[11]

Increased Workloads with Limited Resources

As probation and parole populations have increased over the years, workloads for officers have also increased. The "get tough" era of criminal justice resulted in changes in sentencing and more offenders being sentenced to prison. As "get tough" policies strained budgets and cost billions of dollars, many states began to rethink those policies. Escalating prison costs forced corrections departments to develop alternatives to prison. Many of these programs were based in probation and parole departments, causing caseload sizes and workloads to increase while resources diminished. Probation and parole agencies are often called on to "do more with less." The expectation is effective management and supervision with fewer resources.

Gun Violence

Gun violence continues to be a problem in the United States. As a social problem that costs billions of dollars annually, gun violence affects all members of society both directly and indirectly. Although violent crime has been decreasing since the mid-nineties, gun violence continues to be a problem. Gun violence is especially a problem for youth who are often the victims and perpetrators of gun violence. Data from 2009 reveal that approximately 10,000 people were killed with guns and another 48,000 were treated for serious gunshot injuries.[12] Probation and parole professionals are often at risk for violent attacks or have been threatened by gun violence as they make unannounced field visits and serve warrants. In a recent study of probation and parole officers killed in the line of duty, data indicated that over 80% of those killed were killed with a firearm.[13] Although data for 2011 indicate slight decreases, firearm violence continues to be a social and public health epidemic that poses a challenge to probation and parole officers in their supervision responsibilities.

---

11. William Burrell (2005). "Trends in Probation and Parole in the States." In *Book of the States, 2005 Edition*. Lexington, KY: Council of State Governments, 595–600.

12. *Crime in the United States* (2009). Washington, DC: U.S. Department of Justice, Federal Bureau of Investigations, Criminal Justice Information Services Division, http://www2.fbi.gov/ucr/cius2009/index.html.

13. Robert Thornton (2005). *Guns, Safety and Proactive Supervision*. Washington: American Probation and Parole Association, 9.

What Works in Probation and Parole?

There is a continuing debate about what works in probation and parole to reduce criminal reoffending, reduce threats to public safety, and promote more successful outcomes for probationers and parolees. In a review of correctional programs, McKenzie (2000) and her colleagues classified programs into four categories based on their effectiveness: (1) what works, (2) what does not work, (3) what is promising, and (4) what is unknown.[14] According to her research, treatment programs with multiple components, the incapacitation of chronic offenders, drug courts, prison therapeutic communities, and vocational programs are some correctional programs that work.[15]

Evidence-Based Supervision in Probation and Parole

What are the basic differences between probation and parole programs that work and those that don't? Program administrators have begun to examine programs that work by reducing recidivism and those that don't. Using correctional methods that have proven to be effective based on research is referred to as **evidence-based practice**.[16] Evidence-based policy and practice or "what works" is not a single program but reliable research that identifies effective programs or interventions and the features of those interventions.

> **Evidence-based practices** are practices that have been shown to be effective in reducing offender risk of recidivism.

There are four principles associated with programs that are effective and reduce recidivism rates.

1. Risk principle. The program should be focused on high-risk offenders.
2. Supervision principle. More intense supervision should be placed on high-risk offenders.
3. Treatment principle. Greater treatment options should be developed to deal with high-risk offenders.
4. Referral principle. Increase referrals to treatment programs.[17]

---

14. Doris MacKenzie (2000). "Evidence-Based Corrections: Identifying What Works," *Crime and Delinquency 46*: 457–471.

15. Ibid.

16. Reinventing Probation Council (1999, August). "'Broken Windows' Probation: The Next Step in Fighting Crime," (Civic Report No. 7). New York: The Manhattan Institute.

17. T. Clear, M. Reisig, and G. Cole (2012). *American Corrections*. Belmont, CA: Wadsworth Publishing Company.

In a study of successful programs, research has shown that when these principles are applied to the supervision of high-risk offenders, they are better prepared for life after supervision, and the risk of rearrests declines.[18] Despite the empirical evidence showing that these supervision strategies can improve program effectiveness, many officers do not use these caseload supervision techniques and principles.

Broken Windows Model

Broken windows probation—A recent theory of probation supervision that emphasizes public safety as a priority, supervision in the community, and collaborations and partnerships with the community. The model proposes to bring the community into the supervision process.

Adopted from the broken windows model of law enforcement, this model is used in probation supervision to promote public safety and reduce social disorder. Realizing that traditional probation supervision had failed to make offenders accountable for their actions or promote public safety, a group of probation administrators and leading correctional experts formed the Reinventing Probation Council to address the failures of traditional probation and develop a new vision for probation supervision known as **broken windows probation.**[19]

This new broken windows probation model proposed seven strategies for making probation more effective:

1. Make public safety the primary mission of probation.
2. Supervise probationers in the community, not the office. The office serves as the base for probation, but supervision must take place in the community where it highly visible and positive. Effective supervision is active and engaged but also community-centered.
3. Probation departments must rationally and strategically allocate staff and resources to where they are needed most.
4. Probation departments must strongly enforce probation conditions and quickly respond to violations of conditions. While not all violations will result in revocation, a timely response is critical when there are violations. In order to accomplish this, there must be cooperation between probation programs and the courts.
5. Develop community partners. The probation department should seek community participation and involvement when decisions need to be made regarding new policies, programs, strategies, or the delivery of services.

---

18. Ibid.
19. Ibid.

6. Establish performance based initiatives. Program administrators must know what strategies are effective in correctional supervision, set organizational goals, and evaluate results to determine if the goals have been achieved.

7. Cultivate strong leadership. Potential leaders must be identified who will lead probation into a future of accountability and reengineering.[20]

Paparozzi (2003) makes the following observation regarding the benefit broken windows probation model:

> Perhaps the most significant contribution of broken windows thinking is that it insists on administering community corrections like a business as opposed to an eclectic mix of practices that, upon rigorous examination, is irrelevant to its mission. If the community corrections professional mission begins with the end in mind, it will be impossible to avoid backing into strategies that are irrelevant to where the profession must end up. Without a strong commitment to the broken windows model, it is likely that the profession will be relegated to a position of living under an endless and seemingly mindless swinging of the pendulum of practice.[21]

Specialized Caseloads

This approach involves placing probationers and parolees with special needs and problems in a single caseload that is much smaller than regular probation caseloads. Officers supervising these specialized caseloads target the special needs of the offenders. However, the specialized caseloads go beyond simply placing offenders with similar problems into one caseload. Many of these officers supervising special caseloads develop expertise over time and engage in partnerships with professionals and treatment specialists to provide the offender more comprehensive services.[22]

Offenders that may be better served through specialized caseloads include mental health offenders, drug and alcohol offenders, sex offenders, and domestic violence offenders. Juvenile or younger offenders who are placed on adult probation are often supervised in a special caseload.

---

20. Ibid.
21. Mario Paparozzi (2003). "Historical Lessons and Emerging Trends in Probation and Parole." In *The Book of the States*. Edited by Keon Chi. Lexington, KY: The Council of State Governments.
22. Burrell, "Trends in Probation and Parole in the States," 595–600.

Looking to the Future

At the beginning of the twenty-first century, probation and parole trends emerged that are likely to define their futures. There are three important trends that will impact the future and direction of probation and parole.

Rediscovering Rehabilitation

During the 1970s, there was a return to a classical/deterrence model that focused on punishment and retribution. The attack that began in the 1970s on rehabilitation continued into the 1980s and 1990s when a "get tough on crime" approach dominated correctional policy and practice. Probation and parole supervision was affected by this change in ideology that stressed punishment over treatment. Probation and parole officers assumed law enforcement and surveillance roles. Their primary responsibilities were to enforce the conditions of probation and parole and deal with violators. In the 1990s, there was awareness that some offenders had special mental health and substance abuse needs. There was also a re-entry crisis caused by prisoners returning from prison addicted to drugs, mentally ill, and lacking vocational skills. As incarceration costs increased, there was a search for alternatives to incarceration that were less expensive. In the search for alternatives, there was interest in rehabilitation that Reisig (1998) defines as the attempt to improve and return people to society.[23] These alternatives required offenders to participate in drug treatment, community service, and vocational and academic programs.[24] Drug courts, mental health courts, and specialized caseloads emerged to address offenders' special needs. Reentry programs were implemented to facilitate prisoners' return to the community.

Reisig sums up the re-emergence of rehabilitation in this way:

> Rediscovering rehabilitation is not about being soft on crime; it is about using our economic and human resources wisely.[25]

Partnerships

The future of probation and parole is likely to focus on partnerships between probation and parole agencies and community agencies. Probation and

---

23. Martin Reisig (1998, February). "Rediscovering Rehabilitation: Drug Courts, Community Corrections and Restorative Justice," *Michigan Bar Journal 172*: 172–176.

24. Ibid., 172.

25. Ibid., 173.

parole agencies have always collaborated with community resources such as police departments, drug treatment centers, employment agencies, and mental health counselors. In recent years, those partnerships have become formal. Collaborations with drug courts and mental health courts serve as good examples of formal partnerships.[26] A recent collaboration between probation and parole departments and law enforcement has been Project Safe Neighborhoods. Project Safe Neighborhoods is an initiative that promotes collaborations between local, state, and federal law enforcement agencies, corrections, the prosecutor, and the community with the goal of reducing gun crime and violence.[27]

Community Justice

Probation and parole will continue to be involved with offenders, victims, and community members. The Reinventing Probation Council has recommended a greater emphasis on community probation, where officers supervise offenders in their communities rather than the probation offices. Using community-oriented strategies, probation and parole officers must supervise offenders where they live, work, and have recreation.[28] A brief monthly visit with probationers and parolees is not sufficient to reduce risk and encourage public safety. Officers must be engaged in the community and involve the community in the supervision process. The community may be involved in probation and parole supervision by:

a. Serving as volunteers to assist probation and parole officers in working with offenders.
b. Participating in neighborhood probation and assisting the probation department in coordinating supervision and resources in a particular geographic location to improve public safety.
c. Assisting probation personnel in implementing and coordinating community programming, such as victim/offender mediation, community review boards, victims notification practices, and offender community service.[29]

26. Burrell, "Trends in Probation and Parole in the States," 3.

27. Thornton, *Guns, Safety and Proactive Supervision*, 9.

28. Reinventing Probation Council (2000). *Transforming Probation through Leadership: The Broken Windows Model.* New York: The Manhattan Institute.

29. B. A. Fulton, S. B. Stone, and P. Gendreau (1994). *Restructuring Intensive Supervision Programs: Applying "What Works."* Lexington, KY: American Probation and Parole Association.

Recap and Review

- The correctional population in the United States has been declining since 2008. Much of the decline was due to a declining probation population.
- In 2011, the number of probationers under supervision fell below four million for the first time since 2002.
- The most significant declines in the population were seen in California, Florida, Texas, Michigan, and Georgia. These states accounted for 56% of the decline in probationers under supervision.
- Declines in violent and property crimes and increased use of incarceration have been identified as possible reasons for the decline in the probation population.
- While there has been a decline in probation numbers, the parole population has increased since 2008.
- Although the federal system phased out parole, it has provisions for the supervised release of federal offenders.
- Probation and parole have been attacked as a result of the wider attack on rehabilitation that began in 1970s. Probation and parole continue to be viable correctional alternatives because they are more economical than incarceration.
- Probation and parole officers have faced many challenges, including increased workloads, limited resources, and increased threats from gun violence. The increase in gun violence has been a challenge to probation and parole officers as more officers are being victimized in the community. Eighty percent of the officers killed were killed with firearms.
- Recently, there has been emphasis on programs that work in probation and parole supervision. Evidence-based practice suggests identifying programs that work and adopting the approach of those programs.
- The future of probation and parole is likely to include more emphasis of rehabilitation of offenders and public safety, more use of specialized caseloads, partnerships and collaborations with community agencies and programs, and more emphasis on involving the community in the supervision process.

Questions for Review

1. Identify possible reasons for the decline in the probation population.
2. What states showed the most significant declines in the probation population?

3. Why did the parole population increase?
4. What states showed the largest increases and decreases in the parole population?
5. How did the 1970s attack on rehabilitation affect probation and parole?
6. How has increased gun violence threatened probation and parole supervision in the community?
7. What is evidence-based practice? How has it been applied to probation and parole?
8. What is the broken windows probation model? What are the major principles of this model?
9. What is Project Safe Neighborhoods?
10. How can the community and probation and parole programs work together to reduce risk and promote public safety?

Questions for Discussion

Please use these questions for discussion. Choose the response that you think is most appropriate and explain your reasoning. Why are the other responses not appropriate?

1. As a probation officer, you have been asked to speak to a community group regarding the role of rehabilitation in correctional supervision. Realizing the loss of public confidence in rehabilitation, you decide to:
    A. Skip the talk because you agree with the public.
    B. Focus on new initiatives that combine treatment with concerns for public safety and community involvement.
    C. Show a film about a successful probationer that will distract them from the negative images of probation and parole.
    D. Have a question and answer session, instead of a talk, so you only address questions.

2. In an effort to address the needs of female offenders that might be different from those of men, the probation department supervisor asks you to supervise a special caseload of 50 female felons in addition to your caseload of 150. You respond by:
    A. Telling your supervisor that you see no need to have a special caseload for female offenders.
    B. Looking for another job because you feel that he wants you to quit.

C. Telling him that you would like to accept the responsibility because you understand the importance of addressing these needs. However, you would like to have a smaller regular caseload to devote more time to the specialized one.

D. Refusing to take on this new responsibility even if it means losing your job.

3. You discover that your swim instructor at the local YMCA has served 15 years for cocaine and heroin possession. He approaches you about partnering with you to develop a community action program to teach younger probationers (age 18–25) to become swimmers and those who can swim to become lifeguards so that they can secure employment. What is your response?

A. You tell him that you will think about it but you have no intention of following up.

B. You think that it is a good idea and tell him so. You promise to get back with him after talking to your supervisor.

C. You tell his employer to watch this instructor because you think that he is trying to recruit offenders to sell drugs.

D. You are not really sure what to do. Your supervisor is always looking for ways to partner with community resources, but you are nervous about following up on this idea.

4. The director of parole and parole services has asked you to attend a community resource workshop to represent probation and parole services. While there, a committee member starts to criticize probation and parole services for being ineffective in controlling offenders and protecting the public. He uses Martinson's 1973 study that concludes that "nothing works" to support his position. Everyone looks to you for a response. How do you respond?

A. You are humiliated and inform the group that you agree with him.

B. You leave vowing never to work with this group again.

C. You explain to the group that this research was done in the 1970s and now, new approaches used in probation and parole supervision involve modeling programs that are effective and do work.

D. You get into an argument with this man, which takes up most of the meeting time. As a result, most people leave the meeting.

5. You have been asked to speak to a community group, Citizens Against Community Violence. In the middle of your speech, you are interrupted by a father whose twin sons were recently killed by an offender who was

convicted and imprisoned for murder in 2006 but was released on parole after serving 5 years of a 20-year sentence. He killed again in 2010 and was again given parole. When his sons were killed in May 2013, this offender was out on bail after his third murder. He states that programs such as probation and parole place too much emphasis on rehabilitation of the offender while compromising the public safety of innocent citizens. Thinking about the trends in probation and parole in the twenty-first century and beyond, how do you respond to this father's and the group's concerns regarding the balance between offender rehabilitation and public safety?

6. Following the killing of Trayvon Martin and the subsequent trial and acquittal of George Zimmerman, a citizen group sponsors an ALARM Forum. You are the only representative from the criminal justice system sitting on a panel consisting of a school administrator, a university law student, a parent, an ex-offender, and a member of the religious community. The panel and the group expressed several concerns:

   A. The lack of response by the community to violence in disorganized neighborhoods.

   B. The increasing violence rate among juveniles.

   C. The apparent trend of locking up drug offenders for long periods of time but leaving violent offenders in the community under probation supervision.

   D. The failure to assist ex-offenders in the re-integration back into society.

   E. The role of the community in addressing crime, public safety, and rehabilitation issues. How can the community become more involved?

   As an action item for the meeting, they have asked you to develop ideas for collaboration between the Department of Probation and Parole Services and the community to address many of these issues. What would be the features of your program?

Index of Cases

Index